THE KEYS OF BIBLE STUDY

Unlocking Scripture in an Age
of Forgotten Truth

MARK TROTTER

LIVING
FAITH
BOOKS

Copyright © 2019 by Mark G. Trotter. All scripture quotations are taken from the King James Authorized Version.

First published in 2019 by Living Faith Books.

All rights reserved. This book or parts thereof may not be reproduced in any form, stored in any retrieval system, or transmitted in any form by any means—electronic, mechanical, photocopy, recording, or otherwise—without prior written permission of the publisher and/or author, except as provided by United States of America copyright law.

Living Faith Books
3953 Walnut St
Kansas City, MO 64111

Director: Brandon Briscoe
Designer: Joel Springer
Editors: Melissa Wharton and Hanna Oswald

ISBN: 978-1-950004-03-4
Printed in the United States of America

TABLE OF CONTENTS

Chapter 1 - The Key of David   9

Chapter 2 - The Key of Theme   33

Chapter 3 - The Key of Divisions   73

Chapter 4 - The Key of Context   115

Chapter 5 - The Key of Comparison   141

Chapter 6 - The Key of Application   177

Chapter 7 - The Key of Words   203

Chapter 8 - The Key of Consistency   229

Chapter 9 - The Key of Association   253

Chapter 10 - The Key of Apparent Contradictions   279

Chapter 11 - The Key of Literality   301

Chapter 12 - Unlocking It All   321

FOREWORD

Our Lord Jesus Christ was a champion for common people. It was the big-wig, high-positioned intelligentsia who were so against Christ and caused Him so much grief during His earthly ministry. That's why I love the simplicity of the last sentence of Mark 12:37: "And the common people heard him gladly." And I believe they still do today!

This book was written to let common people know and believe that they truly can understand and know the Bible. By learning and utilizing the God-given, Holy Spirit-inspired, biblically identifiable keys of Bible study, I believe there may come a day when in all humility you will be able to say with David, "I have more understanding than all my teachers" (Psa 119:99).

I must offer this disclaimer from the outset. The principles discussed in the following pages did not originate with me. As mentioned in the previous paragraph, they are clearly identifiable in scripture; ultimately, they originated in the mind of God. I am, however, indebted to those who have influenced me in my understanding of these God-given principles. As I seek to trace the passing of the baton over the last one hundred years or so, it would appear that Dr. R. L. Moyer of Northwestern University influenced one of his students, J. Edwin Hartill, who wrote a book titled *Principles of Biblical Hermeneutics* back in 1947. That book influenced the teaching of a pastor named Mel Sabaka, who influenced pastors Bob Alexander and Jeff Adams, both of whom influenced me in my younger years.

It is my heartfelt desire that the keys of Bible study presented in the following pages will so impact your understanding of the word of God that you to fall in love with it—and that God will use you to be another link in the chain to impact the lives of others.

December 2019
Mark G. Trotter

THE KEY OF DAVID

In the ensuing chapters of *The Keys of Bible Study*, we will examine ten keys that are crucial to developing and possessing a biblical mindset and approach to studying and interpreting the word of God. I refer to them as *keys*, because these are the biblical principles the Holy Spirit uses to unlock the incredible riches contained in the treasure chest of God's holy word.

The Primary KEY of BIBLE STUDY

Before we dive into these ten keys, however, there is something tremendously important we need to talk about. There is a particular key of Bible study that is separate, unique, distinct, and unlike any of the other ten keys we'll be examining. Just as we often refer to Jesus as the *King of kings,* the *Lord of lords,* and the *God of gods,* and just as we often refer to the Bible as the *Book of books,* in terms of Bible study, we could say that this key is the *Key of keys!* This is, without a doubt, the most important key, because this is the key that actually makes all of the other keys work. And though it is my intention through this book to teach *The Keys of Bible Study*, this is a particular key that, quite honestly, can't be *taught... caught...* or *bought!* It is a very real key, that has a very specific biblical name, and a very specific biblical purpose. It is called the **Key of David**.

The Keys of Bible Study

You know what's kind of crazy? As important as this key is, most Christians have never even *heard* of the key of David, much less, know what it is... and much, much less have it in their possession! It is my hope and prayer that by the time you've completed this chapter, you will not only understand what it is, but that God will have so stirred your heart concerning this key that you have a passion to get it! I also hope and pray that by the time you have completed *The Keys of Bible Study*, it will actually be in your possession and remain with you for the rest of your life!

<u>KEY UNDERSTANDINGS:</u>

As we begin talking about this key, there are several vital pieces of information of which we must be keenly aware. First, the key of David today is in the possession of the Lord Jesus Christ—and unless He entrusts us with it, there is no other way to get it! But, secondly, we must also be keenly aware that *who* Jesus entrusts with this key is anything but random! It isn't a matter of luck. It isn't a matter of chance. It isn't a matter of faith. It isn't even a matter of sovereignty! He gives it to *individuals* and He gives it to *churches* that possess the key ingredient to David's walk and relationship with God that made him the only one in scripture to whom God ever referred as a man after his own heart! (1Sa 13:14; Act 13:22) This, of course, is why this key is referred to in scripture as the "key of David."

But before we talk about what that key ingredient to David's walk and relationship with God actually was, let's first take a few minutes to get ourselves biblically acquainted with what the key of David actually is.

First of all, from a biblical standpoint, the key of David is representative of two very important concepts:

1. It is representative of *ACCESS*
2. It is representative of *AUTHORITY*

10

Chapter 1 — The Key of David

What that means from a very practical standpoint is that the key of David is the key to two very important entities:

1. It is the key to *God's WORD*
2. It is the key to *God's WORK*

My goal in this first chapter isn't to fully exhaust the teaching concerning the key of David. With the keys we'll be getting into in the chapters to follow, perhaps you can take the time to implement these keys to study the key of David in further detail. Instead, my goal in this chapter is to provide you with enough biblical information concerning this key to help you understand why possessing it should become your passionate pursuit.

One of the particular things we need to understand from the outset about being entrusted with the key of David, is that it doesn't really have to do with our **minds**. It's not about our intellectual capacity or capabilities in the word of God. It's not about the accumulation of biblical information. No, the key of David, first and foremost, has to do with our **hearts**! It's all about our heart's desire to both know and love God. It's about allowing the word of God to produce in us a biblical transformation that affects how we view the word of God, and the heart with which we approach it!

KEY THOUGHT:

The entrustment of the key of David doesn't have to do with our APTITUDE in the word of God: it has to do with our ATTITUDE toward it!

KEY VERSES:

God talks to us about the key of David in two specific places in scripture: one is in the Old Testament, and one is in the New Testament.

Isaiah 22:20-22

The Keys of Bible Study

And it shall come to pass in that day, that I will call my servant Eliakim the son of Hilkiah: And I will clothe him with thy robe, and strengthen him with thy girdle, and I will commit thy **government** into his hand: and he shall be a father to the inhabitants of Jerusalem, and to the house of Judah. And **the key of the house of David will I lay upon his shoulder; so he shall open, and none shall shut; and he shall shut, and none shall open.**

What we find in this first occurrence of the key of David in scripture, is that this key had been entrusted to this man by the name of Eliakim, the son of Hilkiah. We learn from verse 20 that Eliakim was certainly a good man, one for whom God Himself referred to as His "servant." Isaiah 36:1-3 lets us know that King Hezekiah recognized what a special man Eliakim was, placing him in the position as both the treasurer and master "over the house" (or over King Hezekiah's palace). As we find here in Isaiah 22:21, Eliakim was the one to whom God had determined to commit the **government** (or **authority**) to be "a father to the inhabitants of Jerusalem, and to the house of Judah," and the one to whom He would grant the key of David, which would provide Eliakim both **authority** and **access** to all the treasures in the kingdom. When he opened the door to those treasures, buddy, they were open! And yet, just as surely, when he shut the door to those treasures, they were shut! In other words, Eliakim was the man! Verse 22 says that the key of David had been laid upon his shoulder—simply meaning that the **access** to the treasures of the kingdom were placed under his **authority**.

Keep those facts in mind as we now look at the New Testament reference to the key of David found
in the letter our Lord Jesus Christ dictated to the Apostle John and addressed to the church in Philadelphia.

Revelation 3:7-8

And to the angel in the church of Philadelphia write; These things saith he that is holy, he that is true, he that hath the key of David, he that openeth, and no man shutteth; and shutteth, and no man openeth; I know thy works: behold, I have set before thee an open door, and no man can shut it...

Once again, God let's us know that it is the key of David that provides both **access** and **authority**. The key of David opens what no man can shut... and shuts what no man can open. And from what we learned from Isaiah 22:20-22, this **access** and **authority** is specifically related to the treasures of the king.

So, as we look at these two places in scripture that talk specifically about the key of David, it forces us to step back and ask ourselves a...

KEY QUESTION:

From a biblical standpoint, just what are these treasures that the key of David actually opens?

As we apply the God-ordained method whereby the Spirit of God reveals to us the wisdom of God (1Co 2:9-13), we find that the answer to that question from a biblical standpoint is actually twofold. First of all, those "treasures" are:

1. The treasures in the <u>word</u> of God

Have you ever noticed how Paul refers to the word of God in Ephesians 3:8? He calls it "the **unsearchable riches** of Christ." In Proverbs 2:4, God tells us that we are to seek the wisdom, understanding, and knowledge that is revealed in the Bible as if we were searching for "**hid treasures.**" Colossians 2:3 says that in Christ "are **hid all the treasures of wisdom and knowledge.**"

So, obviously, the first thing we come to understand biblically about the key of David is that it unlocks the treasures contained in the word of God! If we'll ever truly open the treasures God has stored in His book, we're going to need the key to **access** them! And the key that opens them is a key we must get directly from the Lord Jesus Christ: the key of David!

13

The Keys of Bible Study

But what does it actually look like in real life when **access** to the treasures in the **word of God** have been placed under the **authority** of someone who has been entrusted with the possession of the key of David?

Have you ever encountered another believer with such keen insight into the word of God that it actually arrested your attention? I'm talking about people who have the uncanny ability to take **deep** biblical truths, and explain them with such incredible **simplicity**, you find yourself asking, "How in the world did I not see that?" And yet at the same time, these people also possess the uncanny ability to take **simple** biblical truths, and expand and expound them with such **depth**, it is nothing short of amazing.

How do they do that? How do they take what is deep and make it simple and take what is simple and reveal its depth? What is that certain something they possess that causes them to have such keen insight into the word of God? Is it merely the fact that they possess greater intellect and reasoning abilities than the rest of us? I would submit to you that it is not because they possess some kind of intellectual or educational superiority, but it is the simple fact that they possess the key of David! Quite simply, the "eyes of their understanding [have been] enlightened" (Eph 1:18), allowing them to "behold wondrous things" out of the word of God (Psa 119:18), almost as if their eyes had been anointed with a supernatural eyesalve (Rev 3:18).

So, first of all, the treasures the key of David actually opens are **the treasures in the <u>word</u> of God**. But as we continue to seek to discern what the 'treasures' are, we find that secondly, the treasures the key of David opens are:

2. The treasures in the <u>work</u> of God

In Matthew 13:44, Jesus said:

> ... the kingdom of heaven is like unto **treasure hid in a field**; the which when a man hath found, he hideth, and for joy thereof

14

goeth and selleth all that he hath, and buyeth that field.

In this passage, the treasure Jesus is talking about *isn't* the word of God. Notice though, that whatever this "treasure" is to which He's referring, He tells us it is "hid in a **field**." Do you know what a field is in the Bible? Just six verses previous in this same context (Mat 13:38), Jesus specifically tells us that the "**field is the world!**"

So, do you know what the treasure that was hid in the field actually is? It is people! Specifically, the souls of the people of the world! Look again at what Jesus says in Matthew 13:44:

> ... the kingdom of heaven is like unto treasure hid in a field; the which when <u>a man hath found, he hideth, and for joy thereof goeth and selleth all that he hath, and buyeth that field.</u>

And do you know who **the man** in this illustration actually is? It's none other than our Lord Jesus Christ! This passage is revealing the fact that God became **a man** in the person of Jesus Christ, who came down to this world to buy the treasure He saw in that field to make them a part of His everlasting kingdom. But He lets us know in this verse, that to purchase that treasure, it would cost Him everything He had. In other words, it would cost Him His very life. Hebrews 12:2 tells us that it was "for the joy that was set before him [that Jesus] endured the cross." And the joy that was set before Him was the precious treasure of the souls of the men and women in the field of the world. And on the cross, Jesus shed His blood, completely giving His life for every person who would ever live! In other words, He sold all that He had to purchase the treasure that was in the field—or to buy the redemption of every person in the world! Hallelujah!

And the fact is, when Jesus looks out of heaven and sees an individual or a church that possesses the key ingredient to David's walk and relationship with God, He gladly entrusts to them the key that grants them **authority** and **access** to the treasures in the field, just like He did with those who comprised the church of Philadelphia (Rev 3:7–8).

The Keys of Bible Study

Have you ever encountered another believer who possessed an uncanny ability to minister the gospel to people? It's almost as if everywhere they go, doors of opportunity fling open to them, not only to be able to give people the gospel, but to articulate it with such simplicity, boldness, and clarity, that God actually uses them to reach people with the message.

It was this very thing for which Paul was requesting prayer for he and his missionary team when he wrote to the church in Colossae, saying:

> Withal praying also for us, that God would open unto us a door of utterance, to speak the mystery of Christ, for which I am also in bonds: That I may make it manifest, as I ought to speak. (Col 4:3-4)

These kinds of doors don't open, and this kind of clarity isn't manifested simply because a person has been entrusted by God with a winsome personality, a vast education or incredible skills in communication. No, these doors of ministry open to people and to churches because they have been entrusted with the key of David!

But people who possess the key of David don't just have doors of opportunity supernaturally open to them to minister the gospel and see lost people become members of the body of Christ. Those who possess the key of David also have doors of opportunity supernaturally open to them to minister the word of God through their gifts to people who are already members of the body of Christ. Doors of ministry open to them that are both incredible and unexplainable, and God supernaturally directs them to minister in the specific field of His choosing through the key of David opening doors that no man can shut, and He likewise, supernaturally directs them through the key of David shutting doors that no man can open (Rev 3:7–8). Their ministry reflects the fact that they function by a different **power**, or a different **authority**. Quite simply, they are in possession of the key of David.

16

Chapter 1 — The Key of David

When Jesus writes the letter to the church in Philadelphia in Revelation 3:7 and says that He is the one with the key of David, do you understand what He's actually saying? He's saying, "I'm the one with the key to **access** the treasures to be found in the fields of this world. I'm the one with **authority**!"

Jesus said in Matthew 28:18: "All **power** is given unto me in heaven and in earth." In other words, "I'm the one with **authority** in this world... and I'm the one with **access** to the world!" And He says in verse 19: "Because I am, 'go ye **therefore**, and teach all nations'!" In other words, "Because I have this **authority** in the world, and, therefore, have **access** into the entire world, I am sending you to go and make disciples in all nations!"

In that Philadelphian church in the first century, and in the Philadelphian period of church history in the 16th through 19th centuries, do you know what actually happened? This was the time in the history of the church when the Lord Jesus Christ, the one who holds the key of David, took that key and laid it on the shoulder of many of His sons and daughters, granting them His **authority** and **access**, or the open door, to the world! (Col 4:3; Rev 3:8) That's why when we look back historically into the Philadelphian church period (a period from around 1500-1900), we find that it was the time of the greatest missionary movements, the greatest revivals, the greatest preaching, and the greatest demonstration of evangelistic power in the history of the church! And do you know why it was? It was because during that period of time, the Lord Jesus Christ found many believers and churches that possessed the key to David's walk and relationship with God, so He granted them the key to His **word** and the key to His **work**: the key of David! Through that key, Jesus gave them both **authority** and **access** to understand His word—and **authority** and **access** to then take His word across the street... and around the world!

Perhaps we could summarize the key of David this way:

1. The key of David is the key that <u>opens</u> the <u>eyes of our</u> <u>understanding</u> to the <u>word</u> of God.

17

The Keys of Bible Study

2. The key of David is the key that <u>opens</u> the <u>doors of opportunity</u> in the <u>work</u> of God.

In these last days of the church age, as individuals and as churches, we tend to think we need a lot of things. But there's really only one thing that you and I actually need, and there's really only one thing Christ's church actually needs! It is the key of David! And the tremendous reality is, the Lord Jesus Christ is still laying the key of David upon the shoulders of individuals and churches! But, like we mentioned earlier, receiving the entrustment of that key is anything but random! There is a condition for receiving it.

As we also mentioned previously, the reason this key is called the "key of David" is because it is given to those who possess the key ingredient to David's walk and relationship with the Lord. As we look at David's life and the things the Holy Spirit inspired him to write, it reveals some very interesting things about what made David's relationship with the Lord so unique that the Lord actually looked at this guy and said: "That man right there is a man after my own heart!"

Do you know what the key to that relationship was? **It was David's <u>reverential attitude toward and passionate love for the word of God</u>!**

And lest we read that statement and simply file it like a piece of information into our minds, we would do well to allow it to search our hearts, that we might determine whether or not we personally possess the key to David's walk and relationship with God!

May I take the liberty to share with you a personal testimony about this thing of possessing a reverential attitude toward the word of God and passionate love for the word of God?

I didn't grow up in a Christian home. By my early teens, the world, the flesh, and the devil had pretty much taken over my life. Through an extremely bizarre set of circumstances that is too detailed to get into here, when I was a sophomore in high school in Miami,

18

Chapter 1 — The Key of David

Florida, I found myself in a church service where an evangelist was preaching the gospel of Christ's death, burial and resurrection with power and authority. At the end of his message, he extended an invitation to those who desired to confess with their mouth the Lord Jesus. I was under such deep conviction of my sin that I was literally trembling. I desperately wanted Christ to be my Savior, so I responded to the invitation. With firm belief that I was a sinner before a holy God, and that this holy God had given His Son to die for my sin, be buried, and raised from the dead after three days, I called upon the name of the Lord and was gloriously saved (Rom 10:9,13).

I can tell you, that the freedom from the condemnation of my sin and the prospects of possessing and developing an intimate, personal, love relationship with the God of the universe was both astounding and exhilarating to me. By God's mercy and grace, I was a new creature in Christ! And my life was immediately transformed! I brought my Bible with me to school the next day and began reading it every chance I could get. I got plugged into the local church where I had heard the gospel and became an active part of the youth group.

It was shortly after my coming to Christ that Mrs. Dewhurst, my English teacher, required that we purchase one of those black and white speckled notebooks and bring it with us to class on a daily basis. When we got to class each day, she would have written a word, a sentence, or sometimes a short paragraph on the chalkboard, and our assignment for the first 15 minutes of each class was to begin to write in our tablets whatever came to our mind based on what she had written.

Much to my surprise, this assignment would prove to be life-changing in years to come, and a key part of my life's testimony. I might add, though, that at this time I was clueless about how to actually study the Bible and pretty much anything and everything that had to do with God, the Bible, or His Church. I had long stringy blonde hair, dressed like a hippie wannabe, and as I found out later, the people in my church didn't quite know what to think

19

of me. I'll come back to the significance of that black and white speckled notebook in just a minute.

As time went on, I began to grow and piece more and more things together in my newfound faith. I cut my hair, started wearing not-quite-so-radical clothes, and began to talk in a different manner. Before long, though I had grown up with aspirations of being an FBI guy, I came to the place that I couldn't imagine doing anything except telling people about my Lord and His word for the rest of my life. Upon my graduation from high school, though it scared me to death at the time, I enrolled in Bible college in hopes of God somehow turning this beach-combing street urchin into a pastor!

The years went by and I graduated from Bible college, became a college and young adult pastor in a church in Southern California, then a young marrieds' pastor at a church in Atlanta, and then an Associate Pastor at a large church in New Philadelphia, Ohio. By the time Sherry (my wife) and I had been in the ministry six years, we had lived in nine different houses or apartments. The moves were so frequent that I often found myself moving boxes from attic to attic or basement to basement without ever even opening them. I didn't even have a clue what was in most of them!

After six years in the ministry, Sherry and I finally purchased a home and were beginning the process of readying ourselves for yet another move. I had determined I was not going to move those boxes again without at least finding out what was in them! I went down to the basement and began rummaging through the boxes. After working through a few of them, I came upon a box that had "Mark's Junk Box" written on the outside. I thought to myself, "What in the world could possibly be in here?" As I opened it, I realized that it was some of the things left in my bedroom when I went off to college and had come back into my possession after getting married. There were some trophies, a few newspaper clippings from high school football days, and as you might have guessed by now, there was a black and white speckled notebook. Initially, I didn't even remember what it was. I opened it and was immediately taken back to my English class in those early days

20

Chapter 1 — The Key of David

after coming to Christ.

As I began reading, I was amazed to find that regardless of what Mrs. Dewhurst had written on the board, somehow God and His word flowed out of my mind, through my pen, and onto those pages. As I read page after page, I was able to see a long-haired, clueless teenager who pretty much knew nothing about nothing express his undying passion for His Savior and His glorious book. And I must tell you, it not only brought extreme conviction, but also scared me to death! Because here I was, the Associate Pastor of a great church, who now had all of the externals of the Christian life down pat. I had learned how to wear the right hair and the right clothes. I knew all of the right places to say "amen" and "praise the Lord." But that night, through the pages of that journal, I was taken back to the early days of my salvation and was horrified to discover that, though I had learned all of the right things to do in order to look and act the part of being a sold-out, all-in, Bible-believing Christian, somewhere along the way I had lost my heart and passion for my God and His word. To put it in the words Jesus used when writing to the church of Ephesus in Revelation 2:4, I had left my first love. Through that old speckled notebook, I realized that the Lord had allowed me to "remember... from whence [I had] fallen" (Rev 2:5a), and right then and there, I repented (Rev 2:5b) and determined that I would "do the first works" (Rev 2:5c). I determined that by God's grace and power, I would go back to doing the things I was doing when my love for Christ was fresh, vibrant and new.

In my quest to go back to get my love for God and His word, I determined that I would take however long it took me to go through the key characters of the Bible and write down all of the expressions of their love for God and/or His word that I could find so I could meditate on them and pray that God would take the passion of their heart to help restore mine. I desperately longed to have restored to me the reverential attitude and the passionate love for the word of God and the God of the word that I had in those early days.

In my quest, I began looking at the life of a man by the name of Ezra. I found that Ezra was just an absolute spiritual stud! The book of the Bible that bears his name reveals that though the Jews had been in captivity in Babylon for years and years, the pagan king had finally granted them release to go back to their homeland. Ezra, of course, was the one entrusted with the responsibility of leading the troops back to Jerusalem—that glorious place where the God of the Bible was intended to be worshipped by His people, the Jews, in all of His glory.

Near the end of the book, Ezra records that as this remnant was finally closing in on the outskirts of the city of Jerusalem, they had been made aware of the unbelievable atrocities that were taking place in Jerusalem. The Jews who were living in Jerusalem had intermarried with heathen peoples, and were involving themselves in all of their abominable and pagan practices. Ezra was so impassioned and distraught by the news that he says:

> And when I heard this thing, I rent my garment and my mantle, and plucked off the hair of my head and of my beard, and sat down astonied. (Ezr 9:3)

Can you imagine that? The way we might say that today is that he just went berserk! The news he had received left him at such a place emotionally, that physically, it was as if he had turned to stone. He could not so much as move a muscle. Ezra then adds:

> Then were assembled unto me every one that trembled at the words of the God of Israel, because of the transgression of those that had been carried away; and I sat astonied until the evening sacrifice. (Ezr 9:4)

Ezra lets us know that the news of how God's people were living caused Him to sit for hours in the same position, not moving a muscle. That's just how passionate he was for God and His word! And as I saw Ezra's passion, I cried out to God that He would so work in my heart to make me that passionate for His glory!

But I also want you to notice who the scripture says it was who had gathered themselves around Ezra to join him in this expression of passion and sorrow for God's glory. Verse 4 says it was all of those in this remnant "that trembled at the words of the God of Israel." Wow! Do you hear that? There were people in this remnant with Ezra who had so much awe and reverence for the word of God that it made them literally and physically tremble! As I read these words, reflecting on where I was in that moment, I realized that at one time I knew what it was to tremble at the words of God. But I also realized that if God were to assemble the people who so reverenced His word that it actually caused them to tremble, I would no longer have been in that group. And again, I began to cry out to God that He would restore to me that kind of reverence and passion for His word!

I then came to another incredible man who passionately loved God and His word: Jeremiah. I read where Jeremiah was pouring out his heart to God, declaring:

> Thy words were found, and I did eat them; and thy word was unto me the joy and rejoicing of mine heart... (Jer 15:16)

And once again, Jeremiah's incredible passion for the word of God caused me to look within and ask myself: "How long has it been since that has been my response to the things I consume in the word of God? When was the last time I could honestly say that the word of God utterly filled my heart with joy and rejoicing?" And I cried out to God that it would!

I then came to Job. I saw in Job 23:12, that he was able to unhesitatingly declare:

> Neither have I gone back from the commandment of his lips; I have esteemed the words of his mouth more than my necessary food. (Job 23:12)

And wow! I had to ask myself, could I boldly declare with Job that I would never compromise any of the commands He has given to me in His word? And how long has it been since I could genuinely say that I would rather sit down to feast on God's word than to feast

The Keys of Bible Study

on my favorite food? And again, I cried out for God to restore my reverence, passion and hunger for His word.

And then, of course, I came to David. In Psalm 63:1-2, David was able to say to the Lord:

> O God, thou art my God; early will I seek thee: my soul thirsteth for thee, my flesh longeth for thee in a dry and thirsty land, where no water is; To see thy power and thy glory, so as I have seen thee in the sanctuary. (Psa 63:1-2)

And again, the question I was forced to ask myself in response to David's powerful declaration is: "Am I so passionate for God and His word that I can even remotely relate to the thirst to which David is referring?"

As an American, it probably goes without saying that I have never been stranded in the middle of a hot desert where there is absolutely no water, leaving me so dehydrated that my flesh was literally craving water as David talks about here. As I mentioned, however, I did grow up in the hot and humid city of Miami, Florida. And I can tell you that in August during two-a-day football practices, when the temperature on the field was 100°F with 100% humidity (sporting full pads and a helmet, and in those days, no water breaks because they were going to make us tough and get us in shape!), I think I do understand a pretty intense level of insatiable thirst!

During those days, I remember coming into the locker room after practice and going straight to the shower, cupping my hands, and just standing there gulping down as much water as I could. There were times when my belly would be so filled with water that I felt like I couldn't drink another drop—and yet my thirst still had not been quenched!

I thought to myself that must be the idea David is expressing in Psalm 63:1-2. He was so passionate about the word of God that he just couldn't get enough of it! Though he had consumed massive amounts of it, he still thirsted for more. And I realized that

24

Chapter 1 — The Key of David

though I had learned a lot about the word of God in those ten years following my salvation and six years in the ministry, there was no longer a deep passion and longing in me for more and more of it. And so I cried out to God that He would allow me to experience an insatiable thirst in my soul for His word once again!

It took a few months of passionately pursuing God through the pages of His word, but I can humbly say that God graciously shined on me and restored my first love passion for Him and His word.

My dear brother or sister, as I have been bringing you through my testimony of losing my reverential attitude toward the word of God through these verses and passages of scripture, could I humbly and graciously ask you: has the Lord been revealing anything to you about your reverential attitude toward Him and His word?

Based on the passages we just looked at, could I ask you to consider...

Where are the people in the 21st century who so *reverence* the word of God that it actually causes them to *tremble?* Are you one of them?

Where are the people in the 21st century who so *delight* in God's word that it actually brings *joy* and *rejoicing* to their heart and their life? Are you one of them?

Where are the people in the 21st century who so *hunger* for God's book that they would rather have it than the *very food that sustains their life?* Are you one of them?

Where are the people in the 21st century who so *thirst* for God's word that they find themselves with an all-consuming, all-embracing, pre-occupying passion for it that simply cannot be *quenched?* Are you one of them?

These questions are vitally important, because they reveal to us the reverential attitude toward the word of God that causes our Lord Jesus Christ to place the key of David on someone's life, or on a

The Keys of Bible Study

particular church!

And yet, recognize that in David's walk and relationship with God, it wasn't just that he *reverenced* the word of God... it wasn't just that he *delighted* in the word of God... and it wasn't just that he *hungered* and *thirsted* for the word of God. Oh, that was certainly part of it! But do you know what the key actually was? It was his *love* for the Word of God!

And in keeping with the questions we were asking above, I ask you: where are the people in the twenty-first century who can honestly say that they *love* the word of God? And again I ask you, could it be said of *you?*

As I was in the midst of my journey to retrieve my first love, I remember being intrigued with the fact, as I mentioned earlier, that David was the only man in scripture ever referred to as a man after God's own heart. I didn't fully know what that meant, though I certainly knew enough to know that David loved God passionately—so I figured it had something to do with that. But it sent me on a more thorough search of David's life to see what was really behind the passion of his heart and his love for God, to see what I could learn from him in hopes that I, too, might be considered by God a man after his own heart.

I remember being excited about reading the psalms of David with the particular focus of seeing just how David expressed his deep love for God. I had determined that every time I could find where David expressed his love and passion for God, I would begin using David's words and seek to use his heart as a template for verbalizing my love for the Lord.

But, much to my surprise, do you know what I found? All of the times that David expressed his love for God in the psalms actually came to a grand total of *two!* Yeah, two! That's it! And if I may be so brash, those two places didn't really seem to me to be some heart-warming, life-changing, beautiful expression of his love— nor was it some powerfully convicting demonstration of it. These

Chapter 1 — The Key of David

two instances actually sounded to me as if they were simply the declaration of a fact.

Listen to what David said in Psalm 18:1:

I will love thee, O Lord, my strength.

And that's it! I mean, that's the whole verse! And, sure, it's awesome anytime someone tells the Lord they love him—but when we're talking about the man after God's own heart, you kind of expect that it might be a little more expressive and heartfelt than a mere statement of fact! Do you know what I mean?

The other time David expresses his love for the Lord is in Psalm 116:1—and in terms of trying to learn from his passion and heart for the Lord, the truth is, this one isn't a whole lot better! David, seemingly somewhat unemotionally, says:

I love the Lord, because he hath heard my voice and my supplications. (Psa 116:1)

And again, I don't want to sound negative or judgmental about how anyone chooses to express their love for the Lord. I'm just saying, it's not the kind of passionate, intimate, heartfelt, life-changing expression of love I was expecting from the only person in the word of God to whom God ever bestowed the title a man after his own heart!

But then I got to Psalm 119... and wow! You talk about receiving a startling revelation! I don't know what you already know about Psalm 119, but it has 176 verses. It's not only the longest psalm, it's also the longest chapter in the Bible. And in this psalm, David is passionately and emotionally pouring out his heart to the Lord. And what is absolutely amazing in this psalm, is that out of the 176 verses, all but two of them specifically talk about the word of God! And in this one psalm alone, in ten different places, David finds ten different ways to express his heartfelt love for the word of God!

27

The Keys of Bible Study

Would you listen to his heart in Psalm 119:47? David says, "And I will delight myself in thy commandments, **which I have loved**." In other words, David is saying: "Lord, I have made a choice: that Your word is going to be where I find my delight, because I so love it!"

David follows that in the very next verse, Psalm 119:48, saying: "My hands also will I lift up unto thy commandments, **which I have loved**; and I will meditate in thy statutes." The lifting up of his hands to the word of God represents the surrender of David's *heart* and *will* to it. His statement declaring that the word of God was what he had chosen to meditate on represents that his *mind* was likewise surrendered to it. And David makes clear that this was his response to the word of God, because of how he *loved* it!

David expresses a similar sentiment in verse 97, where he says: "**O how love I thy law**! it is my meditation all the day." Because of how he loved the word of God, David says that it had become the complete preoccupation of his thoughts.

In verse 113, David says, "I hate vain thoughts: but **thy law do I love**." David expresses a principle in this verse that is repeated throughout the word of God, and that is, by its very nature, love automatically causes us to hate some things! In this verse, he says that his love for God's word caused him to hate any and all of the world's vain mindsets that run so contrary to God's mind as it is revealed in His word. In verse 163, he says that his love for the word of God also caused him to have an utter hatred for lying: "I hate and abhor lying: but **thy law do I love**."

In verse 119, David says, "Thou puttest away all the wicked of the earth like dross: therefore **I love thy testimonies**." In other words, "Lord, I love Your word, because when it's all been said and done, all of the people who live their lives defying You will be removed from the earth, and the truth of Your word will alone prevail!"

In verse 127, David expresses his love for the word of God as exceeding the love or desire for the finest treasures on earth, saying,

28

Chapter 1 — The Key of David

"...**I love thy commandments** above gold; yea, above fine gold."

In verse 140, David declares his recognition of the pristine purity of the word of God that sets it apart from anything else on the earth, making it yet another reason for his passionate love for it. David says: "Thy word is very pure: therefore **thy servant loveth it.**"

David was so assured and confident in his love for the word of God that in verse 159, He invites the Lord: "Consider how **I love thy precepts.**" And based on his love for the word, he prays that God, in His lovingkindness, would resuscitate life into his entire being.

In verse 167, David declares with unhesitating confidence that his obedience to the word of God wasn't merely an outward adherence to it, but that his obedience was actually bursting forth from the deepest recesses of his inner being, because of his deep, passionate love for it! David says, "My soul hath kept thy testimonies; and **I love them exceedingly.**"

As you can see, David, the man after God's own heart, obviously had a passionate love for the **God** of the **word** (though as we've discussed, biblically it is seldom expressed). But for some reason, as the Holy Spirt inspired David to write what would become the holy scriptures, David can't seem to stop talking about his love for the **word** of **God**!

But what conclusion are we to draw from that? What is the point the Lord wants us to derive from all of this? Are we to conclude that David loved the word of God more than he loved God Himself? Absolutely not! God forbid!

What God is obviously trying to get us to see is that He has always wanted people to love Him—and not just with a nonchalant or haphazard love, but the kind of love Jesus delineated in Mark 12:30: "And thou shalt love the Lord thy God with all thy heart, and with all thy soul, and with all thy mind, and with all thy strength: this is the first commandment." (Note, not "first" in terms of order or sequence, but "first" in terms of importance and priority!) In the

29

The Keys of Bible Study

final analysis, God desires that each of us love Him with all of our heart, and soul, and mind, and strength! And what we learn from the life of David, the man after God's own heart, is that **it is impossible to separate loving <u>God</u> from loving His <u>word</u>!**

My brothers and sisters, *that* was the key to David's walk and relationship with the Lord! It was his heart attitude toward the word of God that caused him to love it! There is no doubt about it: David loved the **God** of the **word <u>because</u>** he loved the **word** of **God**!

That's exactly what happened to our brothers and sisters in the Philadelphian church in the first century, and in the Philadelphian church period in the 16th through 19th centuries. The Lord placed His word in their *hands*... they hid it in their *hearts*... and they *fell in love with it!* And do you know what happened as a result? It caused them to fall in love with the **God** of the **word**, and the **word** of **God** became the key of David in their hands! They possessed the key to David's life, and Jesus put into their possession the key of David. This key gave them unlimited **authority** and **access** to the treasures in His word: the truth of God! And it gave them unlimited **authority** and **access** to the treasures in His world: the souls of people!

As I said at the beginning of this chapter, I'm very excited to share with you the ten keys of Bible study. But listen: without this one key, *the key of David*, we will totally miss the point. It is, indeed, the **key** of **keys!** And our Lord Jesus Christ desperately wants to give us that key! The question is: do we desperately want *it?*

In conclusion, I want you to know how thrilled I am that you were interested enough in God and His word to have even made it through the first chapter of this book. But please allow me to talk to you very briefly and very honestly about where you are in terms of possessing the key of David.

If you don't think that it could be said of you that you love the word of God, chances are that one simple chapter on the subject

30

is probably not going to translate into you truly loving it. *However,* through the things we've talked about in this chapter concerning the key of David, and through the testimony of the men we've talked about who had a passionate heart for the word of God, I believe with everything that is in me that God could be stirring in you at this very moment a holy reverence for His word that causes you to genuinely begin to hunger and thirst for it. And if you will enter into the following chapters of *The Keys of Bible Study,* hungering and thirsting for the word of God along the way, I believe that God can and will take His word that you put in your heart and cause it to become the key of David in your hands.

I know it's the last days, and I know what the Bible says is typically characteristic of us: we are lovers of our own selves and we are lovers of pleasures more than lovers of God (2Ti 3:2,4). Sometimes we seem hopeless. But when a believer gets serious about the **word** of **God** and the **God** of the **word**, I want you to know: God can do some incredible things in us and through us—even in these last days!

Our Lord's letter to the church of the Laodiceans in the first century in Revelation 3:14-22, representative of the church in the 20th and 21st centuries, paints a very indicting picture of believers in our time: Jesus says we are lukewarm, wretched, miserable, poor, blind, and naked! (Rev 3:15-17) But, please hear and heed the words of Jesus to us in Revelation 3:19-20: "As many as I love, I rebuke and chasten: be zealous therefore, and repent. Behold, I stand at the door, and knock: if any man hear my voice, and open the door, I will come in to him, and will sup with him, and he with me."

Do you hear Him knocking? If so, may you then be zealous enough, as Jesus says here, to first of all, repent... and secondly, to open the door of your heart to Him like never before.

THE KEY OF THEME

In the previous chapter, we began talking about an incredibly significant key in the word of God—the *key of David!* We learned that it is a very real key that God grants to those who possess that which was the key to David's relationship with God that caused him to be the only one in scripture who is ever referred to as a man after God's own heart (1Sa 13:14; Act 13:22). That key, of course, was David's love for the word of God. Quite simply, David possessed a very unique love for the God of the word because he possessed a very unique love for the word of God! Historically, God has granted possession of the key of David to those individuals and churches who possessed this same rare quality (Isa 22:20-25; Rev 3:7-8). It is the key that God uses to open the eyes of our understanding in His word, and it is the key God uses to open doors of opportunity in His work.

It is the design and intent of *The Keys of Bible Study* to present the principles of biblical interpretation in such an understandable fashion that God will use them to cause each of us to fall passionately in love with His *word* so we might fall so passionately in love with *Him*, and that it could truly be said of us that we love God with all of our heart and soul and mind and strength (Mar 12:30).

In this chapter, we're going to begin talking about the individual keys which are the foundational tools God has presented in His word to help us to have a *proper understanding* of the word of God stemming from a *biblical interpretation* of the word of God.

The first key of Bible study:
ESTABLISH THE THEME OF THE AUTHOR.

When we're talking about *the theme of the author*, it should be noted that we're not simply referring to the theme of the *human author* of the particular book of the Bible we may be studying. We're referring to the theme of the *ultimate Author* of the entire Bible! The reason the Bible can have over 40 different human authors, who wrote from all kinds of different backgrounds, occupations, and lifestyles; and who wrote from three different continents, in three different languages, over a period of over 1500 years; and yet, read as if it was written by only one Author is because it was! That one Author, of course, is none other than God Himself! The Bible tells us in 2 Peter 1:21 that "holy men of God spake as they were **moved by the Holy Ghost**." In other words, though God used the personality, background and communication style of human authors, the Holy Ghost was so superintending the process that it was actually He who was writing the Bible!

So, when God began the process of revealing Himself and His plan through what would come to be called the Bible, just what was it that was in His *heart?*

- What was He really wanting to communicate?
- What was He actually pointing to?
- What was He really wanting us to see?
- What was He actually wanting to teach?
- What was He intending the theme of His Book to be?

And let it be known, making these determinations is no small thing! The Bible is a big book, and it's easy to get lost in the details

Chapter 2 — The Key of Theme

and come to improper conclusions and interpretations when we don't understand God's overarching point and underlying message. This is one of the key reasons Christianity in the 21st century is so jacked up and whacked out! It's very simply because most of God's people today don't really understand what it is that God intended to communicate through His book.

KEY THOUGHT:

Imagine with me that God just randomly decided to give you a pop quiz and asked you, "What do you think the Bible is really about? What do you think the theme of the Bible actually is?"

What would you say? Take a second right now to think about what your answer would be.

Typically, most people think the theme of the Bible is *salvation*. Others think it's the *cross*, while others think it's the *blood of Christ*— or some combination of all of those things. Sometimes you'll hear people say things like, "There's a scarlet thread that weaves its way through the Bible from Genesis to Revelation!" While that statement is true, is that really the number one thing God was seeking to communicate to us through His incredible book?

KEY ILLUSTRATION:

Perhaps this illustration can help us see the point. There are five men in the Bible who got beamed from the earth directly into the throne room of God. Wow! Can you imagine that? These men were Enoch, Isaiah, Ezekiel, the Apostle Paul, and the Apostle John. But imagine with me that what happened to these guys suddenly happened to you! And in the twinkling of an eye, as it were, you too were immediately beamed from where you presently are, right into God's very throne room! And once God lifts you up off your face (because that's exactly how everybody in the Bible who ever saw God ended up, teaching us that the most comfortable position a human can be in the presence of God is on their face!), you notice up on the wall of jasper behind His throne that there is a calendar.

35

The Keys of Bible Study

Now, I'm not exactly sure what the protocol is in your home when it comes to calendars, but in ours, on special days—like our kids' and grandkids' birthdays, our anniversary, and other significant days— man, we circle 'em, we highlight 'em, we star 'em, we underline 'em, we explanation point 'em, we smiley face 'em, and whatever else we can think of to do to 'em! And, of course, we do that to send the signal to any onlooker that these are tremendously important days to our family!

Well, just imagine with me, that as God sees you looking at His calendar, He says to you, "Do you want to take a closer look at it?" And you say, "Oh, wow! May I?" So God takes His calendar off the wall and hands it to you, and as you begin to flip through the pages, you recognize that this calendar actually chronicles all of the significant days in the history of civilization.

And as you're in the midst of making your way through the annals of history, all of a sudden you come to a particular day, and it's obvious that this day is a day unlike any other! You find that this is a day God has actually circled, highlighted, starred, underlined, exclamation-pointed, and smiley faced!

As you're pondering that day, God says to you, "Do you know what day that is?" You, of course, respond, "Yes, Lord, it's obviously the most significant day in the history of the universe!" And with tears in your eyes, you say, "That's the day when Jesus Christ died on the cross to pay for the sins of the whole world."

God looks at you, and with tears in His own eyes, says, "Yes, you're right. It *is* the most significant day in the history of the universe, but, no—it isn't the day when My Son was brutalized on the cross. Quite the contrary! This is the day when My Son is going to come back to planet earth and cast Satan into the Bottomless Pit, and burn up all His enemies, and every knee is going to bow and every tongue is going to confess that Jesus Christ is Lord to My glory. And for the first time since Adam sinned in the Garden, the whole earth will be filled with His glory, and My Son will finally receive the glory that is due His name!" My brothers and sisters, that is

Chapter 2 — The Key of Theme

the most significant day in the history of the universe from God's vantage point!

Now, let me be quick to clarify for you that by this illustration, I'm not in any way trying to belittle the cross, minimize the blood of Christ, or trivialize that particular day in history when God made the unfathomable sacrifice of His Son for sinners like me and you! A thousand times: no! The finished work of Jesus Christ is so huge to me as a sinful human being that I absolutely have no words to describe my sense of wonder, awe, and gratitude! That day when the Lord Jesus Christ shed His blood on the cross to atone for our sin changed my eternal destiny! That day changed my citizenship! Because of that day, I was translated out of the kingdom of darkness and into the kingdom of His dear Son! So believe me: I'm all about that day—and can't say enough about it! But I also want to make sure we all understand that from God's vantage point, the day He watched His Son brutalized on that cross—as He listened to His Son cry out, "My God, My God, why hast thou forsaken me?"—was certainly not God's most looked-forward-to day!

KEY PRINCIPLE:

The most significant day in the history of the universe to God is the day the Lord Jesus Christ returns in all of His glory to set up His kingdom on the earth—when He will finally receive the glory that is due His name!

That, my friend, is the theme of the Bible! It is **Christ's Kingdom** Glory, or, the glory that will be Christ's when He establishes His kingdom on the earth! That's what the Bible is all about! Another way we could say it is: The theme of the Bible is **the Day of the Lord**.

The reason I gave the calendar illustration is to reveal how we typically think about the Bible. We spend a lot of time in 21st-century Christianity trying to tell people, "It's not about you!" And you know why we have to keep telling people that? It's because

37

The Keys of Bible Study

21st-century Christianity spends so much time teaching people *that it's all about them!*

Typically, we teach people that the theme of the Bible is salvation. In doing so, we'll explain to them that God loves them passionately, and He did what was necessary to prove it: by giving His only begotten Son to shed His blood to pay the price for their sin. And my brothers and sisters, truer words have never been spoken! And again, I'm as thankful for that reality as I can possibly be! But we must make sure we understand that God *actually* offered His Son in order to provide us the opportunity to be citizens in the kingdom over which the Lord Jesus Christ will rule and reign and receive His rightful glory! God graciously provided our salvation through the shed blood of Christ so you and I could be a part of His eternal kingdom, where we will worship Him and bring Him glory forever! Which means that even our salvation isn't, first and foremost, about *us*—it's about *Him!*

Let me tell you why that's such a big deal. If I'm coming to the Bible thinking that the Bible is all about man's salvation, and that salvation is, first and foremost, about *me*, that mentality is going to ultimately lead me to approach the Bible, the church, and the whole Christian life with some level of an entitlement mentality. This mentality will, for all practical purposes, cause me to function as if *God* exists for *me*—rather than *me* existing for *God*. It produces a mentality that unwittingly sends me into the Bible asking the question, "How can I position my life to receive the maximum blessing?" rather than, "How can I position my life to bring Christ the maximum glory?" Though those two statements sound similar, they are actually polar opposites! If I'm looking for how *I* can receive the maximum *blessing*, it fosters a mentality which sends me into the Bible to try to figure out how to **use God** to **please me**, rather than going to the Bible to figure out how I can **please God** so He can **use me**!

And perhaps it's here that we should remind ourselves of the prophetic warning of 2 Timothy 3:1-4, where God gives us His one-word description of the last days (the times in which we are

Chapter 2 — The Key of Theme

presently living!). He refers to them as *perilous!* (2Ti 3:1) He then goes on to list almost 20 different characteristics that make our times so absolutely *perilous*. And do you know what characteristic tops the list? He says it is that men are "lovers of their own selves" (2Ti 3:2). But who would have ever thought that the love of self would so engulf us in these last days that even when we read the Bible, it would cause us to see *ourselves* as the primary figure?

And again, that's what makes understanding the theme of the Bible so important! It keeps the focus on **Christ** and **His kingdom** and **His glory**—and off of **me**... and **my kingdom**... and **my glory**! So it's vitally important from the very outset that we understand that the Bible is all about that day at Christ's second coming, when He establishes His kingdom on the earth and finally receives the glory due His name! And God has found every way imaginable to emphasize and preach that theme through the entire Bible! From cover to cover, that's what the Bible is really all about!

If we look at the Bible from a chronological standpoint, we are brought back to what God revealed to us in Ezekiel 28 and Isaiah 14. In these chapters, we discover that God's record of history actually begins with a battle over a throne! It opens with the Lord Jesus Christ, in all of His majesty and glory, seated upon a throne; and Lucifer, the anointed cherub, declaring his desire to exalt his throne above Christ's, that he might be "like the most high" (Isa 14:13-14). When the Bible ends in the book of Revelation, it ends with somebody seated on a throne... and that somebody is none other than the Lord Jesus Christ, in all of His majesty and glory! And biblically, everything in between those two events is all about God the Father moving throughout history to put His Son on that throne, and Satan doing everything in his power not only to stop Him, but to put himself there! Which leads us to the...

KEY VERSES:

Revelation 11:5 And the seventh angel sounded; and there were great voices in heaven, saying, <u>The kingdoms of this world are become the kingdoms of our Lord, and of his Christ; and he shall reign for ever and ever.</u>

39

Philippians 2:9-11 Wherefore God also hath highly exalted him, and given him a name which is above every name: <u>That at the name of Jesus every knee should bow,</u> of things in heaven, and things in earth, and things under the earth; <u>And that every tongue should confess that Jesus Christ is Lord, to the glory of God the Father.</u>

Psalm 66:4 All the earth shall worship thee, [and shall sing unto thee; they shall sing to thy name. Selah.]

That's how the story of the Bible ends! All of these verses are pointing us to that time when our Lord Jesus Christ, in all of the fullness of His glory, splendor, and might will be ruling and reigning over all the kingdoms of the world and everybody everywhere will be bowing before the King of kings, confessing that He is Lord of lords, and singing His praise in ceaseless worship of His holy name! Hallelujah!

KEY UNDERSTANDINGS:

1. The number seven is a very significant number to God

As we begin to increase the seriousness of our study of God's word, we need to train our minds to recognize that the number seven in the Bible is very significant. The number seven is the number of completion and/or perfection in God's mind, which, of course, is reflected throughout creation, as well as throughout the Bible.

For example, there are seven days in a week. We, of course, call them Sunday, Monday, Tuesday, Wednesday, Thursday, Friday and Saturday. But when we get to Saturday, the **seventh day**, a week is perfectly complete. After the **seventh day**, the next day isn't the eighth day. God starts over with Sunday, the first day of the week.

Notice also, there are seven colors of the rainbow. They are, of course, red, orange, yellow, green, blue, indigo and violet. Once we get to violet, the rainbow is perfectly complete. There isn't an eighth color. The rainbow begins again with the first color... red!

And notice, also, there are seven notes in a musical scale. We often say that there are eight notes in the scale, but it actually pans out like this: the first note is C, the second is D, the third is E, the fourth is F, the fifth is G, the sixth is A and the seventh is B. But when we get to the so-called eighth note in the scale, the eighth note is not a new note! The eighth note in the scale is actually the first note... C! Likewise, we talk about there being 88 different keys which play 88 notes on a piano, and yet, in reality, there are actually only seven different notes. Because, again, in God's mind, seven is the number of completion and/or perfection.

Once you see the pattern of sevens established in creation, it becomes obvious that God wanted us to recognize the establishment of His pattern of sevens in His word!

2. The number seven is associated with key events in the Bible

For example:

- The first 34 verses of the Bible are really nothing more than the details regarding the seven days in what we sometimes refer to as the creative week. God created and made the earth and the universe as we know it in seven days.

- We all know that Noah brought the animals on the Ark by twos, but have you ever noticed that God told Noah to bring the clean animals onto the ark by sevens?

- Jacob served seven years for Rachel.

- In Egypt, you'll remember, there were seven years of plenty and seven years of famine.

- In the Book of Joshua, the children of Israel marched around Jericho seven days, and on the **seventh day**, they marched around it seven times, with seven priests, with seven trumpets leading the way.

- The candlestick in the tabernacle had seven branches.

- Solomon was seven years building the temple, and when it

The Keys of Bible Study

was completed there was a feast that lasted for seven days.

- Job had seven sons, and when the tribulation came into his life, his friends came and spent seven days in silence before they offered seven rams and seven bullocks.

- Naaman the leper washed in the Jordan seven times.

- On the day of atonement in Leviticus 16, the blood was sprinkled on the mercy seat seven times.

- God gave the children of Israel seven feasts.

- On the cross, Jesus spoke seven times.

- In the book of Acts, those in the early church were told to choose out seven men of honest character as the first deacons.

In the book of Revelation, the book that *completes* God's *perfect* revelation to man, it is addressed to seven churches in Asia Minor, from the seven Spirits before the throne. There are seven golden candlesticks. The Lord was holding seven stars in His right hand, and there were seven lamps of fire burning before His throne. There is a seven-sealed book, and a Lamb having seven horns and seven eyes. There are seven angels who sound seven trumpets. There are seven thunders. There is a beast with seven heads, a dragon having seven heads and seven crowns upon his heads. There are seven plagues, seven vials, seven mountains and seven kings. In all, the number seven appears 59 times in the book of Revelation!

Undoubtedly, there is something extremely significant God is wanting to show us about the number seven! But just what is it?

3. God works in history according to a pattern of seven sevens

One of the key things we learn about the God of the Bible and need to file in our understanding of Him is that He is very patterned— and works according to a pattern of seven.

a. God works according to a pattern of seven _DAYS_ (Exo 23:12)

42

Chapter 2 — The Key of Theme

When God laid out the law, Israel was to work six days and on the **seventh DAY** they were to enter a sabbath rest. On the eighth day, the counting started over, so it was actually the first day of a new week.

b. God works according to a pattern of seven _WEEKS_ (Lev 23:15-16)

In Leviticus 23:15-16, God told Israel to count seven sabbaths from Passover, so that Pentecost fell on the 50th day after the completion of **seven WEEKS.**

c. God works according to a pattern of seven _MONTHS_ (Lev 23:24)

In Leviticus 23:24, Israel was told to count six months, and in the **seventh MONTH** was held the Feast of Tabernacles, the Feast of Trumpets and the Day of Atonement.

d. God works according to a pattern of seven _YEARS_ (Lev 25: 1-6)

In Leviticus 25:1–6, God told Israel they were to work the land for six years, but then on the **seventh YEAR,** the land was to enter a sabbath rest.

e. God works according to a pattern of seven _WEEKS of YEARS_ (Lev 25:8-13)

In Leviticus 25:8-13, God established a pattern that after **seven WEEKS of YEARS**, or **7 X 7 YEARS**, or **49 YEARS**, the next year was the year of Jubilee. In that year, not only was the land to rest, but all debts were to be canceled, and all slaves were to be released.

f. God works according to a pattern of seven _DECADES_ (Dan 9:2; Jer 25:11-12)

43

God's judgment upon Israel in Babylonian captivity was a period of **seven DECADES**, or **7 X 10 YEARS**, or **70 YEARS**.

g. God works according to a pattern of seven _MILLENNIA_. (Gen 2:1-3; 2Pe 3:8)

And God working according to **seven MILLENNIA** is the key point that has to do with the theme of the Bible being **the day of the Lord** or **Christ's kingdom glory.** In the first seven days of the creative week recorded in Genesis 1 and 2, God was already pointing in the direction His word would take, as it specifically points to that time when the Lord Jesus Christ will receive the glory that is due His name in His millennial kingdom.

KEY EXAMPLES:

EXAMPLE #1:
The theme of the Bible observed through the record of the first seven days of the creative week.

As we make our way into Genesis 1, one of the things that becomes obvious is that the God of the Bible is very ordered, very patterned, and very structured. That is apparent simply by observing His record of the days of the week.

- Genesis 1:5: "And the evening and the morning were the **first day**."

- Genesis 1:8: "And the evening and the morning were the **second day**."

- Genesis 1:13: "And the evening and the morning were the **third day**."

- Genesis 1:19: "And the evening and the morning were the **fourth day**."

- Genesis 1:23: "And the evening and the morning were the **fifth day**."

- Genesis 1:31: "And the evening and the morning were the **sixth day**."

Chapter 2 — The Key of Theme

I think it's obvious through the first six days of the creative week that God couldn't be more patterned, ordered, and structured!

But then, when we come into Genesis chapter 2, we observe something very interesting as God gives us His record concerning the **seventh day!**

Thus the heavens and the earth were finished, and all the host of them. And on the **seventh day** God ended his work which he had made; and he rested on the **seventh day** from all his work which he had made. And God blessed the **seventh day**, and sanctified it: because that in it he had rested from all his work which God had created and made. (Genesis 2:1–3)

Do you see it? After meticulously laying out the pattern of "the evening and the morning" on the first, second, third, fourth, fifth, and sixth day in chapter one, all of a sudden we come to chapter two where God provides us with the record of the **seventh day**... and having already seen the biblical significance of the number seven, we find that something crazy happens on the **seventh day!** For some reason, the very patterned, ordered, and structured God breaks His pattern... His order... and His structure! When God does things like that in the Bible, it's typically to get our attention so that we slow things down and take a closer look! So let's do that!

Key things to notice about the record of the *seventh day:*

a. It was a day God *RESTED*_

Do you remember how God created and made everything in those first six days? How did He do it? He simply spoke them into existence, right? And with that being the case, would there be anybody anywhere who thinks that when God got to the **seventh day**, He suddenly thought to Himself, "Whew! That was rough! Speaking everything into existence has Me just plum tuckered out! I've been going hard all week—I need a day off! I'll tell ya what: tomorrow, I'm not doing anything but resting!" Is there anybody who thinks that's what actually happened?

45

b. It was a day that had *NO EVENING or MORNING*

Now, that's not to say that the **seventh day** didn't actually have an evening or morning—but it is to say that for some reason, in God's *record* of the **seventh day**, He purposely broke His pattern! Surely, we're not to think that the omniscient God of the Bible got thirty-something verses into His perfect revelation to man and just suddenly forgot the pattern of "the evening and morning" that He had so meticulously established in His record of the first six days! I mean, how could He possibly get to the **seventh day** and leave out such a significant detail... unless it was on purpose!

c. It was a day God *BLESSED*

Is that to say that the previous six days, for some reason, were not blessed? Obviously they were! But with the specific blessing attached to the **seventh day**, we'd have to ask, why is this **seventh day** so special to God? And the "blessedness" and "specialness" of the **seventh day** is only heightened when we see this next detail.

d. It was a day God *SANCTIFIED*

And, of course, the word *sanctified* means *set apart.* Think about that. The **seventh day** was *the day* God Himself specifically *set apart* for Himself. As God approached that **seventh day**, He said, "This is My day!" In light of Him sanctifying this day, perhaps we could say...

e. The seventh day is the *LORD'S DAY!*

It is *His* day. He chose to set apart that day for *Himself!*

What God is doing in Genesis 2:1–3 is giving us a glimpse into how He thinks—and thus, how He reveals truth in His supernatural Book. Because you see, when we take the details of this **seventh day**, and begin to compare them (1Co 2:10,13) with what God reveals throughout the remainder of the Bible in terms of the unfolding of human history, it gets very exciting!

Because God finds another very interesting way to get our attention

Chapter 2 — The Key of Theme

in another passage toward the end of the Bible. In 2 Peter 3:8, the Spirit of God inspires Peter to write, "But beloved, be not ignorant of this one thing..." Let's just stop there for a second. Maybe we could paraphrase that by saying, "Now, there may be some things in this book that you've missed along the way—but just make sure this one doesn't get added to the list! Be sure you don't miss this!" Oh, okay Peter, so what's this "one thing" we better be sure not to miss? Peter tells us: "...That **one day** is with the Lord as a **thousand years**, and a **thousand years** as **one day**!" Obviously, God is letting us know here that as God, He doesn't count time the way we do!

Now, that's clearly a very important truth, but somehow it doesn't seem to merit the fanfare of being that *one thing* we better be sure not to miss! Right?

However, if we were to take that little equation in 2 Peter 3:8 (one day = one thousand years) and plug it into the first time *days* are mentioned in the Bible in Genesis 1 and 2, what it would say to us, is that after 6000 years (each of the first six days X 1000), the following 1000 years (represented in the **seventh day**) would be...

1) A 1000 year period on this planet when God would _REST_ (Heb 4:3–5; Act 3:19–21)

2) A 1000 year period on this planet that has _NO EVENING or MORNING_ (Rev 20:1–5; 21:23)

3) A 1000 year period on this planet that is _BLESSED_ like no other period in history (Psa 29:2; Php 2:9–11; Psa 66:4)

4) A 1000 year period on this planet that God _SET APART_ for Himself

5) A 1000 year period on this planet known as _the LORD'S DAY_ or _the DAY of the LORD_

The Keys of Bible Study

Do you realize that from this point in the Bible (Gen 2:1-3), everything in it will be wrapped around that very THEME—and pointing to that very DAY! What DAY? *The SEVENTH Day!* That 1000 year *"day"* when our Lord Jesus Christ sits on His throne in Jerusalem ruling and reigning over all the earth in all of His splendor, majesty, wisdom, power and glory—and every knee is bowing, every tongue is confessing, and every heart is singing in worship to the King of kings and Lord of lords!

This is what the entire book of Psalms is about—not to mention the books of Isaiah, Jeremiah, Lamentations, Hosea, Joel, Amos, Zachariah, and on and on and on! They're all screaming about that **seventh day**, or that thousand year period... that *1000-year day* when our Lord Jesus Christ finally receives the glory that is due His name! No wonder Peter said, "But, beloved, be not ignorant of this <u>one thing</u>" (2Pe 3:8).

And man, does it ever get interesting when you take that "a day is as a thousand years" equation from 2 Peter 3:8 and start plugging it into some of the passages in the Bible that are rather familiar to us! For example...

We come toward the end of Matthew 16 where Jesus is teaching His disciples, and He says this in verse 27:

> For the son of man shall come in the glory of his Father with his angels… (Mat 16:27a)

This is the second coming of Christ... the day of the Lord... the day God blessed and sanctified (set apart) for Himself in Genesis 2:1–3! He's specifically talking about that very day that is the theme of the entire Bible!

Jesus continues in Matthew 16:27-28:

> For the son of man shall come in the glory of his Father with his angels; and then he shall reward every man according to his works. Verily I say unto you, [*and remember now, He's saying*

48

this around 33 AD!], There be some standing here, which shall not taste of death, till they see the Son of man coming in his kingdom.

Wait now. Say what? Are you kidding me? "Not taste of death, till they see the Son of man coming in his kingdom?" If that's true, do you realize that would mean that there must be some majorly old folks roaming around somewhere on this planet?! Because that was close to 2000 years ago, and He still hasn't come to set up His millennial kingdom!

And that's how the chapter ends! No clarification, and no further explanation. We're just left to think that there were actually people listening to Jesus on that day almost 2000 years ago who wouldn't die before being eyewitnesses of Christ's second coming.

As we come into the next chapter, the first two verses say,

> Jesus taketh Peter, James, and John his brother, and bringeth them up into an high mountain apart…And was transfigured before them: and his face did shine as the sun, and his raiment was white as the light. (Matthew 17:1-2)

Now, it's important to know that any time in scripture when Jesus reveals Himself for who He really is, He always shows up the same way—as blazing, blinding light! You see, He has always been the very glory of the Father; it's just that when He was born into this world, His glory was veiled, as it were, with His body of flesh. And what is happening here on the Mount of Transfiguration is that our Lord is simply pulling back the veil of His flesh, revealing who He really is, in all of His majesty and glory!

And then, verses 3-5 say:

> And, behold, there appeared unto them Moses and Elias talking with him. Then answered Peter, and said unto Jesus, Lord, it is good for us to be here: if thou wilt, let us make here three tabernacles; one for thee, and one for Moses, and one for

The Keys of Bible Study

Elias. While he yet spake, behold, a bright cloud overshadowed them: and behold a voice out of the cloud, which said, This is my beloved Son, in whom I am well pleased; hear ye him. (Mat 17:3-5)

In other words, "Peter, this really isn't a time you need to be talking. So why don't you just close your mouth for a second and listen to what My beloved Son has to say!"

Do you understand what's happening in this passage? Jesus takes Peter, James, and John—three of the men who just happened to be standing there at the end of chapter 16 when He talked about some being there who would not taste death until they saw Him coming in His kingdom—and do you know what it was they actually witnessed on the Mount of Transfiguration? They saw the Lord Jesus Christ, just as He will be revealed when He returns at His second coming to set up His kingdom!

And do you know *when* it was that Peter, James and John were witnesses of Christ's second coming? I purposely left the first part of Matthew 17:1 out earlier. Because do you know what it says? Check this out:

And <u>after six days</u> Jesus taketh Peter, James, and John his brother, and bringeth them up into an high mountain apart, (Mat 17:1)

This is the same pattern God established in Genesis 1 and 2! After six days (and since a day is as a thousand years: after 6000 years!), Peter, James and John saw Jesus come in the glory of His Father, to set up His millennial (or, 1000 year) kingdom... on the ***seventh day!***

And someone might say, "Well, how can you be so sure that this passage is really all about Peter, James and John being witnesses of Christ's second coming?" Well, that's actually not a matter of speculation or debate! Peter actually gives us the interpretation of what was happening in Matthew 17 on the Mount of Transfiguration! Peter himself says,

Chapter 2 — The Key of Theme

> For we have not followed cunningly devised fables, when we made known unto you the **power** and **coming** of our Lord Jesus Christ, but were eyewitnesses of his majesty. For he received from God the Father honour and glory, when there came such a voice to him from the excellent glory, This is my beloved Son, in whom I am well pleased. And this voice which came from heaven we heard, when we were with him in the holy mount. (2Pe 1:16-18)

Having been with Jesus on the holy mount, Peter claims that he was, in fact, an eyewitness of the second coming of Christ! And again, keep in mind, it happened after six days!

Now, someone might say, "Boy, Pastor Mark, I don't know about all of that, because in Luke's account of the transfiguration in Luke 9:28, it says,

> And it came to pass about an eight days after these sayings, he took Peter and John and James, and went up into a mountain to pray. (Luk 9:28)

"And notice here, the timing of the event isn't after six days, but is about eight days! I mean, hey Pastor Mark, doesn't that contradict your point about the timing of the these guys being eyewitnesses of the second coming after six days, which is representing 6000 years of human history?"

Well, I'm not a math whiz, but I do think I might be able to determine what number is after six and is about eight! Seven!

What I'm trying to get you to see is that we can't get past the second chapter in the Bible without God finding this crazy way to let us know how the plan is going to unfold! There will be 6000 years of human history, and then that final 1000 years, represented in the **seventh day**, will be **the day of the Lord!**

So, first of all, we see the theme of the Bible through the record of the first seven days of the creative week. But then...

The Keys of Bible Study

EXAMPLE #2:
The theme of the Bible observed through the identification of the ten men in the first genealogy.

I think most of us would agree that the most "boring" part of the Bible are the genealogies. (Wait. Are we allowed to say that?) And, of course, I jest, because we know the Bible is a supernatural book, and every single word was carefully chosen by none other than God Himself—and everything in His book is there for a reason! (Pro 30:5; 2 Pe 1:21) And man, the reason for this first genealogy is a doozy!

We just looked at how God opens His book and shows us this awesome thing about the day of the Lord, the theme of the Bible, in Genesis 1 and 2. We then get to chapter 3, and God shows us how the world we live in actually got so jacked up, by revealing to us our enemy (the serpent) and the details of how our first parents thrust the entire human race into sin. Then, in chapter 4, He shows us the deadly effects of sin in the world, as Cain murders his very own brother. And when we get to chapter 6, the entire chapter sets the context of Noah's day, which is very important, because Jesus lets us know that the world at the time of the second coming was going to look a whole lot like it did in the days of Noah (Mat. 24:37)! So, Genesis 6 is obviously a very significant chapter. But right in between the account of Cain and Abel in chapter 4 and Noah in chapter 6, God peels off a little space to do something weird in Genesis 5. The entire chapter (32 verses!), is nothing more than a genealogy! And what's interesting is that God spends more time detailing this genealogy than He did detailing the entire record of creation in Chapter 1!

As has already been mentioned, we know and believe that God is never random with anything He does in His book. Whatever is in His book is there for a very particular reason. And when it comes to determining God's reason for this rather elaborate genealogy through the lifespan of each of these men, we could do the math and figure out that there is actually a period of over 1400 years between Genesis chapter 4 and chapter 6, which is tremendously

52

Chapter 2 — The Key of Theme

important in terms of providing a biblical timeline. But why not just find some concise way to just tell us there is over 1400 years between these two chapters... right? I mean, why would God take 32 verses full of nothing but a bunch of names of some guys and how long they lived?

However, when we look at what the names of these ten key men in this genealogy actually mean, it begins to reveal something rather incredible!

First of all, let's identify the names of the ten men found in Genesis 5:1-32. I'll also identify the meaning of each of their names, because that's where this chapter becomes absolutely astounding!

The first man we meet, of course, is **ADAM**. His name means **MAN**.

The second man is **SETH**. His name means **APPOINTED**.

The third is **ENOS**. His name means **DESPERATELY WICKED**.

Fourth in the genealogy is **CAINAN**. His name means **POSSESSION**.

Fifth is **MAHALALEEL**. His name means **PRAISE OF GOD**.

Sixth is **JARED**. His name means **DESCENT**.

The seventh man is **ENOCH**. His name means **DEDICATED** or **TRAIN UP**.

The eighth man is **METHUSELAH**. His name means **MAN OF THE SWORD**.

The ninth is **LAMECH**. His name means **POWERFUL**.

The Keys of Bible Study 🔑

Then, the tenth man is **NOAH**. His name means **REST**.

And what becomes apparent as we begin to consider the meaning of the names of these ten men is that God isn't simply trying to communicate to us that there are 1400 years of human history between Adam and Noah. Again, that's significant, but what He's actually doing here **is providing us an outline of the entire history of man for his 7000 years on this planet!** Let me show you what I mean.

The first man, **ADAM**, meaning **MAN**...

Represents **CREATION**. And specifically, the **CREATION of MAN**. God did that in Genesis 1:26. He said, "Let us make man in our image after our likeness."

Then comes **SETH**, meaning **APPOINTED**.

He represents when **God APPOINTED man with his COMMISSION**. After God creates the man in Genesis 1:26, in the remainder of verse 26 on through verse 28, God APPOINTS man to have dominion over everything in the earth and in the sea, and He APPOINTS or COMMISSIONS him, along with his bride, to "be fruitful and multiply and to replenish the earth." That's his COMMISSION—that's what he was APPOINTED by God to do.

Next comes **ENOS**, meaning **DESPERATELY WICKED**.

Which, obviously, represents the **FALL of MAN**, since man's heart, because of his sinful choice, becomes just that—DESPERATELY WICKED! It is here that mankind, represented in Adam, loses the image of God and the ability to reproduce sons of God. Now all man has the ability to do is to reproduce sons of Adam; God reveals this in Genesis 5:3. After the FALL, "Adam... begat a son in his own likeness, after his image," which of course, was a fallen image. That's a problem!

54

Chapter 2 — The Key of Theme

But the next name, **CAINAN**, means **POSSESSION**.

And now, God is showing us the direction His plan is going to take, and how He will fulfill it. In Genesis 17, God enters into an unconditional covenant with a man by the name of Abram, or Abraham. But God said that covenant wasn't just with Abraham, but also with his seed after him—which, of course, was the nation of Israel. Listen to what God says to Abraham:

> And I will give unto thee, and to thy seed after thee, the land wherein thou art a stranger, all the land of Canaan, for an everlasting possession. (Genesis 17:8)

Through Abraham, God calls out the nation of Israel and promises them a possession. Back in Genesis 17:6, God told Abraham that "kings shall come out of thee."

So, make sure you grab the pieces here: God calls out the nation of Israel, and when you put the promise of a POSSESSION and a king into that equation, you begin to understand what God is trying to get us to see! This nation, or this POSSESSION, is going to produce the king who will rule in Israel, and all of the other Gentile nations of the world will come to Jerusalem to praise the God of Israel!

And you say, "Well, how did you make that connection?"

Quite coincidentally I'm sure, the next name in the genealogy is **MAHALALEEL**, meaning **PRAISE of GOD**.

1 Kings 10 is absolutely incredible! During the reign of Solomon, the nation of Israel is the **PRAISE of GOD**! All of the kings and queens of the Gentile nations are coming to bow their knee before the king of Israel—the son of David, seated upon his throne—and present him with gifts. And we find that MAHALALEEL represents the glory days of the nation of Israel—the time when they were, in fact, the PRAISE of GOD!

55

The Keys of Bible Study

But no sooner are we out of 1 Kings 10, before chapter 11 begins their DESCENT.

And again, quite coincidentally I'm sure, the next man in the genealogy is **JARED**, meaning **DESCENT**.

In 1 Kings 11, the nation of Israel begins a downward spiral of **DESCENT** that ultimately leads them to be taken into captivity in Babylon—and there is no more king in Israel! And once again, it looks like the plan of God isn't going to be able to be fulfilled. And there is a long period of silence where God doesn't speak *to* or *through* anyone for almost 400 years.

The next man in the genealogy is **ENOCH**, whose name means **DEDICATED** or **TRAIN UP.**

After those 400 silent years, all of a sudden, almost out of nowhere, a very **DEDICATED** man comes on the scene! In fact, Jesus said of this man,

> Among them that are born of women there hath not risen a greater than John the Baptist. (Matthew 11:11)

And John has some instruction for the nation of Israel. Or, in other words, he has some **TRAINING UP** that God has commissioned him to accomplish. John the Baptist comes on the scene saying:

> Repent ye: for the kingdom of heaven is at hand... Prepare ye the way of the Lord, make His paths straight. (Matthew 3:1-3)

And what is God's purpose in desiring John the Baptist to TRAIN UP the people? What is he actually preparing them for? He was getting them ready for the first coming of Christ, who we see represented in the next name in the genealogy.

Next up is **METHUSELAH**, meaning **MAN of the SWORD**.

We know what that SWORD is, right? Ephesians 6:17 tells us to

56

equip "the sword of the Spirit, which is the word of God."

John 1:1 says: "In the beginning was the Word, and the Word was with God, and the Word was God."

John 1:14 says: "And the Word was made flesh [or, became a man], and dwelt among us."

And the **MAN of the SWORD** was here! John 1:14 says that Christ came the first time full of grace and truth. But when He comes the next time, it's not going to be like that at all! Mark 13:26 says He's coming with great power and glory! Revelation 19:15 says that the MAN of the SWORD will then use that sharp SWORD that goes out of his mouth, to smite the nations! Peter referred to that time as "the power and coming of our Lord Jesus Christ" (2Pet. 1:16). Jesus referred to that time as "the kingdom of God come with power" (Mar 9:1).

And, of course, the meaning of the name of the next man in the genealogy, **LAMECH**, just happens to mean **POWERFUL**.

At the second coming of Christ, He comes in **POWER**, smites the nations, and puts His enemies under His feet. But do you know what happens next?

The next name in the genealogy, **NOAH**, meaning **REST**, provides a major clue!

The second coming of Christ will usher in a period of **REST** on the earth that we call the Millennium, which is the time when the kingdom has finally come, and our Lord Jesus Christ finally gets the glory that is due His name... and not only will the earth be at REST, but for the first time since man sinned in the garden, God is going to be at REST.

Are you seeing what God just did through the meaning of the names of the ten men in this first genealogy in the Bible? As only the omniscient God of the Bible could possibly do, He walks

The Keys of Bible Study

us step by step through the entire history of man on the earth—ending, of course, with the theme of the Bible! God RESTING on the SEVENTH DAY, or the DAY of the LORD! (Gen 2:2; 2Pe 3:8)

Do you think all of that is just a coincidence? Listen, I'll be the first to admit it—I am a man of very average intelligence. Do you think I could possibly have the ability to somehow spin the names in this genealogy to make them line up with every single thing the Bible reveals will happen through the annals of the 7,000 years of human history on this planet? There's not a chance!

What I'm wanting you to see is that in every way imaginable, the God of the Bible lets us know that the THEME of the Bible is about is His Son coming in His kingdom and finally receiving the glory that is due His name!

So not only do we see the THEME of the BIBLE through the first seven days of the creative week, but also through the ten men in the first genealogy in the Bible. But those aren't the only ways God lets us know his theme!

EXAMPLE #3:
The theme of the Bible observed through the witness of creation.

God has designed the universe in such a way so that every single day paints a picture which specifically points to the day of the Lord. Let me show you what I mean...

In John 9:5, Jesus made a monumental statement: "As long as I am in the world, I am the light of the world." It's obvious that Jesus is likening Himself to the sun. And, of course, His point is that what the sun is to the world physically, He is to the world spiritually.

Then, in Acts 1:9, Jesus is on a hillside giving final instructions to His disciples when all of a sudden, He began to ascend out of this world. In light of John 9:5, had we been on that hillside on that day,

Chapter 2 — The Key of Theme

we could have leaned over to someone next to us and said, "Hey, just in case you were wondering, there goes the light of the world!"

This is a very significant event, because it is at this very instant, as the light of the world went out, as it were, that we entered into what the New Testament refers to as the *night*. That's why Romans 13:12 says,

> The night is far spent, the day is at hand. (Romans 13:12)

And it's why 1 Thessalonians 5:5 says,

> Ye are all the children of light, and the children of the day: we are not of the night, nor of darkness. (1 Th 5:5)

Paul's point here is that as believers, we live in a spiritual nighttime, but we are not of the night, or of darkness. And that's why Paul says in Philippians 2:15:

> That ye may be blameless and harmless, the sons of God, without rebuke, in the midst of a crooked and perverse nation, among whom ye shine as lights in the world. (Php 2:15)

Do you know why He was careful to phrase it the way he did? He says that we "shine as lights in the world." This is because even though Jesus isn't physically on this planet, He is still "the true Light, which lighteth every man that cometh into the world" (Joh 1:9). The fact is that, though we are the only light the world presently has (Mat 5:14), we actually have no light of our own. In this biblical nighttime, we simply reflect the light of the Son.

Does that sound like anything you've ever heard of in creation? It sounds like the *moon* to me! Sometimes we'll talk about how brightly the moon is shining, but most of us realize that the moon isn't actually shining, because it has no light of its own! The moon is simply a dead rock that shines as a light in the midst of the darkness of the night by reflecting the light of the sun!

59

The same is true of us! Without the true Light, the Lord Jesus Christ, we have as much light to shine to the world as a dead rock! But our Lord has us here, in the dark nighttime of the Church Age, reflecting His light in the world until that glorious day when, once again, the Light of the world will dispel the spiritual and moral darkness of the night by rising in the eastern sky at His glorious second coming!

And do you realize that every 24 hours, this message gets preached by the witness of creation itself?

The very last chapter of the very last book of the Old Testament brings the whole message of creation together! Check this out...

> For, behold, the day cometh, that shall burn as an oven; and all the proud, yea, and all that do wickedly, shall be stubble: and the day that cometh shall burn them up, saith the Lord of hosts, that shall leave them neither root nor branch. (Malachi 4:1)

We can clearly see that this is none other than **the day of the Lord**! Our Lord describes this day in Malachi exactly the way the Apostle Paul delineated it in 2 Thessalonians 1:7–10! And our Lord continues His description of this day in Malachi, saying:

> But unto you that fear my name shall the Sun of righteousness arise with healing in his wings... (Mal 4:2)

And please don't allow yourself to just read over that! Did you catch how our Lord referred to Himself? He called Himself the **Sun** (capital S!) **of righteousness!** And did you hear what He said He is going to do on that day? He is going *arise* on this planet, and bring *healing* to the people in the last days of the tribulation period who fear His name!

So, it goes like this... We are presently living in what the Bible refers to as *the night*. But there is coming a time in the very near future when *the Sun of righteousness*, the Lord Jesus Christ, is going to rise in the eastern sky, and it will be *the day of the Lord!*

60

Chapter 2 — The Key of Theme

Creation itself has been preaching that message for the last 6000 years, because every day the evening (the night) gives way to the morning (the day), as the sun rises in the east. What an incredible reality that even creation itself preaches the very theme of the Bible on a daily basis!

Have you ever noticed what Paul says about creation in Romans 8?

> For we know that the whole <u>creation groaneth and travaileth</u> in pain together until now. And not only they [in other words, not just everything in creation], but ourselves also, which have the firstfruits of the Spirit [all of us who know Christ!], even we ourselves groan within ourselves, waiting for the adoption, to wit, the redemption of our body. (Rom 8:22-23)

What is it that creation is actually *groaning* and *travailing* about? It's groaning and travailing because of its longing for **Christ's kingdom glory!** It's groaning and travailing in anticipation of that time when everything in creation is brought back to its original condition before man thrust it into chaos and wickedness through his choice of sin! It's groaning and travailing for the "times of restitution of all things" (Act 3:21).

Paul goes on to say in verse 23 that, because we have the Holy Spirit living inside of us, we join creation in groaning and travailing because we are so filled with a passion and a longing to finally shed this vile, corruptible body of flesh. We long to finally experience the redemption of our body, to live for all eternity in a glorified body that is incapable of sinning, forever bringing Christ the glory that is due His name! And oh, I ask you, where are the believers in the 21st century who know firsthand this groaning and travail? Oh, my brothers and sisters, may we be filled with that kind of passion and longing for Christ's kingdom glory! May the theme of the Bible (and the theme of creation!) genuinely become the theme of our lives!

The Keys of Bible Study

EXAMPLE #4
The theme of the Bible observed through the preaching of all of the Old Testament prophets.

And yes, I did say *all* of the Old Testament prophets! And that, too, is not a matter of speculation or exaggeration! The Bible makes that abundantly clear in Acts 3:19-21. But before we actually look at these verses, please allow me to set their context.

As we come into Acts 3, it is very important to recognize that though our Lord had already ascended to the Father's right hand (Act 1:9-11), He was still offering the kingdom to the Nation of Israel through the preaching of the apostles. What unfolds in Acts 1-7 was a very interesting period of time in the history of Christianity, because what Acts 3:19-21 is about to show us is that if Israel would have presented to the Lord a national repentance, history would have looked extremely different than it has! (We will get into this in more detail when we talk about the DIVISION Key of Bible Study in the next chapter.)

When we reach Acts 3, Peter and John encounter the lame man who was asking for alms at the temple gate. This is the account where Peter says to him, "Silver and gold have I none; but such as I have give I thee." And, of course, what he had to give the man was healing! So Peter heals the man in the name of Jesus, and all the people see it and are amazed, as if Peter were some kind of god himself! So Peter clears off some space to make sure that everybody fully understood that the lame man had not been healed by anything but the power of Christ! As Peter comes to the conclusion of his message, notice that he is still offering the kingdom to Israel.

> Repent ye therefore, and be converted, that your sins may be blotted out, when the times of refreshing shall come from the presence of the Lord; And he shall send Jesus Christ, which before was preached unto you: Whom the heaven must receive until the times of restitution of all things... (Act 3:19-21a)

62

Chapter 2 — The Key of Theme

The *times of REFRESHING* and the *times of RESTITUTION of all things* are what happens when Christ establishes His kingdom! Everything gets put back the way it was in the garden. Everything goes back to it's rightful owner, the Lord Jesus Christ! Everything that is out of whack in the world begins to function properly. Everything that is wrong in the world is made right. That's what Peter is talking about here. He's talking about our King, the Lord Jesus Christ, returning to this planet to totally set it aright.

But watch this unbelievably significant concluding statement Peter makes about Christ's coming in the last part of verse 21:

> ...which God hath spoken by the mouth of <u>all his holy prophets since the world began</u>. (Act 3:21b)

Peter is letting us know that every single one of God's prophets throughout the annals of Old Testament history have actually been preaching about the second coming of Christ—even before He came the first time! Rather than preaching with a focus on the day of Christ's *birth*, at His *first coming*, all of God's holy prophets in the Old Testament were preaching about *the day of the Lord*—or, His *second coming!* The theme of their preaching was actually the theme of the Bible!

A great case in point is what Jude lets us know about the preaching of Enoch.

> And Enoch also, the seventh from Adam, prophesied of these, saying, Behold, the Lord cometh with ten thousands of his saints, (Jud 14)

First notice that Enoch was the seventh from Adam, and remember what we've already learned about the number seven in the Bible! And now let me ask you: do you remember anything about the Lord coming with ten thousands of His saints at His first coming? Absolutely not! Because this isn't a prophecy regarding the first coming of Christ; it's a prophecy regarding His second coming! Enoch was actually preaching about the second coming of Christ

The Keys of Bible Study

thousands of years before He came the first time!

When we go back into the ministries of Isaiah, Jeremiah, Ezekiel, Daniel, Joel and all the rest, we find that every last one of them were actually preaching about the day of the Lord! They were all preaching about what happens on that **seventh day**, that seventh thousand-year period we call the Millennium, which Peter describes as *the times of refreshing* and *the times of restitution of all things.* And Peter clearly lets us know that the theme of the preaching of all of the Old Testament prophets was the day of the Lord! In fact, it's referred to in the preaching and prophecy of the Old Testament over 800 times!

Let's look at the preaching of the prophet Zechariah.

Zechariah 12:3 says...   "And **in that day**..."
Zechariah 12:4 says...   "**In that day,** saith the Lord..."
Zechariah 12:6 says...   "**In that day**..."
Zechariah 12:8 says...   "**In that day**..."
Zechariah 12:9 says...   "And it shall come to pass **in that day**..."
Zechariah 12:11 says... "**In that day...**"
Zechariah 13:1 says...   "**In that day...**"
Zechariah 13:2 says...   "And it shall come to pass **in that day**..."
Zechariah 13:4 says...   "And it shall come to pass **in that day**..."

After all of these references to **that day**, the obvious question we have to ask ourselves is, "**What day?**" Zechariah answers that question in the first verse of the next chapter.

Zechariah 14:1 says...   "Behold, **THE DAY OF THE LORD** cometh..."

And after making sure everyone knew exactly the day to which he was referring, he then continues his verbal rampage.

Zechariah 14:4 says...   "And His feet shall stand **in that day** upon the mount of Olives..."
Zechariah 14:6 says...   "And it shall come to pass **in that day**..."

Chapter 2 — The Key of Theme

Zechariah 14:8 says... "And it shall be **in that day**..."
Zechariah 14:9 says... "And the Lord shall be king over all the earth: **in that day**..."
Zechariah 14:13 says... "And it shall come to pass **in that day**..."
Zechariah 14:20 says... **"In that day..."**

God has found every way possible to let us know that the theme of the Bible is **that day** when our Lord Jesus Christ returns to the earth to establish His kingdom and receive the glory He deserves!

EXAMPLE #5:
The theme of the Bible observed through the stories in the Old Testament and the songs in the book of Psalms.

We just looked at the repetition of the simple phrase *in that day* in the book of Zechariah, where Zechariah specifically lets us know he was using that phrase in reference to the day of the Lord! But one of the things we must train our brain to recognize in our study of the scriptures, is that nearly every time we find the phrases *in that day, on that day,* or *that day,* it is a reference to the theme of the Bible: the second coming of Christ!

And believe me, those phrases show up in some pretty strange places that we usually wouldn't otherwise associate with the second coming of Christ and the establishment of His millennial kingdom on the earth! But these phrases are what I like to refer to as biblical "icons." When we see them, they automatically alert us to the fact that the prophetic context of the passage is actually pointing to the day of the Lord. In other words, when we see these phrases, we recognize that God has chosen to strategically inject *that day* into the account, not only to refer to the specific day the event happened historically, but also to let us know that He is using it to paint a graphic picture of what will take place on this planet when Christ comes to the earth to receive the glory due His name!

For example, one of the most familiar stories of the entire Old Testament is found in Exodus 14. It is the infamous account of the

65

The Keys of Bible Study

miracle God performed at the Red Sea in delivering the children of Israel out of their bondage in Egypt. And I'm sure you remember in this story that Pharaoh and the armies of Egypt were in hot pursuit of the helpless and untrained children of Israel. The children of Israel had gotten as far as the Red Sea and had absolutely no idea what to do or where to go, when God miraculously parted the waters and they came through to the other side on dry land. When Pharaoh's armies followed suit, the waters fell upon them, and once and for all God had finally delivered His people out of their bondage in Egypt.

But as we're reading this account, we see this:

> Thus the Lord saved Israel <u>that day</u> out of the hand of the Egyptians; and Israel saw the Egyptians dead upon the sea shore. (Exo 14:30)

And God drops that little icon, as it were, into the text, alerting us to put our mental and spiritual brakes on and to start examining the passage in more detail—knowing that He is using it to picture **that day** when Christ comes back to the earth to establish His everlasting kingdom.

Recognizing that prophetic context of this passage, we start snooping around and all of the sudden the Spirit of God begins to open our eyes to what is being pictured here! We notice in verse 19 that it makes reference to *the angel of God*. This is a biblical phrase, along with the phrase *the angel of the Lord,* that is used to refer to an Old Testament appearance of the Lord Jesus Christ! (This will be key to your understanding of the Bible as well, so make a mental note of that! The *angel of God* and the *angel of the Lord* in the Old Testament are none other than appearances of the Lord Jesus Christ Himself!)

In verse 24, we notice that in Moses's record of the event, he also makes reference to "the morning watch." This is another key biblical phrase, because Jesus let us know that "the morning watch"

66

Chapter 2 — The Key of Theme

or "the fourth watch of the night" is when He would return to establish His kingdom glory on the day of the Lord (Mar 13:35, 6:48).

And interestingly enough, in this account of the parting of the Red Sea in Exodus 14, verse 24 also talks about "the pillar of fire." When Paul tells the Thessalonian church about the the day of the Lord, he talks about Christ coming "in flaming fire taking vengeance on them that know not God, and that obey not the Gospel of our Lord Jesus Christ" (2Th 1:8).

When we put all of the pieces of this story together, what we have prophetically in Exodus 14 is the Lord Jesus Christ appearing with flaming fire on behalf of the children of Israel... in the morning watch... at a time when the children of Israel's backs are against the wall... and they have nowhere to go... and don't know what to do... and the Lord Jesus Christ just absolutely annihilates their oppressors, just as He will at His second coming!

And again, these are some of the things that bring to light the supernatural quality of the Bible! I mean, how about a God who can so orchestrate the record of Old Testament history that it pictures the future fulfillment of the theme of the Bible?

We come to another little Old Testament story in Joshua 6—the historical account of Joshua and the battle of Jericho. As we get into the story, our attention is immediately drawn to the repetition of the number seven. I mean, it's hard to miss that there are *seven priests*, with *seven trumpets*, who march around the city of Jericho for *seven days*, and on the **seventh day**, they march around it *seven times*, and God gives Israel the victory over their formidable foe without the use of a single weapon!

Now, if we had not already connected this victory to what will happen on the **seventh day** when Christ comes to give the victory to Israel over their formidable foe at His second coming, in verse 15 God makes sure we don't miss it by injecting into the passage the *on that day* icon!

67

The Keys of Bible Study

> And it came to pass on the <u>seventh day</u>, that they rose early about the dawning of the day, and compassed the city after the same manner seven times: only <u>on that day</u> they compassed the city seven times. And it came to pass at the seventh time, when the priests blew with the trumpets, Joshua said unto the people, Shout; for the Lord hath given you the city. (Jos 6:15-16)

Sure, everything in this passage actually happened in history exactly as it is detailed in Joshua 6, but when God sets the context through the iconic phrase, *on that day* and *on the **seventh day***, we find that the story of Joshua and the battle of Jericho is actually a perfect picture of Jesus and the battle of Armageddon that will take place on the **seventh day,** also known as *the day of the Lord!* (Note that *Jesus* is actually the Greek rendering of the Hebrew name *Joshua!* And note that the name *Joshua* is also translated *Jesus* in Acts 7:45!)

Back in Joshua 6:4, we also find in this story of Joshua and the battle of Jericho the Ark of the covenant. The Ark is also an Old Testament picture that always represents the Lord Jesus Christ. When John sees the Lord Jesus Christ in Revelation 8, coincidentally enough, before Him are *seven angels* which have *seven trumpets.* And by the time the *seventh angel* blows the trumpet for the *seventh time,* it ushers in the **seventh day,** or *that day,* when our "Joshua," the Lord Jesus Christ, returns to the earth to defeat the enemies of Israel. Listen, y'all! You can't make this stuff up!

Let's talk about another biblical icon which points us to the **seventh day,** or the day of "rest" on this planet that we call the Millennium. Have you ever noticed the little word *Selah* that is periodically found in the Psalms?

Historically speaking, the placement of the word *Selah* in the Psalms (songs) denotes a rest in the musical score. However, from a prophetic standpoint, God strategically places that word in the scripture every time He wants to point us to that time when He and this entire planet will be at *rest!* Every time we find the word in scripture, it is always used to set the prophetic context to the

68

Chapter 2 — The Key of Theme

Lord's day of rest.

Let's take, for example, Psalm 3. Three times in this psalm, David includes the word *Selah*, denoting a rest in the music. We could also say that three times in this psalm, God identifies for us the prophetic context of the passage by injecting the word *Selah* into the text (3:2,4,8), pointing us to the thousand year day of rest when Christ returns at His second coming to establish His kingdom on the earth!

David begins in verse 1, saying:

Lord, how are they increased that trouble me! many are they that rise up against me. (Psa 3:1)

There is coming a time at the end of the tribulation period, as the previous psalm (Psalm 2) prophesies, when all of the nations of the world are going to converge on the tiny nation of Israel to wipe her off the map! And in that day, as David goes on to explain, there will be

...many which say of [Israel's] soul, There is no help for him in God. (Psa 3:2)

That will actually be the consensus of the whole world! But then comes the insertion of the word *Selah* into the text! God lets us know that just when it seems that all hope is lost and it looks like the nation of Israel doesn't have a prayer, He's suddenly going to turn their day of calamity into rest!

David then continues,

But thou, O Lord, art a shield for me; my glory, and the lifter up of mine head. 4 I cried unto the Lord with my voice, and he heard me out of his holy hill. Selah. (Psa 3:3-4)

Another rest! David picks back up in verse 5 saying:

69

I laid me down and slept; I awaked; for the Lord sustained me. 6 I will not be afraid of ten thousands of people, that have set themselves against me round about. 7 Arise, O Lord; save me, O my God: for thou hast smitten all mine enemies upon the cheek bone; thou hast broken the teeth of the ungodly. 8 Salvation belongeth unto the Lord: thy blessing is upon thy people. Selah. (Psalm 3:5-8)

Hallelujah! The nation of Israel will be blessed with supernatural deliverance, as the Lord Jesus Christ comes out of heaven and destroys their enemies and gives them rest!

We find another beautiful example of God's usage of the word *Selah* in Psalm 9:

Arise, O Lord; let not man prevail: let the heathen be judged in thy sight. Put them in fear, O Lord: that the nations may know themselves to be but men. Selah. (Psalm 9:19-20)

Are you already seeing it? At the end of the tribulation period, all of the heathen nations are going to be assured that they are going to prevail against Israel, and the Lord will indeed "arise" from His throne in the third heaven and come to this earth in judgment against them, showing that He is God, and they are merely men! And at that point the Lord will establish His thousand year day of rest.

We find that the God of the Bible just keeps using every way possible to let us know that His word is really all about is His Son getting the glory that is due His name, that He won't receive until He returns at His second coming to usher in the everlasting kingdom!

KEY TAKEAWAY:

In terms of studying the Bible, understanding the "big picture" is absolutely essential before we ever begin the tedious work of breaking it down into understandable individual pieces. The reality

Chapter 2 — The Key of Theme

is that we'll never really end with a proper biblical interpretation of any book of the Bible, or any particular passage, or any individual verse for that matter, if we don't begin with a biblical understanding of its theme. Without understanding God's emphasis on Christ's kingdom glory throughout the Bible, we will invariably turn the spotlight of scripture upon ourselves (2 Ti 3:2; Php 2:21).

And yet, as important as this key of Bible study is—and obviously, I must think it's tremendously important since I just devoted an entire chapter to it and positioned it as the very first key—there is a takeaway from this chapter that I believe is even more important than the key itself! It is this:

Until Christ's kingdom glory becomes the passion and theme of our lives, we will totally miss the point of the Bible, our salvation, and thus, the purpose for our very existence.

You may need to go back and read that paragraph again! But recognize that Christ's kingdom glory will never be observed as the *theme of our life* without us first observing it as the *theme of the Bible!* It simply will not happen apart from the transforming power of the word of God. That's why we must know the keys of Bible study like we know the back of our hand! And we only have nine more keys to learn!

THE KEY OF DIVISIONS

As we were talking about the first key of Bible study in the previous chapter, we learned that the beginning place for understanding the word of truth is to establish the theme of the author. Many students of the Bible allow themselves to get biblically disoriented from the very outset by the simple fact that they really don't understand the overarching message God is seeking to communicate to us through His book.

As we sought to examine the Bible from 30,000 feet in the previous chapter, it became obvious that God is purposely and passionately seeking to make clear to us that His book is really all about Christ's kingdom glory. From Genesis to Revelation, God's passion and intention is to get His Son on His throne in Jerusalem, ruling over all the kingdoms of this world with every knee bowing and every tongue confessing that Jesus Christ is Lord to the Father's own glory! That, my friend, is what the Bible is about! It's not about *us;* it's about *God!* Now, in this chapter, we're going to look at...

The second key of Bible study:
MAKE THE RIGHT DIVISIONS.

Have you ever asked yourself why so many people who claim to be Christian believe so many different things that all come out of

The Keys of Bible Study

the same book? I mean, how is it possible that people who claim to know God and believe the Bible, can interpret it so divergently?

For example, some people dogmatically assert that the biblical day of worship is on Saturday, and they can take you to verses that certainly *look* like that is the day God ordained for us to worship Him! Others are just as dogmatic that the biblical day of worship is Sunday... and they can take you to verses that give every indication that that's the case!

Some say speaking in tongues is for today, and they have passages and verses they point to which cause them to believe the issue is completely clear biblically! Other people say speaking in tongues is definitely *not* for today—and they have their string of verses to prove their position!

When it comes to whether or not a person can lose their salvation, again, people will take you to verses that would certainly appear to say we *could*—and yet, others can take you to different verses that would give every indication that we *couldn't!*

And we could go through any number of other doctrines in the Bible and find these same kind of opposing viewpoints. So what are we to make of all of this? I mean, how are we to reconcile what appears to be very significant doctrinal discrepancies in God's word and God's people?

This is exactly why it is imperative that we learn how to use the Division Key of Bible study. The reason we can often go to verses that look like they're teaching one thing but are teaching something completely different is because of a violation of the biblical principle of **making the right divisions.** That's what this chapter is designed to teach: how to make the right divisions in our study of God's word.

<u>KEY VERSE</u>: 2 Timothy 2:15

"Study to show thyself approved unto God, a

74

Chapter 3 — The Key of Divisions

workman that needeth not to be ashamed, RIGHTLY DIVIDING the word of truth."

<u>GENERAL OBSERVATIONS</u> Regarding 2 Timothy 2:15:

Let's begin by simply making some GENERAL OBSERVATIONS from the things we see in this verse.

NEGATIVE OBSERVATIONS:

1. It is possible to be <u>DISAPPROVED</u> of God when it comes to the word of truth.

This is vitally important for us to understand. Paul tells us that when it comes to God's word of truth, it is possible for us to be very disappointing to God, and to actually be "disapproved" of Him when it comes to what we think we're gleaning out of it!

2. It is possible to be <u>ASHAMED</u> before God when it comes to the word of truth.

And we know that, because He tells us in this verse what to do so we are *not* ashamed!

3. It is possible to <u>WRONGLY DIVIDE</u> the word of truth.

And, of course, we know that because Paul specifically instructs us to divide it *rightly!* One of the ways the word of truth is wrongly divided in the last days is by not even recognizing that there are *divisions* in His book!

The reason it's important to note these **negative observations** is because we're living at a time in history that if someone stands up on Sunday morning or in some other teaching environment and is speaking from the Bible, people just automatically assume that what he's saying is true because, after all, it's coming out of the

75

Bible! That is precisely why it's so important for us to understand that it's possible to be disapproved of God... it's possible to be ashamed before Him... and it's possible to wrongly divide the word of truth!

POSITIVE OBSERVATIONS:

1. To be approved of God and not ashamed requires STUDY.

In the 21st century, we do good to just get people to *read* the Bible! But God says that if we are going to be approved of Him, and not ashamed before Him, it's going to require study!

2. To be approved of God and not ashamed requires WORK.

Again, one of the reasons we have such difficulty with doctrine in the last days is because to get into the word of God and actually cull out what God is saying requires that dirty, nasty, four-letter word... work! It requires employing good study habits, which is a lot of work!

3. To be approved of God and not ashamed requires making RIGHT DIVISIONS.

It's very important not only to recognize there are divisions in God's word, but also to learn the biblical keys God has provided for us so we can *rightly divide* it! And that, of course, is the purpose of this chapter.

KEY THOUGHTS:

#1 A common error made by many students of the Bible is believing that the Bible is a Christian book.

And you may be thinking right now, "Did I read that correctly? Did

Chapter 3 — The Key of Divisions

that say one of the 'errors' students of the Bible make is thinking that it is a 'Christian book?'" Yes, you read it correctly! Because, actually, in the strictest sense of the word...

Christianity is a 2,000-year parenthetical in a book revealing the plan and working of God covering a 7,000 year period of time.

In the previous chapter, we saw that God told us through Peter that there is "one thing" of which we must not be ignorant, and it is this: that with our Lord, *"a day is as a thousand years"* (2Pe 3:8). And we saw that if we took that biblical equation (one day = one thousand years), and we applied it to the seven days revealed in Genesis 1 and 2, it would indicate that God's plan for human history is that it is a 7,000 year period (one day = 1000 years X 7 = 7000 years), of which the last 1000 years is "the day of the Lord". In other words, it is that specific thousand-year day to which the whole Bible is pointing. So, if we're going to come to the word of God and really understand how God has laid it out, we must understand that there is a 2000 year period of time where He deals with "Christianity"—but there is another 5000 years the Bible details that is not specifically "Christian" (4000 years of the Old Testament, plus 1000 years for *the day of the Lord*). Making that distinction is absolutely crucial to making right divisions in the word of truth! And you'll understand that in more detail as we continue in this chapter.

#2 All of the Bible is written <u>FOR</u> you, but not all of the bible is written <u>TO</u> you.

You may need to go back and read that statement again very slowly, and think about it for just a second.

Perhaps an illustration can help make the point. Let's say, for example, you shared with me some of the personal struggles you were going through, and in response, I said: "Hey, I'd like for you come over to my house, because I want to share with you a letter I received from my grandfather not long before he died, because with what you're dealing with in your life right now, I really believe that some of the wisdom my grandfather put in this letter will help you!"

77

The Keys of Bible Study

So you come to my house and start reading through the letter, and you get down to the bottom of it where it talks about the fact that upon my grandfather's death, he is bequeathing to me $10 million. And all of a sudden, you look at me and say, "Hey! When do we collect our $10 million?" And, of course, I'm gonna say, "I was just letting you read this letter so you could glean from my grandfather's wisdom for your situation! But this letter was addressed to me! So that promise of the $10 million... that wasn't intended for you! I'm just letting you letting you benefit from what he wrote to me!"

And in that same way, when it comes to the Bible, we have to understand which parts are written **to us**, and what part is written to **somebody else**! That's what we're talking about when we're talking about "rightly dividing the word of truth." Again, make sure you understand that **all of the Bible is written <u>FOR</u> you, but not all of the Bible is written <u>TO</u> you.**

Now, when some people hear that, they'll contest, "But doesn't the Bible tell us in Hebrews 13:8 that Jesus Christ is the same yesterday, today and forever?" And yes, it most certainly does! And it means exactly what it says! Our Lord Jesus Christ absolutely does not change! We can bank on the fact that He is immutable (Heb 6:17-18). But make certain you recognize that though He does not change, the way He deals with people does.

If we take our Bible and open it to the table of contents, do you know what we discover right from the get-go? We see God has actually laid out the Bible with at least two key *divisions.* The first division is what is called the Old Testament, and, of course, the second division is what is called the New Testament. And just the simple fact that one is called "old" and one is called "new" makes it quite obvious that God deals with people differently in one testament as opposed to the other. And because He does, we must make certain in our study of the Bible that we make a clear distinction ("division") between the Old and New Testaments. Now, I know that's very basic, but as basic and as obvious as it is, I'm not so sure that the ramifications of this principle are actually understood by many Christians today!

78

Chapter 3 — The Key of Divisions

But even people who clearly see and observe the significance of the division between the Old and New Testaments often fail to recognize that there are also key divisions within the New Testament itself! In Hebrews 9:15-17, God gives us a "blockbuster principle" when it comes to making right divisions in the New Testament. He tells us this...

> And for this cause he is the mediator of the new testament, that by means of death, for the redemption of the transgressions that were under the first testament, they which are called might receive the promise of eternal inheritance. For where a testament is, there must also of necessity be the death of the testator. For a testament is of force after men are dead: otherwise it is of no strength at all while the testator liveth. (Hebrews 9:15-17)

Now, in these verses, you'll notice He talks about the *first testament*. The *first testament*, of course, would be what we now commonly refer to as the Old Testament. But notice in this passage that the *first testament* is set in contrast to what He refers to as the *new testament*. What many people fail to realize in these verses is that God very specifically and dogmatically wanted us to factor into our understanding and interpretation of the Bible that **the New Testament wasn't actually put in force until the death of Christ!** Don't allow that principle to escape you! Observing and implementing it in our study of the Bible will be one of the key differences between rightly dividing the word of truth and wrongly dividing it! Perhaps the principle could be best explained this way...

By the time most people in our culture turn 50, they've gone to an attorney to craft a legal document known as a last will and testament. It's a binding document that basically says, "This is what I want to happen with all my stuff when I die." But one of the key factors concerning that last will and testament is that it sits under lock and key and isn't actually put in force until *after we die*. We must die in order for that testament to be enforced. And in that same way, Hebrews 9:15-17 provides for us a...

79

The Keys of Bible Study

KEY PRINCIPLE:

A testament is not a testament until the death of the testator.

The testator, of course, is the one who has written the testament, or the one to whom the testament is actually referring. The reason this is such a key principle in terms of our study of the Bible is because it lets us know that even though there is a clear division between the Old and New Testaments, there are also clear divisions that need to be observed *within* the New Testament itself! We must be very careful to recognize where the *death of the testator* actually takes place in the New Testament. The reality is, though we consider the Gospels (Matthew, Mark, Luke and John) to be part of our "New Testament", in the strictest and most biblical sense, according to the principle of Hebrews 9:15-17, the "New Testament" is not actually the "New Testament" until the death of Christ... the testator!

What that means in terms of **making the right divisions** is that as we're working our way through the Gospels, we must recognize that up until the death of Christ (which doesn't actually happen until the last few chapters in each of the Gospels), there is something very Jewish taking place! Those chapters preceding Christ's death have to do with a kingdom that the Lord was offering to the nation of Israel. And though God is most definitely making a transition from law to grace in the Gospels, in many ways He is still operating with the Jews according to an "Old Testament economy." We are going to go into much more detail about that; in fact, most of the remainder of this chapter will be reserved for that purpose. But for now, allow the Spirit of God to begin to infuse your thinking with this key principle from Hebrews 9:15-17: **A testament is not a testament until the death of the testator.**

Hopefully, it's beginning to become more and more apparent that there are obvious divisions in the word of God! If we don't recognize them and skillfully apply them in our Bible study, we will find ourselves in the midst of a breeding ground for false doctrine. We'll find ourselves going into parts of the Bible and believing

80

things we shouldn't believe, but feel completely justified believing, because it appears we have verses to support our belief! But the problem is that we're reading verses that aren't written *to* us, and yet we're ignorantly and indiscriminately trying to make them *apply to us,* because we didn't recognize the clear divisions God has made in His word. But don't miss this: any time we go into a portion of scripture that's *not addressed to us* (i.e. when we're reading letters written to somebody else!) and we're trying to make them *apply to us,* bank on this: it will become a hothouse environment for breeding for false doctrine. This is the key reason so many in the last days believe so many different things, even though we use the same book.

KEY EXAMPLES:

The books of MATTHEW, JAMES and HEBREWS.

As you look at this list of New Testament books, do you recognize anything in particular all of them have in common? It's simply this: though all three of them are found in our New Testament, they are all written to Jews.

Let's talk, first of all, about The Gospel According to Matthew. As you know, there are four Gospels, but do you know that each of them are written to different groups of people for the purpose of presenting Christ in four different ways, each specific to that particular group of people? The Gospel of Mark was written to Gentiles to present Christ as a Servant. The Gospel of Luke was written to Greeks to present Christ as a Man. The Gospel of John was written to the world to present Christ as the Son of God. But the Gospel of Matthew is the Gospel written to the Jews, to present Christ as the King—specifically, the King of the Jews. Because of that, one of the greatest breeding grounds of false doctrine for those of us who call ourselves Christians is the Gospel of Matthew. Do you know why that is? It's because we're reading somebody else's mail, and we don't even realize it! Sure, it's written for us, but it's not written to us! It's written to the *Jews* for the purpose of presenting Christ as the *King of the Jews!*

81

The Keys of Bible Study

Secondly, we come to the book of James. The first verse of the book of James says something tremendously significant! It says: "James, a servant of God and our Lord Jesus Christ, to the twelve tribes which are scattered abroad…" Okay, let me ask you a simple question... which tribe are you from? Unless you're a Jew, you're not from one of the twelve tribes James is addressing! So, what that tells us in the very first verse of this book is that once again, we're reading somebody else's mail. And the false doctrines some people get into by trying to apply to themselves truths that God clearly intended for Jews who make up the twelve tribes of Israel is nothing short of astounding! And once again, it's a classic case of not recognizing that this is a book of the Bible that is written *for* us—so there's a tremendous amount we can apply *practically*—but because it's not written *to* us, we must be very careful about what we're applying **doctrinally.**

The third example of a New Testament book written to Jews is the book of Hebrews. You would think that would go without saying since the very title of the book is *Hebrews,* and yet most students of the Bible look completely past it, not realizing the very title of the book lets them know it's not addressed to them.

Once again, recognizing that this is a book of the Bible written specifically to *Hebrews,* we must exercise extreme caution not to build our doctrinal framework as *Christians* living in the church age off of a book that's not even addressed to us! That just makes good, logical sense—but again, many people have never factored that key principle into their study of the Bible.

When we step back from the New Testament and look at it as a whole, there are four books that are a hothouse environment for false doctrine. Three of them are the ones we just talked about: Matthew, James, and Hebrews. As has been clearly stated, these are books written *for* us; they just don't happen to be written *to* us. That doesn't mean there aren't incredible principles and concepts in them that we can apply to our lives practically... it just means we're going to have to exercise extreme caution in these books—lest we step out of bounds doctrinally—because they are written to Jews,

Chapter 3 — The Key of Divisions

not the church. In terms of our Bible study, always keep that key detail in mind: we aren't Jews... we are the church! And God deals differently with Israel than He does the church.

These books which are written to the Jews that happen to be found in our New Testament also include another very interesting component. After the church has been removed at the rapture and the world is brought into the seventieth week of Daniel's prophecy (that last week of years remaining in Daniel's prophecy that we refer to as the Great Tribulation), these three books will also have a very unique application to Jews alive at that time.

At the beginning of the tribulation period, the Antichrist will appear on the scene and through his miraculous powers and dazzling diplomacy, he will be successful in deceiving the whole world that he is the Christ, or the Messiah (Rev 12:9). But halfway into the tribulation, the Antichrist is going to go into the Temple and sit down on the throne, purporting himself to be God (2Th 2:4). He will then make an idol (image) of himself, and command that the whole world bow down in worship to him (Rev 13:15). But if there's one thing that Israel has learned throughout the millennia, it's that God isn't very fond of idolatry. And buddy, when the Antichrist makes that image of himself and commands people to worship it, the eyes of the Jews are immediately going to be opened to the fact that despite his miraculous power, he is not the Christ! That's why Jesus told the Jews in Matthew 24:15 that when they see the "abomination of desolation" take place (which is the biblical terminology for this reprehensible act of the antichrist coming into the Temple and posing as Christ!), they better run for the hills... literally! (Mat 24:16) They'll run into the mountainous region of Petra, and there God will feed them the same miraculous way He fed them in the wilderness after delivering them from their bondage in Egypt.

And again, what's interesting about these New Testament books written to Jews is that when the eyes of the Jews are opened during the tribulation period and they understand that this charismatic and powerful guy who has united the world isn't *the* Christ, but

83

is rather the *Antichrist*, do you know what they'll be able to do? They'll be able to pick up a Bible, and much to their surprise, they'll find that there are books in the New Testament that are actually written *to them,* and they'll begin to read these books (namely Matthew, James and Hebrews) and find that they provide all the biblical instruction they need for approaching the last three and a half years of the tribulation period! These three books contain that unique prophetic application.

So, the books of Matthew, James and Hebrews are three of the four books that have been and will be a breeding ground for false doctrine in the church age. But there is one other key New Testament book that also poses some major doctrinal miscues.

ANOTHER KEY EXAMPLE:

The book of ACTS.

Now, I want you to think with me about the placement of the book of Acts in our New Testament. It begins with Matthew, Mark, Luke and John… the four Gospels. Next is the book of Acts—and then, of course, we come to the book of Romans. And the book of Romans in the lineup of New Testament books is very significant, because it's the first one that is written to a Christian church. It also opens up a section of letters in our Bible that the Apostle Paul wrote to churches and pastors of churches.

But have you ever considered the dilemma we'd have if we didn't have the book of Acts, or if the book of Acts wasn't placed exactly where it is in our New Testament? Do you understand what a big deal it would be if our New Testament just went from the four Gospels straight into the book of Romans?

Let me take you back to a very significant dialogue our Lord was having with His twelve disciples in Matthew 10. And notice that the passage begins, "When [Jesus] had called unto him his twelve disciples…" And though they had already been following Him and

Chapter 3 — The Key of Divisions

were being discipled by Him for some time, it is at this time our Lord gives them power against unclean spirits, to cast them out, and to heal all manner of sickness and disease. In this particular passage, He is giving them apostolic power. And He's doing that because He's about to send them out!

After referring to them as the "twelve **disciples**" in verse 1, verse 2 turns right around and says: "Now the names of the "twelve **apostles** are these..." Do you know what the word *apostle* means? It means *sent one*, or *one who is sent*. And it is this spot in the New Testament that the twelve *disciples* begin to be referred to in scripture as the twelve *apostles*, because it is at this point that Jesus sent them out. Notice, after listing their names in verses 2-4, verse 5 says: "These twelve Jesus **sent forth**..."

But notice this monumental thing Jesus tells the apostles as He sends them forth:

Go not into the way of the <u>Gentiles</u> and into any city of the <u>Samaritans</u>, enter ye not. (Matthew 10:5b)

Wow! Jesus told his apostles not to go to the Gentiles or the Samaritans. And then in contrast, he tells them where to go instead:

But go rather to the lost sheep of the house of <u>Israel</u>. (Matthew 10:6)

In other words, Jesus is saying: "I'm sending you out, but I want to be very clear—I want you going exclusively to the Jews! I don't want you to go to the Gentiles, and I don't want you going to the Samaritans (those who are half Jew and half Gentile)! I want you going specifically to the nation of Israel!"

And then in verse 7, He says: "And as ye go, preach, saying, The **kingdom of heaven** is at hand."

Now, the fact that you're reading this book is a good indication that you have a testimony of salvation. And if you are indeed born

The Keys of Bible Study

again, it was because you responded in obedience to the message of the gospel that Paul declared in 1 Corinthians 15:3-4. But do recognize this: if you're saved, do you know what message you *didn't* respond to? You *didn't* respond to the "kingdom of heaven" message Jesus sent forth the apostles to preach to the lost sheep of the house of Israel! That's why Matthew 10:1-6 is such a significant passage! Though we were most definitely *lost,* we have never been *the lost sheep of the house of Israel!* And the message that saved us was not the *kingdom of heaven* message that was being preached to Israel in the early part of the first century!

At this point, make sure you take away from this passage two key things: 1) The apostles were sent forth at this time exclusively to *the lost sheep of the house of Israel*; and, 2) They were to preach a *kingdom of heaven* message. Neither of these has anything to do with us as Gentiles or the church!

It's important to realize that the essence of the four gospels is really all about that: a *kingdom of heaven* message being delivered to *the lost sheep of the house of Israel.* That's why, as we were talking about earlier, it is so vital to our understanding to know when the New Testament actually kicks in. Remember, it doesn't really begin until *the death of the testator.* But prior to that, the New Testament is first and foremost a *Jewish* thing... and secondly, and yet just as foremost, it is a *kingdom* thing! And what's notable is that nowhere in any of the four Gospels does our Lord Jesus Christ ever redirect the apostles to a different *audience* or to a different *message!*

With that understanding, let's pretend for a second that the book of Acts isn't in our New Testament. We would go from Matthew, Mark, Luke, and John right into the book of Romans. I don't know if you know this or not, but the Romans just happen to be Gentiles!

So without the book of Acts, we would come out of the four Gospels into this letter written to Gentiles who comprised the church at Rome, and who had responded to a completely different message than the apostles were told to preach to the nation of Israel—and we wouldn't have the slightest clue as to how we got there! It would make absolutely no sense! And that, my friend, is one of the key reasons the book of Acts is in our Bible, and it is the key reason it's placed *where it is* in our Bible: to show us how we got from Matthew 10:5-6 to the book of Romans!

So, if we are going to rightly divide the Bible, one of the key books we must understand is the book of Acts! But to understand the book of Acts and how to rightly divide it, there are some key things we're going to have to understand about this book. Because, you see, there is a very specific key in the book of Acts that is paramount to understanding it! We'll talk about that key in just a bit. But first, let's talk about the book of Acts in a general sense. There are two key things we must make sure we understand about the book of Acts.

TWO IMPORTANT FACTS ABOUT THE BOOK OF ACTS

1. The book of Acts is not a doctrinal treatise regarding church theology. It is a historical account of the <u>acts</u> of the <u>apostles</u>.

And hence the name! The title of this book isn't really The Book of Acts. The actual title of this book is The Acts of the Apostles. What that shows us is that the book of Acts is actually a history book. It is a historical account of the *acts* of the apostles. It is not, first and foremost, a doctrinal book!

You may be thinking, "Well, what about 2 Timothy 3:16? Because doesn't it say that all scripture is given by inspiration of God and is profitable for doctrine?" And sure, the book of Acts is most definitely profitable for doctrine! But God was very careful to let us know before we can even get into the very first verse of the book of Acts, that though this book is profitable for doctrine, that *isn't* its primary intent! The primary intent is to provide the history of what took place after Jesus ascended to His Father, up to and including the establishment of Gentile churches.

87

And let me provide a key example. Let's say that we were going to go (as some denominations do) to the book of Acts to get the most important doctrine of all—our doctrine concerning salvation! Now, does the book of Acts provide doctrine concerning God's plan of salvation? Sure it does! It actually provides ten of them! So, while we could ask, "Can we get our doctrine of salvation from the book of Acts?" a better question would be, "Which doctrine of salvation in the book of Acts are we going to follow?" Because I can assure you, since our eternal destiny is determined by it, we definitely don't want to follow the wrong one!

Can we go into the book of Acts to get doctrine, or teaching? Absolutely! Because the book of Acts is most definitely *scripture* that was given to us by *inspiration of God*—so as 2 Timothy 3:16 tells us, it must be *profitable for doctrine!* But we also need to be keenly aware that if we're just leisurely strolling through the book of Acts and we indiscriminately start grabbing doctrine for the church or for our lives without making proper divisions—oh buddy, we're going to get ourselves into a whole heap of trouble doctrinally. And the reason why is the second thing that we need to understand about the book of Acts...

2. The book of Acts is a transitional book.

Where the book of Acts begins in Acts 1 and where it ends in Acts 28, is as far as the east is from the west! There is a major transition God is making in this book! Actually, there are seven significant transitions that are taking place in the book of Acts of which we must be keenly aware!

SEVEN KEY TRANSITIONS IN THE BOOK OF ACTS

The first one, we've already discussed, is that the book of Acts transitions us...

1. From the four GOSPELS to ROMANS.

As we study the actual instruction and teaching found in the four gospels and compare it to the instruction and teaching found beginning in the book of Romans, it is more than apparent that something significant has changed! Without the book of Acts strategically placed between the four Gospels and the book of Romans, it would be impossible to ever understand what had happened, and why!

2. From an OLD TESTAMENT structure to a NEW TESTAMENT structure.

This transition is made because the testator has died and ascended to the Father, putting the New Testament into action, or *force*.

3. From God working primarily with the JEW to God working primarily with the GENTILE.

The book Acts is also the book of the Bible that lets us know how it is that we went from Jesus specifically saying "don't go to the Gentiles, but to the Jews," to Paul writing specific instructions to Gentile believers in the church in Rome!

4. From God's base of operations being in JERUSALEM to His base of operations in ANTIOCH.

In the early chapters of the book of Acts, it's obvious that God's power and work is based in Jerusalem (Act 2:41-47), but by Acts 13, it's obvious that Antioch has become the new hub from which Christianity will spread to the world. In fact, part of Paul's ministry is collecting funds from the church in Antioch to send back to the poor saints in Jerusalem (Rom 15:26; 1Co 16:3).

5. From God working to accomplish His plan through the NATION of ISRAEL to God working to accomplish His plan through the CHURCH.

After God called out Abraham, the progenitor of the nation of Israel, it was obvious throughout the Old Testament that the plan

The Keys of Bible Study

of God on the earth was intended to be fulfilled by this chosen people and nation. Were it not for the history specifically recorded in the book of Acts, we would never be able to comprehend just how it was that God put the nation of Israel and His promises to them on hold and in order to carry out His purposes and plan on the earth in a 2000 year dispensation through the church.

6. From the ministry of PETER to the ministry of PAUL.

If we were to use a Bible program to do a word search of the word *Peter* in the book of Acts, it would reveal something quite interesting. In the first half of the book, we'd find verse after verse that had Peter's name in it. Fifty-six times to be exact! But by the time we get to chapter 13, with one exception, his name just totally drops out of the book! Likewise, if we were to search the words *Saul/Paul*, we would find that there would be none in the early chapters, but just as Peter's name starts fading out of the book of Acts, Paul's name begins fading in and becoming the predominant name in the middle to the end of the book (153 times in all!). This reveals the fact that there is a transition in the book of Acts from the ministry of the apostle to the Jews (Peter) to the apostle to the Gentiles (Paul).

7. From a "KINGDOM of HEAVEN" message to a "KINGDOM of GOD" message.

And this is that specific key that I mentioned earlier which is so paramount to understanding how to rightly divide the Book of Acts, and the entire Bible for that matter! So, please, pay very close attention.

Do you remember what our Lord told the twelve Apostles they were to go and preach in Matthew 10? It was a *kingdom of heaven* message, right? What we find in the book of Acts is that there is a transition that takes place in this book between a message concerning the *kingdom of heaven* to a message concerning the *kingdom of God*. So, obviously, if we're ever really going to understand the Bible, and

90

Chapter 3 — The Key of Divisions

how to rightly divide it, it is imperative for us to understand some things about the *kingdom of heaven* and the *kingdom of God.*

We see those two familiar phrases quite often in our New Testament, especially in the Gospels. And for the most part, if you pick up a commentary, what most commentators are going to say about the *kingdom of God* and the *kingdom of Heaven* is that they are actually synonymous terms in the New Testament, and that the two phrases are used interchangeably. Really? Can we do that? I mean, can we actually say that? Let me ask you something, have you ever used the words "God" and "heaven" synonymously? Have you ever just randomly interchanged those words, because in your mind, you felt they were the same thing? Not on your life! When we say *God,* we don't mean *heaven.* And when we say *heaven,* we don't mean *God.* That doesn't even make a little bit of sense!

I'll admit that there is at least somewhat of a legitimate reason people might be confused into thinking they're synonymous, or that they're used interchangeably. And that's because we can be reading in one particular place in one Gospel, and it'll be talking about the *kingdom of heaven,* but then when we look at the parallel account of that same story in another Gospel, it will sometimes refer to it as the *kingdom of God.* So, in that respect, it is very understandable how people might conclude that these two kingdoms must be the same thing. But the truth of the matter is—they simply aren't!

Yes, sometimes they do show up in parallel passages—but do you know what God is showing us through that? He's actually revealing to us that there are times when these two kingdoms are present on the earth at the same time! But don't allow yourself to be confused: there is a definite distinction between these two kingdoms. They are sometimes present on the earth at the same time, because the Lord Jesus Christ is the actual embodiment of these two kingdoms—but even then, as we're about to see, they are very distinct.

As we start to see this unfold biblically, let me just say this: the entire Bible is wrapped around these two kingdoms. It is too exhaustive of a study to do it in this setting, but we could literally walk through the entire Bible, from Genesis 1:1 all the way through the end of Revelation, and see how these two kingdoms have unfolded, and will unfold, through the annals of history and on into eternity.

But for the purpose of learning how to rightly divide the word of truth, it is important that we allow ourselves to be exposed to enough of the truth of what these two kingdoms are, so that we can rightly divide not only the truth of the book of Acts, but God's entire *word of truth!*

Let's look, first of all, at...

The Biblical Identification of the KINGDOM of GOD.

One of the keys we're going to be talking about in chapter 7 is the WORD Key, and we'll learn about the importance of the individual words God has chosen to use in His word. The fact is, God chooses His words very carefully! None of them are random. Every word of the Bible is completely pure (Pro 30:5). And the reason He calls these two kingdoms something different is the simple fact that they *are* something different!

Most of today's Christians believe that God has preserved His word in the so-called "original manuscripts". (Strangely enough, these have not been preserved! There is not an "original manuscript" to be found anywhere on this entire planet! More will be said on this in Chapter 7, as well.)

Because of this, we'll hear scholars start to explain the *kingdom of God,* and they'll say, "Well, the word k*ingdom* in the Greek is… and the word *God* in the Greek is… and when we put that together, it means…" And then, they'll follow that same procedure with the *kingdom of heaven,* seeking to explain it by parsing out the Greek dictionary definition of the presumed key words, *kingdom* and *heaven.*

By the time they're done, it sounds really deep and scholarly and impressive, but the reality is that it actually hasn't done one thing

Chapter 3 — The Key of Divisions

to give us a legitimate biblical understanding concerning these two kingdoms! What it has actually produced is a diversion that will ensure that they never really comprehend the biblical meaning and significance of these kingdoms! What they've attempted to do is go to the original languages of the New Testament so *they* can reveal the word of God to us, rather than the prescribed way 1 Corinthians 2:9-13 says *the Spirit of God* reveals His truth to us: by *"comparing things spiritual with spiritual,"* or by comparing scripture with scripture! So, rather than do some extra-biblical exegesis, let's just study what the Spirit of God revealed to us about these kingdoms, simply by looking at what the Bible says in all of the places it specifically talks about and describes them!

First of all, let's compare scripture with scripture concerning the *kingdom of God.*

In Romans, Paul tells us that,

> ...the kingdom of God is not meat and drink; but righteousness, and peace, and joy in the Holy Ghost. (Rom 14:17)

In other words, it's not something you can reach out and touch. Did you ever reach out and touch righteousness? Did you ever reach out and grab a handful of peace or joy? No! But you can grab ahold of a piece of meat or a drink!

Next, Jesus tells us,

> ...The kingdom of God cometh not with observation: 21 Neither shall they say, Lo here! or, lo there! for, behold, the kingdom of God is within you. (Luk 17:20b-21)

You can't see it by just looking for it with your eyes. With this kingdom, Jesus says, you can't say, "I see it!" Jesus says very specifically, "the kingdom of God is within you."

Paul writes in 1 Corinthians 4:20 that the *kingdom of God* is "not in word, but in power." In other words, it's not just a bunch of words—

93

The Keys of Bible Study

but boy, whatever it is, there's a lot of power in it!

In 1 Corinthians 15:50, he tells us "that flesh and blood cannot inherit the kingdom of God."

And John 3:3-5 tells us that we enter the *kingdom of God* by a *spiritual birth.*

Now, I want you to recognize what we just did. We simply went to the Bible, compared scripture with scripture, and allowed the word of God to provide its own definitions as we allowed the Spirit of God that lives in us to reveal to us what the *kingdom of God* is! He more than adequately did His job, didn't He? In five simple passages, we learned a whole lot about what the *kingdom of God* both *is* and *isn't!* And above everything else, our key takeaway is that...

The kingdom of God is a SPIRITUAL kingdom!

So, if that's what the *kingdom of God* is, what might you expect the *kingdom of heaven* to be?

The Biblical Identification of the KINGDOM of HEAVEN (Also known as the <u>KINGDOM of ISRAEL</u>)

Now, we could go to any number of places in the Old Testament to see this. However, I've chosen to begin with a passage in Isaiah 9 that is somewhat familiar to most of us because of its Christmas implications, and I think that can help all of us begin to get our minds wrapped around it.

The passage begins this way:

For unto us a child is born, unto us a Son is given: (Isaiah 9:6a)

Isaiah is describing here the birth of Christ—obviously, at His first coming. And yet, watch the next next phrase:

94

Chapter 3 — The Key of Divisions

and the government shall be upon His shoulder: (Isaiah 9:6b)

Did that happen in the first coming of Christ? I mean, sure, we all know He was and is the King of kings at all times, but in His first coming did He ever sit in all of His glory upon a throne? As I recall, He didn't even have a place to lay His head! Did He ever wear a crown, other than a blasphemous crown of thorns they jammed upon His head at His crucifixion? Did He ever hold a scepter, other than the reed they scoffingly put in His hand as they were unmercifully beating Him? Did He ever wear regal garments, other than the purple robe they mockingly placed upon His back that had been ripped to shreds by the scourging He suffered at the hands of Roman soldiers? Of course He didn't!

And then, moving on to the next verse, Isaiah writes:

Of the increase of his government and peace there shall be no end, upon the throne of David, and upon His Kingdom, to order it, and to establish it with judgment and with justice from henceforth even for ever. The zeal of the Lord of Hosts will performs this. (Isa 9:7)

In other words, once He takes up His authority and right to rule... once He sits on the throne of His glory... once He sets up that kingdom... it will blend into the everlasting kingdom! And I love how Isaiah closes this prophetic declaration! He dogmatically says, "The zeal of the Lord of Hosts will performs this." In other words, no matter what it looks like at any given time in history, you can rest assured: the Father is going to make sure that His Son, the Lord Jesus Christ, sits on a throne on the earth, ruling and reigning in an everlasting kingdom over everything in existence! Hallelujah!

So I ask you, what kind of kingdom is this actually describing? Is this a mere spiritual kingdom of which Isaiah is prophesying? Absolutely not! He's talking about a very literal kingdom, where a very literal king will sit on a very literal throne and will rule over a very literal earth! He is describing for us the *kingdom of heaven*— which is sometimes referred to biblically as the *kingdom of Israel.*

The Keys of Bible Study

The kingdom of heaven is a literal, physical, governmental, Davidic (Jewish) kingdom promised throughout the Old Testament and the Gospels to the nation of Israel, from which the Lord Jesus Christ will rule and reign over all the earth on His throne in Jerusalem.

That, my friend, is a biblical definition and identification of the *kingdom of heaven!* And all through the Old Testament, God continuously makes reference to a kingdom that will be established in Israel. In the book of Isaiah alone, there are over 100 verses which refer to that kingdom! In the book of Jeremiah, again, over 100 verses refer to it. Ezekiel devotes 12 entire chapters to it! Daniel talks about it in chapters 2, 7, 9, and 12! Again, the Old Testament is all about that *kingdom* and the *King* who will rule from that throne!

But those are just the Old Testament references to that kingdom! There are numerous New Testament references to it as well. But here's something very important you must know about the phrase *the kingdom of heaven.* It appears in the New Testament 33 times in 32 verses. We won't take the time to list them all, but you know what I think you'd find astounding about every one of them? All of those 33 references just happen to be in one book! And when you hear that, does it not cause you to step back, and think to yourself: "Wait. What? All of the specific references to 'the kingdom of heaven' in the New Testament are all found in only one book? That's crazy!" And I totally agree! Now, we may not know what that's actually teaching us initially, but we do know one thing for certain... it's teaching us *something!*

That one book in which all of the 33 references to the *kingdom of heaven* are found in the New Testament is the Gospel of Matthew. And isn't that interesting? Because, remember, the Gospel of Matthew is that Gospel that was written specifically to the *Jews* to present Christ as the *King of the Jews,* and the kingdom over which He will rule is called *the kingdom of heaven.*

96

Now, you might be thinking, "Well, if it is a physical kingdom on the **earth**, why then is it referred to as *the kingdom of heaven?*"

NOTE:
Though it is a kingdom on the EARTH, it's called the <u>kingdom of HEAVEN</u> because, from God's vantage point in the third heaven, the EARTH is in the midst of the HEAVENS! And the earth, in the midst of the Heavens, is the capital of the universe—or in other words, the place from which GOD has chosen to enact His plan.

So, in a very general sense, that is a biblical overview of the *kingdom of God* and the *kingdom of heaven.* The *kingdom of God* is the **spiritual kingdom**, and the *kingdom of heaven* is the **physical kingdom.** Hopefully, that will provide us with a working knowledge of how to distinguish between these two kingdoms biblically. And because distinguishing between these two kingdoms is so critical to rightly divide the word of truth, and because there is such a major transition that takes place concerning these kingdoms in the book of Acts which is so critical to rightly dividing the entire Bible, the remainder of this chapter will devoted to revealing...

HOW THESE TWO KINGDOMS UNFOLD IN THE BOOK OF ACTS

Seeing how the *kingdom of heaven* and the *kingdom of God* unfold in the book of Acts is nothing short of astounding! And not only is it astounding, it is critical to our understanding, not only of the book of Acts, but of the entire Bible. I am convinced that without a working knowledge of the things we're about to uncover, we will fall very short in terms of rightly dividing the word of truth.

The Keys of Bible Study

The book of Acts begins this way:

> The former treatise have I made, O Theophilus, of all that Jesus began both to do and teach, (Act 1:1)

And, of course, the treatise he's referring to here is none other than the Gospel of Luke (Luk 1:3). But notice in this first verse that Luke refers to the things written in his Gospel as all of the things "that Jesus began both to do and teach." Which is to say, Jesus is *still doing* something, and *still teaching* something—only now that He's gone, He's using the Apostles to do it!

Luke continues on, saying:

> Until the day in which He was taken up, after that He through the Holy Ghost had given commandments unto the apostles whom He had chosen: 3 To whom also He shewed Himself alive after His passion by many infallible proofs, being seen of them forty days, speaking of the things pertaining to the kingdom of God: (Act 1:2-3)

Do you remember which kingdom that is? It's the **spiritual kingdom**, right? And notice what Luke says! Jesus took *40 days* to talk to these guys about the spiritual kingdom. Wow! Evidently, there was quite a bit of ground to cover!

Notice also that there is a piece of information which is very important for us to know about this 40 day period. Luke 24:45 gives us a very key cross reference. It lets us know that during this 40-day period, "Then opened [Jesus] their understanding, that [the apostles] might understand the scriptures." Do you understand the significance of that? First of all, Jesus is God, and He is without a doubt the greatest Teacher in the entire universe! And the greatest Teacher in the universe takes 40 solid days to teach these guys. But, recognizing, of course, that a teacher's ability to instill knowledge is ultimately only as good as his students ability to receive it, God did something supernatural to ensure that the apostles fully understood what He was talking about!

98

Chapter 3 — The Key of Divisions

You see, these guys were the foundation of the church (Eph 2:20), so their comprehension of the scriptures was obviously crucial for the ongoing ministry of Christ through them in the process of building His church. And for that purpose, our Lord Jesus Christ supernaturally opened their understanding, that they might understand the scriptures! Check that out... not only did they have a supernatural Teacher, but He provided them with supernatural understanding of the things He was teaching them! Do you have any idea the biblical truth they were able to both learn and assimilate during those 40 days? Because the previous verse, Luke 24:44, talks about how He had actually taken them through everything that was "written in the Law of Moses and in the Prophets and in the Psalms concerning" Himself! Man! Wouldn't you have loved to have been able to sit under that teaching?

Jesus takes them back to the Pentateuch (the first five books of the Bible, the things "which were written in the law of Moses"), and basically says to them, "Let me show you where I am in these books! And let me show you where the spiritual *kingdom of God* was at that time. And then, let me bring you through the prophets (Isaiah-Malachi), and show you where I am in those books, and where the kingdom of God was at that period of time. And then, let me do the same thing with you through the Psalms."

The greatest Teacher who ever lived—God, in the person of Jesus Christ—takes 40 days to teach the apostles about the *kingdom of God,* and as He's teaching them, He's supernaturally opening the eyes of their understanding so they can actually process all the information He's giving them. And as he does this, He meticulously and systematically works them through the entire Old Testament.

Then, we pick up in Acts 1:4:

> And, being assembled together with them, commanded them that they should not to depart from Jerusalem, but wait for the promise of the Father, which, saith he, ye have heard of Me; 5 For John truly baptized with water; but ye shall be baptized with the Holy Ghost not many days hence. 6 When they

99

The Keys of Bible Study

therefore were come together, they asked of Him, saying, Lord, wilt thou at this time restore again the kingdom to Israel? (Act 1:4-6)

Do you think the kingdom they're asking about was the kingdom He had just been talking to them about for that 40 day period? Not on your life! Luke has already made clear they had been granted supernatural understanding concerning that teaching! They even refer to the kingdom they're asking about by a different name! And yet, if you pick up a commentary on this chapter, the vast majority of commentators are going to say something to this effect: "These poor deluded, self-absorbed disciples! For 40 days, Jesus has been talking to them about this kingdom, and they just can't get the attention off of their own sorry selves! Jesus had told them that when the kingdom came, they were going to sit on twelve thrones. And these selfish, self-seeking guys just can't get their preeminence in the kingdom out of their heads!" Again, do you think that's what is actually unfolding here? That's ludicrous!

What the Apostles are actually saying to the Lord here is this: "Okay, so we've got this *kingdom of God* thing down now. We understand that spiritual kingdom. But, Lord, is this the time that you're going to restore the kingdom to Israel?" Or, in other words, "Is this the time that the physical kingdom is going to come in?"

And watch what Jesus's reply is:

And He said unto them, It is not for you to know the times or the seasons, which the Father has put in His own power. (Act 1:7)

Jesus is holding them off. He doesn't answer their question, because He doesn't want to commit Himself. And do you know why He doesn't want to commit Himself? It's because at this point in the book of Acts, the real answer to their question is: "It depends!" They ask: "Is this the time you're going to restore again the kingdom to Israel?" And to paraphrase His reply, Jesus is basically saying: "Don't concern yourselves with that right now—because it depends!"

100

Chapter 3 — The Key of Divisions

What did it depend upon?

The answer unfolds like this: through the earthly ministry of Jesus, John the Baptist came to the nation of Israel and their religious leaders preaching about the kingdom God wanted to give to Israel... and they lopped his head off. We might refer to that as strike one.

Jesus, through the Gospels, had fully manifested who He was as Israel's Messiah, and that He had come to offer the kingdom to Israel—and in Matthew 12, the religious leaders of Israel attributed the power through which He worked to Beelzebub, or Satan—and in so doing, committed the "unpardonable sin." We could refer to that as strike two!

Ultimately, after our Lord Jesus Christ fulfilled every last detail of the prophecies of the Old Testament concerning Israel's king, the nation of Israel called for His death, and crucified their Messiah. And that, my friend, is what we could refer to as strike three!

However, do you remember those ten incredible words Jesus prayed to His Father on the cross? Jesus prayed, "Father, forgive them; for they know not what they do" (Luk 23:34). And a question we may need to ask ourselves concerning His prayer is who is the *them* He wants the Father to forgive, who knew not what they were doing? Do you know who it is? It was the nation of Israel.

When Jesus prayed that prayer from the cross, is there any doubt in your mind whether or not the Father was going to answer it? Certainly not! And because He did answer that prayer, God the Father was going to give Israel one more opportunity concerning the establishment of the kingdom to Israel. And whether He would restore the kingdom to Israel at the time in which the apostles were referring by their question would depend! It would depend on what the Nation of Israel would do with their next opportunity.

So again, understand that in Acts 1:6, the enlightened and informed apostles say: "Okay, Lord, so we understand this whole thing about the spiritual kingdom, the *kingdom of God*... but you haven't told

101

The Keys of Bible Study

us anything about the *kingdom of heaven*! Is this the time You're going to set up that physical kingdom on the earth that has been promised to the nation of Israel?" And verse 7 says: "And he said unto them, It is not for you to know the times or the seasons..."

But you know what's interesting? Twenty years after Israel had made their decision concerning their final offer of the kingdom (which will be detailed momentarily) and it was apparent that God was going to put that kingdom on hold, Paul writes to the Thessalonians in 1 Thessalonians 5:1, "But of the times and the seasons, brethren, ye have no need that I write unto you." And verse 2 begins: "For yourselves know perfectly..."

So, check that out... Jesus tells the Apostles 40 days after His resurrection, "It's not for you to know the times and seasons." And yet, twenty years later, the Spirit of God inspires the Apostle Paul to say, "You don't even need for me to address the subject of the 'times and the seasons,' because that's something you already know perfectly well!" Obviously, something significant had taken place somewhere in that twenty year period between Jesus' words to the Apostles in Acts chapter 1, and Paul's words to the Thessalonians. And it all has to do with this final offer of the kingdom the Father would be granting to the nation of Israel. So let's see how this continues to unfold in the book of Acts.

After this final dialogue with the Apostles concerning the two kingdoms in Acts 1:3-7, Jesus once again affirms the promise of the empowering of the Holy Ghost and reminds them of their mission (1:8), and then ascends into heaven to retake His seat at the Father's right hand (1:9-11). The chapter ends with the selection of Matthias to replace the recently deceased Judas (1:12-26).

As we enter into Acts 2, it's the infamous day of Pentecost. And the main thing of which we need to be cognizant here is that what is unfolding is all still very Jewish in nature, and the *kingdom of heaven* (the physical kingdom) is still being offered to Israel.

Verse 5 says: "And there were dwelling at Jerusalem Jews..."

Chapter 3 — The Key of Divisions

Verse 14 says: "But Peter, standing up with the eleven, lifted up his voice, and said unto them, Ye men of Judaea…"

In verse 22, Peter says: "Ye men of Israel…"

In verse 36, again he says: "Therefore, let all the house of Israel know assuredly…"

As you can see, the audience on the day of Pentecost was Jewish, and the entire event centered upon God's specific dealings with Israel. And when you begin to look at the messages Peter is preaching in Acts Chapter 2, 3, 4 and 5, do you know what those messages are? They are second coming messages… addressed to Israel… admonishing them to believe on the very Messiah that they had allowed to be crucified! And it is apparent through these messages that what God was looking for was a national repentance, so the *kingdom of heaven/Israel* could be restored to Israel!

Let me show you an example from Acts 3 that will be somewhat familiar, because we looked at in the previous chapter dealing with the THEME Key. Peter says in verse 19:

> Repent ye therefore, and be converted, that your sins may be blotted out, when the times of refreshing [the kingdom… the Millennium!] shall come from the presence of the Lord. (Act 3:19)

And do you actually hear what Peter is saying? He's telling the nation of Israel that if they'll repent, God will go ahead and get this kingdom thing rolling! He continues:

> And he shall send Jesus Christ, which before was preached unto you: Whom the heavens must receive until the times of restitution of all things, which God hath spoken by the mouth of all his holy prophets since the world began. (Act 1:20)

Again, the point Peter is trying to stress here is, "Listen, God's still giving us an opportunity! And if we, as a nation, will repent, the

The Keys of Bible Study

Father will go ahead and bring the kingdom to Israel at this time!"

So we work our way through the rest of Acts chapter 3, and then chapters 4, 5 and 6... and then we come to what may be the most significant chapter in the book of Acts, in terms of understanding how to rightly divide it... chapter 7! Because it is in this chapter that Israel is going to receive their final offer of the kingdom.

In Acts 7, a deacon in the early church by the name of Stephen has audience with the High Priest and ruling council of Israel. Listen, if these ole boys will repent, the entire nation of Israel will follow! They had that kind of clout. And had the nation of Israel repented, be it known, things would have unfolded historically a whole lot differently than they have!

As Stephen begins preaching in verse 2, he says: "...Men, brethren, and fathers, hearken: The God of glory appeared unto our father Abraham..." Stephen begins his message by taking these guys back to their roots. He takes them back to the first Jew, the father of the nation of Israel... the infamous Abraham.

All the way through Acts 7, Stephen just keeps saying: "Do you remember that? Do you remember back in the Old Testament, when this and that happened with our forefathers?" And he just keeps bringing them through their history, trying to get them to see that God has always been moving to get His Son, the Lord Jesus Christ, on that throne in Jerusalem, ruling over all of the world!

And again, don't miss the significance of the fact that Stephen has audience with the leaders of Israel here! This is their shot! If they'll respond to the conviction of the Holy Ghost through Stephen's preaching, the Father will kick into motion what was necessary for the *"kingdom of heaven"* to be restored to Israel!

But as Stephen is preaching to them, he can tell by their faces that they would have none of what God was offering through his message, and he calls them on it!

104

Chapter 3 — The Key of Divisions

Ye stiffnecked and uncircumcised in heart and ears, ye do always resist the Holy Ghost: as your fathers did, so do ye. 52 Which of the prophets have not your fathers persecuted? and they have slain them which shewed before of the coming of the Just One; of whom ye have been now the betrayers and murderers: 53 Who have received the law by the disposition of angels, and have not kept it. (Act 7:51-53)

And look at what it says in verse 54: "When they heard these things, they were cut to the heart..." Oh yeah, the conviction of the Holy Ghost was certainly there. But rather than repent, "they gnashed on him with their teeth." In other words, they snarled and clenched their teeth at him.

But he, being full of the Holy Ghost, looked up steadfastly into heaven, and saw the glory of God, and Jesus standing on the right hand of God. 56 And said, Behold, I see the heavens opened, and the Son of man standing on the right hand of God! (Act 7:55-56)

Wow! You talk about some insight and vision! Stephen is actually seeing into that other half of reality that Paul talked about in 2 Corinthians 4:18, which can't be seen with our physical eyes. And it's interesting, that as God does allow him to see into this realm, Stephen says he saw Jesus *standing* at the right hand of God. If we all took our handy-dandy little Bible program on our devices, and we plugged in the phrase "right hand", all kinds of references would come up. And you know what we would find repeated in them over and over again? That our Lord Jesus Christ is *"seated* at the right hand... s*eated* at the right hand... s*eated* at the right hand."There is one place, however—and only one place—in all of scripture, where our Lord Jesus Christ is *standing* at the Father's *right hand...* and it just happens to be *this* place in the Bible, where the Jews are getting their last offer of the kingdom. And as they begin to attack Stephen, he looks up, and is able to see beyond this earthly realm, into the eternal realm, and at that very instance... he sees Jesus STANDING.

105

The Keys of Bible Study

I personally believe that Jesus is *standing* here—and *only here*—because if the nation of Israel would have repented, He was poised and ready to return!

And someone may say, "Boy, that would sure mess up a lot of the prophecies in the Bible, wouldn't it?"

Well, recognize that at this point, there's no written New Testament, right? So, it's certainly not going to mess up the New Testament! And as far as the Old Testament is concerned, do you realize that at this point, every single biblical prophecy about the second coming of Christ could have been fulfilled? The Jews have to be in the homeland at the second coming… and at this point, the Jews were in the homeland! The antichrist, Satan, has to be in the bottomless pit… and at this point, Judas, the "son of Perdition," had already gone to the bottomless pit! The right nation has to be in power at the second coming of Christ, and that's Rome… and at this point, Rome was in power!

All of the prophecies regarding the second coming at this point in time could have been fulfilled. And had the nation of Israel received the message of Stephen in Acts 7, sure, the Bible would have looked different… and history would have likewise looked different! That's why we talked earlier about the fact that in the church age, we are presently living in a parenthesis. And it is because of what happens right here in Acts 7 that we actually enter into that parenthetical. It is at this point in the book of Acts that God begins to make all seven of the transitions we talked about earlier. And they come as a result of the nation of Israel's refusal to accept God's final offer of the kingdom.

But watch what happens after the stoning of Stephen in Acts 7…

As we come into chapter 8, verse 5 says something tremendously significant! It says, "Then Philip went down to the city of Samaria, and preached Christ unto them."

Do you remember what Jesus told the Apostles in Matthew 10?

106

Chapter 3 — The Key of Divisions

He specifically told them not to go to the Samaritans! So we have to ask ourselves: what in the world is Phillip doing in Samaria?

You know why he's there? Because God is beginning the transition, not only in the book of Acts, but concerning His plan! And God Himself directs Philip to Samaria for the purpose of arresting our attention concerning this monumental change in direction from what Jesus had clearly stated in Matthew 10:5-6 about not going to the Samaritans or the Gentiles.

And if that weren't enough to arrest our attention, surely what it says down in verse 12 would!

> But when [the Samaritans] believed Philip preaching the things concerning the kingdom of God, and the name of Jesus Christ, they were baptized, both men and women. (Act 8:12)

Notice, they got baptized *because* they believed. But notice also what message it was that they believed! This is huge! The message they believed wasn't about the *physical kingdom* promised to the Jews. No! It was a message concerning the *spiritual kingdom* that Jesus said we must enter by a *spiritual birth.*

Obviously, something major has changed. We now have a bunch of Samaritans who have been born into the *kingdom of God* by way of a spiritual birth—and what's more, by the time we can get out of this chapter (Acts 8), a full-fledged Gentile has also been born again! He is identified as a eunuch from the African nation of Ethiopia, and as Philip ministered Christ to him from Isaiah 53, the Spirit of God opened his eyes, and he then opened his heart and confessed Christ and his belief in Him—and he immediately followed the Lord in believer's baptism!

Do you know what happens in the very next chapter (Acts 9)? We meet a guy by the name of Saul who is converted in the first part of the chapter, who then makes his way to Damascus. In the meantime, God comes to Ananias in a vision, and basically says (my paraphrase), "Listen, there's a dude named Saul that I want

107

The Keys of Bible Study

you to go hang out with for a little while, because I want to use you in his life." And Ananias says, "Oh, wow! I've heard about this guy! Isn't he the guy who persecutes and kills people like me? Are you sure you want me to hang out with him?" And God says, "Yeah, and here's why." And God says to Ananias in verse 15 (not paraphrasing!), "Go thy way: for he is a chosen vessel unto me, to bear My name before the Gentiles, and kings, and the children of Israel."

So, check it out… the first part of the book of Acts is centered around the Jews and the nation of Israel, and the message that is being preached to them is a *kingdom of heaven* message, in which God was essentially saying, "If you'll repent, I'll send Jesus right now!" But after their final rejection at the stoning of Stephen, God begins the transition by first going to the *Samaritans...* then to a *Gentile...* and then we find Him calling out the apostle to the *Gentiles* (Rom 11:13).

When we come into the next chapter, Acts 10:1 says, "There was a certain man in Caesarea called Cornelius, a centurion of the band called the Italian band." And, once again, God is screaming out a very significant message concerning how things will function according to the "new testament"—because Italians, just like Ethiopians, are very much *Gentiles!* And by this point in the book of Acts, the seven transitions we talked about earlier are all in full operation.

So, because God has made this transition, do you know what has to happen? God has to give Peter, the apostle to the Jews, a special vision to help him understand that He had transitioned to the Gentiles, and that He no longer viewed them as unclean. God has to tell him, "No, Peter. Don't you dare call unclean what I'm calling clean." And the remainder of chapter 10 is all about God letting Peter (and us!) know that His plan in the church age will be to work predominantly through Gentiles... in and through the church!

Identifying RIGHT DIVISIONS in the Word of Truth:

The subject of rightly dividing the word of truth could actually be an entire book. The purpose of *The Keys of Bible Study*, however, is simply to launch the student of the word of God into the basic understandings of hermeneutical principles that can be continuously expanded upon through a lifelong pursuit of God through the pages of His word.

With that being said, please allow me to provide a few critical understandings that will hopefully provide a beginning place for you in your understanding of making right divisions, as well as help you to stay within proper doctrinal bounds as you move forward in your studies.

Identifying Basic Right Divisions from the Layout of the Books of the Bible

The information under this heading is by no means the end-all in terms of rightly dividing. It is merely the beginning place I mentioned above to help us understand the big picture of the right divisions that must be noted through the order of the books of the Bible from Genesis through Revelation.

1. The Bible as a Whole (Genesis through Revelation)

As we discussed in chapter two as we were dealing with the very first key of Bible study, the Key of Theme, the entire Bible points towards the second coming of Christ (i.e. the Millennium, the "day of the Lord," the establishment of Christ's kingdom on the earth, etc.), when He finally receives the glory due His name. This theme must be factored into everything we read in both the Old and New Testaments in order to make right divisions.

2. The Old Testament (Genesis through Malachi)

In the Old Testament, God is working through the *nation of Israel* to get the *physical* aspects of the kingdom in order. This organization is seen through the *literary divisions* of the Old Testament.

   A. The books of the LAW (Genesis through Deuteronomy)

109

The Keys of Bible Study

   B. The books of HISTORY (Joshua through Job)

   C. The books of POETRY (Psalms through Song of Solomon)

   D. The books of PROPHECY (Isaiah through Malachi)

3. The New Testament (Matthew through Revelation)

In the New Testament, God is working through the church to get the spiritual aspects of the kingdom in order. This organization is seen through the following basic breakdown of the New Testament.

   A. The GOSPELS (Matthew through John)

   B. HISTORY (The Acts of the Apostles)

   C. PAUL'S Letters to CHURCHES (Romans through Thessalonians)

   D. PAUL'S Letters to PASTORS/LEADERS (1 Timothy through Philemon)

   E. HEBREW Letters (Hebrews through Jude)

   F. PROPHECY (Revelation)

4. Further Divisions to be Noted in the New Testament

   A. Four Gospels to the Stoning of Stephen (Matthew through Acts 7)

It should must be noted that though the text of the New Testament begins with the four Gospels, many well meaning students of the Bible miss the fact that Hebrews 9:16-17 teaches us that a testament is not actually in force until the death of the testator. Christ, of course, is the Testator of the New Testament, but we must keep in mind that His death doesn't come until the end of any of the four gospels! The content of the gospels (as well as Acts 1-7) is Jewish in nature, in which the kingdom of heaven (the literal, physical kingdom in which Christ rules and reigns from Jerusalem over all the earth for a period of a thousand years) is being offered to Israel. Over the course of Christ's teaching in the four gospels,

Chapter 3 — The Key of Divisions

and during the teaching of the apostles and other leaders in Acts 1-7, most of the subject matter is specifically being *addressed to* and *relates to* the Jews and/or the nation of Israel.

There are, however, teachings in this portion of the New Testament (Matthew through Acts 7) that become valid for our instruction and application, because they are repeated in the Letters of Paul (Romans through Philemon). The rule of thumb in determining which portions *are* and *are not* to be applied to us is simply this: if it *agrees* with Paul's teachings (Romans through Philemon) it *applies* to us; if it *doesn't agree* with Paul's teaching (Romans through Philemon), it *doesn't apply* to us.

B. Transition from the Stoning of Stephen to the Church of Antioch (Acts 8 through 12)

I have listed this as a separate division because directly after the stoning of Stephen in Acts 7, God is in the midst of making the seven key transitions in the book of Acts that were discussed earlier in this chapter. Once again, we must be very careful in applying doctrine to ourselves out of transitional periods unless we find it repeated in the Church Epistles (Romans through Philemon).

C. Church of Antioch to the Revelation of the Body of Christ (Acts 13 through 28)

After the stoning of Stephen in Acts 7, God's offer to the nation of Israel to receive her King and the establishment of the kingdom of heaven on the earth was put on hold. After making the key transitions in chapters 8-12, we could say that we officially enter the Church Age in Acts 13. Once we enter Acts 13, God holds up the church of Antioch in Syria, as it provides for us a model of church leadership (13:1), church procedure (13:2), and the fulfillment of the church's commission (13:3). In Acts 13-28, God reveals to us the history of His offer for the Gentiles to enter the kingdom of God by way of a spiritual birth, and the history of the reproduction of New Testament disciples and churches

111

The Keys of Bible Study

D. Church Epistles (Romans through Philemon)

This is the section of the Bible/New Testament specifically written to and intended to be applied both doctrinally and practically by those of us living in the Church Age. The instruction in these books of the Bible is the revelation of that which was hidden in the Old Testament (the mysteries) and pictured in many of the Doctrinal/Prophetic Applications of the Old Testament. The instruction in these books of the Bible is very straight forward, and every bit of it is intended to be taken literally, and should serve as the basis for everything we believe and practice in our local New Testament churches.

E. Tribulation Epistles (Hebrews through Revelation)

The nine books from Hebrews through Revelation comprise about 16 percent of our New Testament. In these books, there are many doctrinal truths and practical instructions that should be noted, learned, and applied because they agree with the teachings of Paul in the Church Epistles. As we compare the spiritual things found in Hebrews through Revelation with the spiritual things found in Romans through Philemon, the Spirit of God reveals to us many doctrinal and practical realities that have bearing on our lives.

It is important to realize, however, that the books from Hebrews through Revelation have a very specific application to the tribulation period. They might most aptly be called "Hebrew Christian Epistles" or "Tribulation Epistles." These books are not directly written to the body of Christ in the Church Age, nor are they aimed doctrinally at the Church, even though local churches are sometimes addressed in their content. Their specific application has to do with a period of time *after* the rapture of the church. Just as the gospel of Matthew serves as a bridge from the Old Testament to the New Testament, and just as the book of Acts serves as a bridge from Israel to the Church, the book of Hebrews serves as a doctrinal bridge out of the Church Age into the tribulation period.

May I state again that this section is intended to simply provide

112

an overview of right divisions and serve as a beginning place for understanding them. Be it known, however, that there can be no complete right division without considering the crucial biblical ramifications and implications of *dispensations, covenants,* and *periods of prophecy.* As you progress in your biblical understanding and training in the word of God, these will be subjects you will want to explore in more depth through the training ministry of your local church or through the Living Faith Bible Institute, to which I am connected.

My dear brothers and sisters, we've covered a whole lot of ground in this chapter! I hope you've been able to see how God has laid out His book so that it makes total sense! But to get there, and not get swept away into false doctrine, it's going to require three inviolable things: 1) Lots of *study,* 2) Lots of *work,* and 3) Knowing how to *rightly divide* the word of truth.

"Study to shew thyself approved unto God, a workman that needeth not to be ashamed, rightly dividing the word of truth." 2 Timothy 2:15

THE KEY OF CONTEXT

The next key of Bible study is related to the Key of Division we discussed in the previous chapter, in that it emphasizes having a keen awareness of who the particular audience is in a verse or passage, and the subject matter of what is actually being written to them. However, the Key of Context includes some very significant distinctions and ramifications that must also become a part of the fabric of how we train our brain to study the scriptures.

The third key of Bible study:
KEEP VERSES IN THEIR CONTEXT.

If you've ever had to endure the frustration of someone taking something you said out of context and making it sound like something you didn't mean, you're in good company—because it happens to God all the time! Churches have been divided, denominations have been formed, and sadly, many people are in hell today because of a violation of this tremendously important and far-reaching key of Bible study.

KEY VERSE: 2 Peter 3:16

"As also in all his epistles, speaking in them of these things; in which are some things hard to

The Keys of Bible Study

be understood, which they that are unlearned and unstable WREST, as they do also the other SCRIPTURES, unto their own destruction."

Yes, the key verse is 2 Peter 3:16, but as to not violate the very key of Bible study under consideration, we must be sure we keep verse 16 in it's context! Let's at least look back at the preceding verse to get a running start into verse 16. Peter says,

> And account that the longsuffering of our Lord is salvation; as our beloved brother Paul also according to the wisdom given unto him hath written unto you; As also in all his epistles, speaking in them of these things; in which are some things hard to be understood… (2Pe 3:15-16)

Have you ever been reading Paul's writings in the New Testament and thought to yourself, "What in the world is he even talking about here?" Or, "Man, I'm not sure I have a clue as to what any of what I just read even means!" Well, isn't it comforting to discover that there were times when even the great Apostle Peter felt that way? Peter goes on to say in this verse, that in some of those "hard to be understood" places in Paul's epistles, "they that are unlearned and unstable *wrest*, as they do also the other scriptures, unto their own destruction."

There are several things that are noteworthy in this verse. First of all, notice that as early as the last part of the first century, the apostle Peter was already recognizing the epistles of Paul as *scripture!* That, my friend, is no small thing, because many scholars, Bible teachers, and churches try to tell us that nobody really knew what writings were to be included in the canon of scripture until 397 AD at the Council of Carthage. Peter lets us know in this passage, however, that Christians (the priesthood of New Testament believers, 1Pe 2:5,9) already understood what was inspired scripture before the end of the first century! Recognize that when Peter refers to Paul's epistles as scripture, he is inferring upon them the same inspiration and authority as the entire Old Testament. That is quite an inference—and a very important observance!

116

Secondly, notice that Peter tells us in verse 16, "they that are unlearned and unstable wrest...the scriptures." In other words, Peter is telling us, they take them out of context. That word *wrest* is obviously the root from which we get the word *wrestle*. In a wrestling match, a person grabs their opponent and twists and turns them any way they can to get them where they want them. And that's exactly what Peter is saying "unlearned and unstable" people do with the scriptures. They grab a verse or a passage and twist it and turn it to get it out of its context, so they can make it say whatever they want it to say. And it is extremely dangerous, because as Peter says at the end of verse 16, they do this unto their own destruction.

The fearful reality of verse 16, however, is this: people can end up going to hell, claiming Bible verses in the New Testament! That is why it is vitally important for us to understand how to **keep verses in their context**!

KEY THOUGHTS:

#1 There are many cults and false systems of religion in the world that use the Bible as their supposed source of "truth."

The false teaching that originates in these systems is usually actually rooted in biblical truth! And yet, it is truth that has been taken **out of context**. In other words, it is a biblical truth that has either been **misplaced** and/or **misapplied**.

#2 *A TEXT without a CONTEXT is a PRETEXT.*

In other words, coming to a particular *text* in the Bible and failing to put it in its *context* provides opportunity for a student of the Bible to be misled in their own interpretation of a verse or passage, and likewise allows false teachers to mislead people by teaching something different than the author's intended purpose in an individual verse or the particular passage being considered.

The Keys of Bible Study

So, how do we come to a particular verse or passage in the word of God and utilize biblical principles to actually put it into its proper context?

KEY PRINCIPLES:

1. The Principle of Audience.

Identifying the **audience** being addressed in a particular passage is crucial to keeping verses in their context. A very important principle, and a very key way to keep this principle simple, is understanding the following:

The Bible is written to three groups of people: Jews, Gentiles and the Church.

We find all three of these groups listed in **1 Corinthians 10:32**, where Paul says,

> Give none offence, neither to the Jews, nor to the Gentiles, nor to the Church of God. (1Co 10:32)

So, the first question we ask ourselves as we're considering a particular verse or passage is very simple: To whom was this written?

As we go back into the books of the Old Testament, obviously, the **audience** is typically strictly **Jewish**. But not in every case! As we come into the little book of Obadiah, for example, we find that this Old Testament book was actually written to **Gentiles**! We learn that from the very first verse in the book. It's addressed to the nation of Edom, and the Edomites were Gentiles! This means that as we're reading this particular book, we must approach it understanding that it might read a little differently than the other Old Testament books in which God is addressing His people, the Jews... and that it will obviously have a different application.

In the previous chapter, we observed how the key to understanding

118

the context of the Gospel of Matthew is found in identifying the fact that this Gospel is written to the Jews to present Christ as the King of the Jews. So for us to attempt to make personal application of this book to our lives—or to attempt to make application of this book to the church or to attempt to derive from it doctrine for the church without understanding the intended **audience**—is almost a guarantee of entering into false doctrine.

Now, that is certainly not to say that New Testament books which are not specifically written to the church (Matthew-Acts and Hebrews-Revelation) have no value or inspirational application to us, because they often do! In these non-church directed books of the New Testament, however, recognize that we only make personal application of the truths we find repeated in a church-directed epistle (Romans-Philemon).

We observe this particularly in the book of James, which, as we also saw in the previous chapter, in that it's addressed to the Twelve Tribes of Israel. Obviously, there's absolutely no debate about who James' **audience** is: the Jews! And while there are certainly things from the book which we can apply to our lives as Church Age believers, we must be careful to pay attention to the passages with strictly Jewish context.

The same is true when we come to the book of Hebrews. The very title of the book itself lets us know that its **audience** is *not* Gentiles or the church, but Hebrews (the Jews). And again, making application of the book of Hebrews to ourselves individually or to the church corporately without a clear understanding of the intended and clearly stated audience is an invitation to confusion, misapplication, and false doctrine.

As was also mentioned in the previous chapter, when we're reading things that have application to the Jews, we must realize that we're reading somebody else's mail, as it were. Applying things that have specific application to the Jews may seem like a rather insignificant thing, but our Lord Jesus Christ gives an incredibly stern warning regarding it as he speaks to the church in Smyrna. Our Lord says:

The Keys of Bible Study

> I know thy works, and tribulation, and poverty, (but thou art rich) and I know <u>the blasphemy of them which say they are Jews, and are not, but are the synagogue of Satan</u>. (Rev 2:9)

And, of course, the question we have to ask ourselves is, "Just who are these people who **say they are Jews, and are not**?" Because whoever they are, our Lord lets us know that they had been used of Satan to develop a blasphemous, pseudo-Jewish system of worship. He calls it here a *synagogue,* and specifically, *the synagogue of Satan!* We learn from Jesus's statement that, historically, there were those who were guilty of committing this *blasphemy* in the church in Smyrna around 95 AD when our Lord dictated this letter to them, as well as in the Smyrna Church Period of church history (180-325 AD) represented in this letter (Rev 2:8-11).

But what did that actually look like in practical terms? I mean, what were these people actually doing or saying that caused our Lord to refer to it with such drastic terminology? What we discover historically is that there were those in the church in Smyrna, and again in the Smyrna Church Period, who were taking the instruction of scripture that had been written to the Jews—and was intended to be applied by Jews—and were making it apply to them! They were, thereby, effectively saying they were Jews. This violation caused them to "give place to the devil" (Eph 4:27), and it became a doctrinal place where Satan was able to set up shop. And again, what we find historically is that any time people misapply teaching directed to the Jews, it becomes a place from which Satan is able to develop a false religious system that becomes a *synagogue,* or an operational headquarters, if you will, that he uses to propagate his false teaching.

In these last days, there are at least three major *synagogues* that have plagued and are plaguing the church. I refer to them as the three "C's" of false doctrine: Catholicism, Calvinism, and Charismaticism. What all three of these false systems of teaching have in common is they are the result of taking biblical teaching *written to* Israel, and intended to be *applied by* Israel, and trying to make it apply to those

Chapter 4 — The Key of Context

of us who are not only Gentiles, but also part of the church. Let me show you what I mean.

Catholicism believes that Peter, the Apostle to the *Jews*, was the first Pope because Jesus gave to him *the keys of the kingdom of heaven* in Matthew 16:19. The *kingdom of heaven,* however, just happens to be the kingdom promised to the *Jews* who comprised the nation of *Israel!* (Act 1:7) Catholicism sees their "church," therefore, as the fulfillment of the *kingdom of heaven* on the earth, and has, therefore, felt justified through the centuries to imprison, persecute, torture, and even murder those who didn't agree with them, or those who impeded the establishment of their "church" (*a synagogue of Satan*) as the sole governmental and spiritual authority on the earth. Again, practically speaking, Satan was able to build that entire *synagogue* of false teaching as a result of people historically, who, in effect, said they were Jews when they weren't.

Calvinism is another system of teaching that has been propagated by them which say they are Jews, and are not. (In the final analysis, Calvinism is simply another form of Catholicism, and interestingly enough, was first propagated by Augustine. In the 4th century, he just happened to craft his doctrines regarding predestination which were then embraced by the Roman Catholic Church. And by John Calvin's own admission, Augustine was the one from whom he learned the entire system of teaching that now bears Calvin's name!) This is the basic essence of the Calvinistic teaching which has come to be called *replacement theology.* This is the false teaching which says that the New Testament teaches that God is finished with the Jews, and that the church has actually replaced Israel in the unfolding of God's plan—which means that the promises given to the Jews/Israel are now intended for those of us who comprise *the church of God.* Though there are Calvinists who do not embrace all of the teaching included in replacement theology, most modern Calvinists certainly do.

And then, just as both Catholicism and Calvinism are based on a faulty understanding of the principle of **audience**, the same is true of the *synagogue* of false teaching embraced and propagated by

121

The Keys of Bible Study

those within the Charismatic ranks. Charismatics fail to recognize that the sign gifts in the New Testament were given at a time of transition in the early church when the written New Testament had not yet been completed. During this time of transition, there were God-ordained gifts of the Holy Spirit which were given for the purpose of confirming that New Testament apostles and prophets were, in fact, speaking *of* God and *for* God. God confirmed their new message by giving the Jews exactly what 1 Corinthians 1:22 says they require: a sign. Hebrews 2:3-4 lets us know that the preaching and teaching of the New Testament…

> …at the first <u>began to be spoken by the Lord, and was confirmed unto us by them that heard him</u>; 4 <u>God also bearing them witness, both with signs and wonders</u>, and with divers <u>miracles</u>, and <u>gifts of the Holy Ghost</u>, according to his own will. (Heb 2:3b-4)

Those just happen to be the very things the entire Charismatic system of teaching are built upon. But all of those were intended for the Jews, to help them comprehend that God had made a shift from how they were accustomed to Him working according to the revelation of the Old Testament scriptures. Gentiles didn't need or require that… the Jews did!

We should note that, historically, when the New Testament revelation of God had been completed around 95 AD with the Apostle John receiving the Revelation of Jesus Christ (the last book of the New Testament), the sign gifts ceased to operate. Why? Because there was no longer a need to confirm the message of God. The completed Bible is its own confirmation of itself!

So, if there was no longer a biblical need for God to confirm His message through signs and wonders, miracles, and gifts of the Holy Ghost—and if the historical record reveals that they did, in fact, cease—how in the world did the Charismatic movement become one of most powerful and far-reaching doctrines in both the 20th and 21st centuries?

The modern Charismatic movement began on New Years Day 1901 at a Bible college in Topeka, Kansas. It unfolded like this: for a

122

Chapter 4 — The Key of Context

period of a few weeks, the school's founder and president, Charles Parham, had been asking the small student body to consider various questions about what he called "the sign of the baptism of the Holy Ghost," totally neglecting the Jewish nature and purpose of the sign gifts biblically. And once again, a group of people who were functioning as if they were Jews (when they weren't!) provided Satan all the latitude he needed to develop this elaborate *synagogue* of false teaching that has swept the world throughout the entire Laodicean Period of church history (1901 - Rapture; Rev 3:14-22).

These three false religious systems—Catholicism, Calvinism and Charismaticism—are all indicative of the elaborate theological paradigms that can be developed when people violate the principle of audience in identifying the context of a verse or passage, by saying they're Jews when they aren't.

Speaking of claiming promises directed to and intended for Jews, most of my efforts in the past decade have mainly focused on training pastors and leaders in one of the poorest countries in the world: Malawi, Africa. Surprisingly, a system of teaching that has been exported from the U.S., Kenya, and Nigeria—often referred to as the Prosperity Gospel—has swept into Malawi and many other extremely impoverished African nations, teaching, in effect, that God wants His people rich. This teaching is running rampant in a nation where the vast majority of the people will go their entire lifetime never holding a full-time job, and where the average annual income is often less than $250!

Obviously, Malawians are vulnerable to this teaching because of their desperate financial and material situation. But once again, recognize that Satan has been able to build this *synagogue*, or this so-called *theology,* upon divinely inspired declarations which God gave to the **Jews** of the nation of **Israel** in the **Old Testament**, promising that He would prosper them financially and bless them materially for obeying His word and exercising faith in His promises. Like those who embrace Replacement Theology, these false-gospel prosperity preachers proclaim that the promises God gave to His people the Jews are promises He now intends to be

123

The Keys of Bible Study

fulfilled in His people the Church—and thus, the financial and material blessing for their obedience and faith. This false teaching both originated and survives because of people who *say they are Jews* when they just flat-out *are not*.

Do you realize the amount of clear biblical, church-age teaching you have to violate to believe and/or teach the Prosperity Gospel? Colossians 3:1-2 clearly tells us,

> If ye then be risen with Christ, seek those things which are above, where Christ sitteth on the right hand of God. Set your affection on things above, not on things on the earth. (Col 3:1-2)

God is essentially saying, "Now that you've been saved, here's how you're to live your life." Notice, as New Testament believers, God specifically tells us *not* to seek financial gain or material things, and *not* to set our affection (our heart and mind) on them.

This same sentiment is expressed in Philippians 3:18-19, where Paul talks about a group of people he calls "the enemies of the cross of Christ." And who are they? He goes on to provide the answer: it is those

> …whose end is destruction, whose God is their belly [their fleshly desires], and whose glory is in their shame, who mind earthly things. (Php 3:19)

God makes abundantly clear that a life wrapped up in materialism or material blessings is what is characteristic of *the enemies of the cross of Christ*. As church-age believers, the kingdom through which God is now operating is a spiritual kingdom (the *kingdom of God*), not the physical kingdom promised to the Jews (the *kingdom of heaven*). Simply put, it is a violation of New Testament teaching to take verses or passages in which God is specifically promising material blessing to Old Testament Jews and trying to make them apply to New Testament Christians. It is a classic example of those to whom Peter was referring in 2 Peter 3:16 when he talked about

124

how those who are unlearned and unstable wrest the scriptures.

So, the first principle in understanding biblical context is properly determining the **audience**.

2. The Principle of <u>Content</u>

Biblical context is determined by keeping the specific verse being examined and interpreted within the context that has been revealed within the content of the whole book of the Bible in which it is located.

Which is to say, as we consider the biblical key of keeping verses in their context, we must recognize that it is not as easy as simply looking at the verse before and after. That's a great start, but if we're really going to study the word of God, and actually be workmen who are diligently seeking to *rightly divide the word of truth*, keeping verses in their context is a little more extensive and involved than that.

To put a **verse** in its true and complete biblical context, we must broaden our understanding to also consider the **passage**, asking ourselves: what is this passage teaching? Then, beyond just understanding the passage, we must also consider the **chapter**, asking ourselves: what is this chapter teaching? Then, beyond the chapter, we must also consider the entire **book**, asking ourselves: what is this book of the Bible teaching? And then, even beyond the book, we must consider the **Bible**, asking ourselves: why is this particular book in the Bible? In other words, we must determine what God's intention and purpose was for including this book of the Bible into the canon of scripture.

The Keys of Bible Study

At the end of that process, our understanding of a verse's context should look like this:

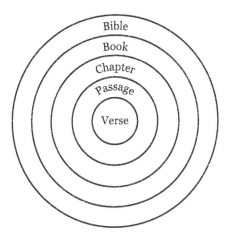

When we're talking about **keeping verses in their context,** this is how we must begin to train our minds to think. There's a chance you're thinking that this is a lot of work, and you'd be right! That's why God refers to those who *study* His word in 2 Timothy 2:15, as *workmen*. It really is a lot of work, but I'll also tell you this... as you employ the keys of Bible study, it also becomes a lot of fun! As God begins to open the treasures in His word to you, you're going to become so excited about the things He's revealing, you'll wish you had even more time to study.

KEY EXAMPLES:

Because this approach to setting the context of a verse is new for many, please allow me to provide a few examples to illustrate exactly how to utilize these principles. In these examples, I've chosen what I consider to be verses that, without putting them in their context, can be used to land people in eternal destruction (2 Pe 2:16), or lure people into believing and preaching false doctrine. With each example, we'll follow the same progression; we'll start with the outside circle (Bible), and begin working our way down

Chapter 4 — The Key of Context

to the innermost circle (verse), asking ourselves these questions...

- Why is this book in the **Bible**?
- What is this **book** actually teaching?
- What is this **chapter** actually teaching?
- What's happening as we get into this **passage**?
- Based on the information gathered by those first four questions, what does the **verse** actually say?

EXAMPLE #1: Acts 2:38

This is a verse that zealous people will often have on bumper stickers on their car or that churches will place on their marquees, in hopes that people will look up the verse and follow their false doctrine of including baptism as a condition for receiving salvation. And if undiscerning people do look up the verse without understanding how to put it in its context, it most definitely could prove problematic!

> Then Peter said unto them, Repent, and <u>be baptized</u> every one of you in the name of Jesus Christ <u>for the remission of sins, and ye shall receive the gift of the Holy Ghost</u>. (Act 2:38)

Allow me to illustrate the operation of the religious zealots of water baptism who emphasize and prioritize the teaching of Acts 2:38 as the means of biblical salvation:

Some guy comes to our church on a Sunday and gets saved by grace through faith in Jesus Christ (Eph 2:8-9) by confessing with his mouth the Lord Jesus and having a heart belief that God the Father raised Christ from the dead (Rom 10:9). He's obviously ecstatic about what God has done in saving him, and he's anxious to tell others about it at work the next day. As he comes into the break room, he says, "Hey guys! I wanted to let you know that I went to church yesterday, and I got saved!" Most of his coworkers don't really know how to respond to his testimony, but they're at least kind in appearing to share in this new convert's excitement.

A little while later, however, one of his coworkers comes over to him and says, "Hey, I heard you what you said about getting saved yesterday. Could I ask you something, though? Did you repent of your sin *and* get baptized in water yesterday?" And the new believer responds, saying, "Oh, I don't even know about all of that. All I know is God convicted me of being a sinner, and I told Him I believed that He died, was buried, and rose again, and I called upon Him to save me!"

His coworker responds by saying, "Well, you believe the Bible, don't you?" And the new believer responds, "Well, sure! I just told you; I followed the Bible's instruction and called on the name of Jesus to save me!" And the baptism zealot says, "Well, let me show you what it says over here in Acts 2:38. It says that Peter said unto them, first of all, to repent. And I assume that's what you were just explaining to me that you did when you called on His name. But, I want you to notice, Peter didn't stop there! Notice, he goes on to say, 'AND be baptized every one of you in the name of Jesus Christ for the remission of sins, and ye shall receive the gift of the Holy Ghost.' So, listen friend, if you haven't been baptized yet, your sins haven't really been forgiven, and you don't have the Holy Ghost living in you. And if you don't have the Holy Ghost in you, Romans 8:9 says you're 'none of his'. So, I hate to burst your bubble, friend, but according to the Bible, you aren't really saved yet."

And that's often how it happens. I believe that whole scenario epitomizes the danger of taking verses out of their context. Because you'll have to admit, their argument is pretty convincing—and as you can only imagine, would especially be so to a brand new believer!

So, how do we employ the principles of keeping verses in their context to answer this specific verse?

Chapter 4 — The Key of Context

Well, we begin by asking ourselves the question:

- Why is this book of the **Bible** (the book of Acts) included in the canon of scripture?

And with some of the things we've already talked about concerning the book of Acts in the previous chapter, this shouldn't be too hard for us to answer. The actual title of this book is *The Acts of the Apostles.* And what that lets us know is that this book of the Bible, first and foremost, isn't a doctrinal treatise of church theology. In other words, this isn't a book of the Bible in which we're going to attempt to build our personal theological framework or our create our church's doctrinal statement. The very title of the book lets us know before we even enter the first verse that it is predominantly intended for the purpose of providing the history of what happened after Christ rose from the dead and ascended to the right hand of His Father in heaven all the way to how local churches began to multiply on the earth. That's why this book is in our Bible: to give us a historical account of the acts the apostles did after our Lord ascended back to the Father.

Having made that determination, we now move deeper into the context by seeking to determine:

- What is the **book** of Acts actually teaching?

And again, as we saw in the previous chapter, the book of Acts is the book God gave to help us see some monumental transitions that were taking place during this time in the unfolding of His plan. We saw seven transitions which are made in this book:

1. From the four **Gospels** to the book of **Romans**

2. From and **Old Testament structure** to a **New Testament structure**

3. From God working primarily with the **Jews** to working primarily with the **Gentiles**

129

The Keys of Bible Study

4. From God's base of operations being in **Jerusalem** to being in **Antioch**

5. From God working through the **nation of Israel** to working through the **church**

6. From the ministry of **Peter** to the ministry of **Paul**

7. From a **Kingdom of Heaven** message to a **Kingdom of God** message

So, to establish the biblical context of this controversial—and perhaps even confusing—verse (Act 2:38), we must understand that the book of Acts is first and foremost a *historical* book and that, secondly, it is a *transitional* book.

Having established and understood those two things about God's purposes through the book of Acts, we now move deeper into our search, asking ourselves:

• Why is this **chapter** in this book?

And as we examine it, we find that Acts 2 is a historical account of a very important day in the history of the nation of Israel and in the history of the church; it is the day of Pentecost. And on the day of Pentecost, Peter, the apostle to the Jews, is the one who is preaching. And as we are making our way toward Peter's "controversial" words in Acts 2:38, we must determine who the audience is that Peter is actually addressing. (Remember, that's one of the key ways we determine context!) Watch how this chapter makes that abundantly clear:

Luke is careful to identify the audience in verse 5. He writes, "And there were dwelling in Jerusalem, **Jews**..."

In verse 14, Luke says, "But Peter, standing up with the eleven, lifted up his voice, and said unto them, **Ye men of Judaea**, and all **ye that dwell at Jerusalem**..."

130

Chapter 4 — The Key of Context

As Peter is in the midst of preaching his message to the residents of Judaea and Jerusalem, he says to them in verse 22: "**Ye men of Israel**, hear these words..."

And as Peter begins the conclusion of his message, notice that he once again makes his audience abundantly clear in verse 36, saying: "Therefore let **all the house of Israel** know assuredly, that God hath made that same Jesus, whom ye have crucified, both Lord and Christ."

Peter is getting up in the face of and pointing his finger at the Jews in and around Jerusalem who had called for the Lord's death, telling them that it was by their wicked hands the Messiah had been crucified (Act 2:23,36). Throughout the entire second chapter of Acts, the context is very Jewish, and is specifically aimed at the Jews of the nation of Israel who were guilty of calling for Jesus's death.

So, having established the overarching context of the chapter of the verse in question, we now proceed by specifically asking ourselves:

- What is happening in the **passage**?

In the passage (2:36-38), Peter is in the midst of his famous sermon on the day of Pentecost. In it, he absolutely nails the Jews' hides to the wall, informing them that they were responsible for killing their very own Messiah and Lord (2:36). And as the Spirit of God revealed to these Jews through Peter's preaching what they had actually done, verse 37 says,

> Now when [the Jews] heard this, they were pricked in their heart, and said unto Peter and to the rest of the apostles, Men and brethren, what shall we do? (Act 2:37)

And having answered the first four questions in determining context...

1. The purpose and placement of the book of Acts in the Bible;

131

The Keys of Bible Study

2. The purpose and teaching of the book of Acts;

3. The purpose and teaching of Acts chapter two; and

4. The purpose and teaching of the passage…

…we should now be ready to answer the fifth question:

- What does the **verse** in question actually mean in its context?

So, let's look at it. The particular **verse** we're seeking to put in its context (verse 38, i.e. *"Repent and be baptized"*) is Peter's answer to the question they've just asked in verse 37 about what they needed to do, now that they had crucified their very own Messiah. And may I remind you, that the *they* who are asking the question in verse 37 just happen to be *Jews*. And the question the Jews are asking *Peter* (the Apostle to the Jews) is about what they, the *nation of Israel*, needed to do now that they understood they were guilty of crucifying their Messiah, the very Lord of glory (2:36).

Please allow me to call to your attention here that the question they're asking about what they needed to do in this situation *is not* the same question that was being asked by the Philippian jailer in Acts 16:30. What Luke is detailing in Acts 16 is his divinely inspired account of when Paul and Silas had been imprisoned in Philippi, and God brought an earthquake that broke open the doors of the prison, allowing them the ability to simply walk out in freedom. Had Paul and Silas escaped, Roman law at this time would have inflicted upon the keeper of the prison the death penalty. That's why when the jailer was awakened out of his sleep and saw the doors of the prison open, he reached for a sword to take his own life on the spot, presuming that Paul and Silas had taken the opportunity to escape. By the question the jailer asked Paul and Silas when he saw that they had not left, it's apparent that they had been witnessing to the jailer earlier that evening to no avail. But when the jailer saw this expression of true Christianity being lived out before his eyes, the jailer was brought under immediate conviction. This is what prompted his infamous question in Acts 16:30: "Sirs, what must I do to be saved?"

132

Chapter 4 — The Key of Context

But pay close attention! This is not the same question that the Jews were asking back on the Day of Pentecost in Acts 2:37. When a member of the Christian Church, the Church of Christ, or the Disciples of Christ whips out this passage without establishing the context, most people just typically assume that the question being asked in Acts 2:37 is the same question the Philippian jailer was asking. But that isn't the question the people in Acts 2:37 were asking at all! It is a totally different **context**! The question they were asking is: what do *we*, the Nation of Israel, do now that *we* have crucified *our* Messiah? And to make it anything other than that—or to try to apply the condition of baptism for the remission of sin or the gift of the Holy Ghost—to anyone other than those Jews in the first century who were guilty of crucifying the Lord Jesus Christ is not only to grossly take this verse out of context; it is to preach and teach absolute heresy.

What Peter said to these Jews on the Day of Pentecost who were guilty of calling for their Messiah's death was intended strictly for them. And what did these Jews in the first century who had witnessed the ministry of Christ, and yet called for Him to be crucified rather than Barabbas, need to do to have their sin remitted and receive the Holy Ghost? They needed to do exactly what Peter told them; they needed to "repent <u>and</u> be baptized." It says what it means, and it means what it says.

Based on the biblical context of Acts 2:38, is this the message of the gospel that Paul and Silas gave to the Gentile Philippian jailer? Is it the method of salvation for every person wanting to be saved in the church age? Absolutely not! Paul clearly describes church-age salvation for those of us who are not first-century Jews:

> That if thou shalt confess with thy mouth the Lord Jesus, and shalt believe in thine heart that God hath raised him from the dead, thou shalt be saved. (Rom 10:9)

The Philippian jailer was a Gentile just like most of us, and he asked a personal question: "What must **I** do to be saved?" And what was the answer? It wasn't, "Repent and be baptized." No, Paul

The Keys of Bible Study

and Silas told him to simply "**Believe** on the Lord Jesus Christ" (Act 16:31). It was that simple, and that hard. Man always wants to add some condition to God's free gift of salvation—whether it be through water baptism, keeping the seven sacraments, holding out faithful to the end, and on and on and on.

Please understand that this is no small issue! To put baptism (or anything other than confession and belief) as a condition for salvation is actually to add to the finished work of Christ. And to add to the work of Christ not only screams that the work of Christ wasn't sufficient; it actually nullifies the power of the gospel to save, because it is no longer even the gospel! It is what Paul referred to as "another gospel" (2Co 11:4; Gal 1:8-9).

This isn't simply a matter of, "Well, some denominations believe baptism is a part of salvation, and we don't." No! We're talking about what is actually the *true saving gospel,* and what is a *false gospel* which is powerless to save.

This is certainly not to say that water baptism isn't significant, because it most certainly is! But the reason it's significant isn't because it's a vital condition for our *salvation*. It's significant because it is a vital part of our *obedience* to Christ's lordship *following* our salvation (Mat 28:19-20; Luk 6:46).

And someone is no doubt pondering right now: "Well, why did God place baptism as a condition for the salvation of these first century Jews who had crucified their Messiah and Lord in Acts 2?" Well, as we've seen, the transitions in the book of Acts had not yet been made, including the transition from the Old Testament to the New Testament. And in keeping with the Old Testament ceremonial washing that was associated with the shedding of *innocent blood* (which obviously foreshadowed the ultimate fulfillment of the shedding of the blood of the Lord Jesus Christ), God wanted these Jews who were responsible for shedding Christ's *innocent blood* to fulfill the Old Testament picture by being baptized.

134

Chapter 4 — The Key of Context

EXAMPLE #2: Galatians 5:4

This is a verse which many individuals and denominations use to teach that it is possible, having once been saved, to lose your salvation. And unless this verse is put in its context, it would certainly give every indication that you could!

> Christ is become of no effect unto you, whosoever of you are justified by the law; ye are fallen from grace. (Gal 5:4)

Those who espouse the teaching that it is possible to lose your salvation will often hold this verse up as a proof text, or to describe someone who isn't walking according to God's word. You will hear them say something like, "Well, so and so was saved, but now they've fallen from grace." In their interpretation, they mean that this person has lost their salvation and needs to get saved again!

But is that really what Paul was saying to these believers in the region of Galatia and to us? Is it possible for those of us who have been placed in Christ to do something (or to *not* do something) that would cause us to lose our salvation? Is that consistent with the New Testament teaching for those of us in Christ's church? Is it even consistent with the teaching of the book of Galatians?

Just what are we to do with Paul telling the Galatians they were *fallen from grace*? Well, first and foremost, we need to make sure that we place it in its biblical **context**! And so we begin in that outermost circle in the above illustration, making sure we answer the question:

- Why is the book of Galatians in the **Bible**?

As we study this book, it's not difficult to see that God chose to include the book of Galatians into the canon of scripture to teach the body of Christ that Gentiles are free from Old Testament Law and Judaism (the teachings of the Jews).

135

The Keys of Bible Study

We learn this from what prompted the book of Galatians to be written in the first place. We pick up that vital piece of information back in Acts, where Luke tells us,

> And certain men which came down from Judaea taught the brethren, and said, Except ye be circumcised after the manner of Moses, ye cannot be saved. (Act 15:1)

It had unfolded like this: Paul and his missionary team had come into the region of Galatia (which is modern day Turkey) and proclaimed the good news that salvation is by grace through faith, apart from adherence to any of the rules, regulations and laws of the Old Testament. It was the same message you and I responded to which provided our salvation! And glory to God, as Paul proclaimed that message throughout Galatia, people were born again by grace alone, through faith alone, in Christ alone, resulting in the planting of local churches.

Shortly thereafter, however, as we just read in Acts 15:1, men from Judaea had come down into this region and were teaching these born again Gentiles that even though they had placed their faith in Christ, it was still incumbent upon them to keep the laws of the Old Testament, represented in circumcision. Historically, we now refer to these false teachers as *Judaizers*—a term that encapsulates the fact that they were zealous for the Jewish faith and, specifically, the teaching that Gentiles needed the mixture of Jewish law-keeping with their belief in Christ in order to truly be saved. With that historical backdrop, God reveals His whole purpose in including the book of Galatians in the Bible in Galatians 2:21, where Paul says: "I do not frustrate the grace of God: for if righteousness come by the law, then Christ is dead in vain."

Paul is seeking to make clear in this verse that we *frustrate the grace of God* when our actions illustrate that we believe we can be made righteous by something we *do* (or something we *don't do*). It frustrates his grace because if those things had the potential to make us righteous, it would mean that the death of Christ wasn't even necessary, and that He actually died in vain! It would mean

136

Chapter 4 — The Key of Context

that God could have just bypassed the whole suffering and death of His only begotten Son and simply commanded and demanded that we perform strict adherence to the law.

That's why God put this book into the canon of scripture: to teach us that righteousness is not *achieved*, but *received*—that salvation is imparted to Gentiles completely by *grace*, and not by *law-keeping*.

Which leads us to the next question in determining context:

• What is the real teaching of this **book**?

As we examine the actual content of this book, we find that this isn't a book to teach people how to be saved; it's a book to teach saved people how to be spiritual. Just that piece of information alone will do a whole bunch to keep us between the white lines doctrinally in this book. It provides the basic framework we need as we move deeper into the process of determining context, as we examine the content of the various chapters and seek to answer the question:

• Why is this **chapter** in this book?

As we look specifically at Galatians 5, we find that the purpose of this chapter is to teach us *how to walk*; verses 16 and 25 reveal this to us.

This I say then, <u>Walk in the Spirit</u>, and ye shall not fulfil the lust of the flesh....If we live in the Spirit, let us also <u>walk in the Spirit</u>. (Gal 5:16,25)

The fact is, if we're going to be *spiritual* (the purpose of the **book**), we must *walk in the Spirit* (the purpose of the **chapter**). We find in this chapter that Paul wanted to emphasize a particular truth when it comes to walking that even 12-month-old babies understand: namely, that before we can *walk*, we must first learn to *stand!* The problem the Galatians had is they could do neither! Because verse

The Keys of Bible Study

4 tells us that they had *"fallen."* That's the context of the chapter.

As we move even deeper into determining the context of Galatians 5:4, we ask ourselves:

- What is the context of the particular **passage** where the verse is found?

We find that Paul's admonition concerning the Galatians' fallen state in this passage (or, the solution to their problem) wasn't for them to "get saved again". That's not what he tells them! He tells them to get up! He tells them to get back up on their spiritual feet, so they can resume the position of standing. The false teaching of the Judaizers had knocked them down. They had *fallen,* and from that position it would be impossible for them to *walk.* So Paul admonishes them in this passage to stand up. Look at the first verse in this chapter:

> <u>Stand</u> fast therefore in the liberty wherewith Christ hath made us free, and be not entangled again with the yoke of bondage. (Gal 5:1)

Trying to add the keeping of the law to their newfound faith is what had tangled the Galatians up and caused them to fall. So Paul says, "Look guys! If you're ever going to get back to the grace walk that God intended the Christian life to be, you're going to have to get back to where you're standing on your own two spiritual feet, so you can walk in the Spirit (Gal. 5:16). So you can walk, not in the power of the flesh and your own works, but in the power of the Spirit—what God does through you!"

So now, having set the context for why the book of Galatians is in the **Bible**, what the **book** is actually teaching, what the **chapter** is actually teaching, and what the **passage** is actually teaching, we are now ready to understand the real teaching of the **verse**.

Chapter 4 — The Key of Context

We find that Paul is most certainly not saying (as false teachers try to lead us to believe) that from the sin in our life we fall out of God's grace into an unsaved state. No, no, no... a thousand times, no! As the context clearly reveals, what he's actually saying to the Galatians (and to every believer in the church age) is that through your attempts to do righteousness by the law, you have fallen from the very thing you trusted to make you righteous. And that, of course, is grace.

And you know what the crazy thing is about Galatians 5:4? The people who use this verse to teach that you can lose your salvation think that the verse is referring to those who have lost their salvation. The reality is, however, that this verse is actually directed to them! It's directed to those who teach that you can lose your salvation, or that there's something we have to *do* or *not do* to be righteous or spiritual! God's indictment in this passage is upon *them.* What He's saying in the verse is this: by adding the keeping of the law to your salvation, you've fallen from the very and only thing which saved you and actually makes you spiritual: grace. This brings us back to the theme of the entire book—don't frustrate the grace of God.

Setting the context of a verse in the Bible is just that easy... and just that hard! Just like 2 Timothy 2:15 says, understanding the Bible requires that we become a *workman,* and it requires *study.* But understanding **how to keep verses in their context** (the Key of Context) keeps the process very *simple* (2Co 11:3).

139

THE KEY OF COMPARISON

We have very dutifully been working through just how it is that we can come to the treasure of God's Word and have the keys we need to unlock the truth contained within. We now come to...

The fourth key of Bible study:
UTILIZE GOD'S PRINCIPLE OF COMPARING SCRIPTURE WITH SCRIPTURE.

Notice, first of all, my emphasis on this being *God's principle* of comparing scripture with scripture. It is worded that way very specifically, because this principle is not something I invented or developed, nor is it something those who invested in me invented or developed. The Key of Comparison, just as with the previous keys we've discussed, is a principle of biblical interpretation that is clearly observed and/or identified in scripture. And though all of the keys of Bible study have been extremely significant, I must say: this key has been one of the most life-changing and ministry-changing for me. I sincerely hope it can become that for you!

KEY VERSE: 1 Corinthians 2:13

"Which things also we speak, not in the words which man's wisdom teacheth, but which the Holy Ghost

teacheth; comparing spiritual things with spiritual."

As we begin this explanation of the Key of Comparison, notice several key things about verse 13. First of all, notice that Paul sets the things he was speaking and teaching in contrast to the things man's wisdom teaches. Secondly, notice that the things Paul said God used him to "speak" were not "in the words which man's wisdom teacheth," but were in the words "which the Holy Ghost teacheth." He goes on to let us know that these words "which the Holy Ghost teacheth" are actually taught by "comparing spiritual things with spiritual."

The question, of course, is: just what are these **words** which the Holy Ghost teacheth, and what are the **spiritual things** that are to be compared with **spiritual things**, so that those **words** can be understood?

To answer that question, let's take a minute to first put verse 13 in its context by acquainting ourselves with the entire passage…

> And I, brethren, when I came to you, came not with excellency of speech or of wisdom, declaring unto you the testimony of God. 2 For I determined not to know any thing among you, save Jesus Christ, and him crucified. 3 And I was with you in weakness, and in fear, and in much trembling. 4 And my speech and my preaching was not with enticing words of man's wisdom, but in demonstration of the Spirit and of power: 5 That your faith should not stand in the wisdom of men, but in the power of God. 6 Howbeit we speak wisdom among them that are perfect: yet not the wisdom of this world, nor of the princes of this world, that come to nought: 7 But we speak the wisdom of God in a mystery, even the hidden wisdom, which God ordained before the world unto our glory: 8 Which none of the princes of this world knew: for had they known it, they would not have crucified the Lord of glory. 9 But as it is written, Eye hath not seen, nor ear heard, neither have entered into the heart of man, the things which God hath prepared for them that love him. 10 But God hath revealed them unto us

Chapter 5 — The Key of Comparison

by his Spirit: for the Spirit searcheth all things, yea, the deep things of God. 11 For what man knoweth the things of a man, save the spirit of man which is in him? even so the things of God knoweth no man, but the Spirit of God. 12 Now we have received, not the spirit of the world, but the spirit which is of God; that we might know the things that are freely given to us of God. 13 Which things also we speak, not in the words which man's wisdom teacheth, but which the Holy Ghost teacheth; comparing spiritual things with spiritual. (1Co 2:1-13)

This is a very monumental and interesting passage. With the subject matter of this passage clearly established, I wish I could tell you how many sermons I've heard through the years from verse 9 concerning heaven! Preachers somehow dive into this passage, grab a hold of verse 9, wrest it out of its context (2Pe 3:16), and preach about how our *eyes* have never seen anything like they'll see in heaven; our *ears* have never heard anything like they'll hear in heaven; and our *hearts* have never been able to conceive of the things in heaven that God has prepared for those of us who love him.

Though all of that certainly makes for good "preaching", and though I'm quite certain all of those things are absolutely true about heaven, there's just one problem. You couldn't find heaven in this passage with a spotlight, a jackhammer, and a stick of dynamite! Heaven isn't mentioned or even alluded to in six chapters in either direction of this passage. But as we saw in the previous chapter, this is the kind of thing that happens when a verse is taken out of its context. And though it makes for good "preaching", it does such a disservice to God's holy Word!

This passage is actually talking about the wisdom of God—not heaven! And the meaning of verse 9 in its context is that when it comes to God's wisdom, nobody can see it with their natural human *eyes*. Nobody can hear it with their natural human *ears*. And nobody's natural human *heart* can receive it, or even conceive of it!

143

The Keys of Bible Study

Throughout this entire passage, notice that Paul has been setting up a series of very important contrasts:

- The *wisdom of men* (2:5) versus the *power of God* (2:5)
- The *wisdom of this world* (2:6) versus the *wisdom of God* (2:7)
- The *things of a man* (2:11) versus the *things of God* (2:11)
- The *spirit of man* (2:11) versus the *Spirit of God* (2:11)
- The *spirit of the world* (2:12) versus the *spirit which is of God* (2:12)
- The *words which man's wisdom teacheth* (2:13) versus the *words which the Holy Ghost teacheth* (2:13)

By simply focusing on the left side of the contrasts listed above, we could summarize the teaching of this passage concerning *man's wisdom* this way:

Man has a *wisdom* with which he operates in the world. This *wisdom* has to do with *things* that specifically relate to *man*, and are taught to and known by a man through a spiritual process. In this process, the *spirit of the world* uses **words** to *teach* this *wisdom* which find entrance into man's spirit. From a very practical standpoint, we might refer to these **words** as the the teaching of man's wisdom from men like Plato, Aristotle, Socrates, Voltaire, Confucius, and the like.

If we focus on the right side of the contrasts listed above, we could summarize the teaching of this passage concerning *God's wisdom* (2:7) this way:

God, likewise, has a *wisdom* with which he operates. This *wisdom* has to do with *things* that specifically relate to *God*, and are taught to and known by believers through a spiritual process. In this process, the *Spirit of God* uses **words** to teach His wisdom. Paul says that *we have received the spirit which is of God* for this purpose: *that we might know the things that are freely given to us of God (2:12)... yea,*

144

the deep things of God (2:10). Paul reemphasizes this point in verse 13, telling us that *the things which are freely given to us of God* are taught to us by the **words** *which the Holy Ghost teacheth.*

So again, the question is, what are these **words** *which the Holy Ghost teacheth?* Just as importantly, where are these **words?** Well, verse 10 lets us know that **what** these words are is what *God hath revealed... unto us by his Spirit* (2:10). And where the **words** the Holy Ghost uses to teach us are found is in the **revelation** the Spirit of God Himself gave to us in the **word of God**!

And how is it that the Holy Spirit actually *reveals* His revelation (the word of God) to us (2:10)? Verse 13 says it is through the spiritual process whereby we take the spiritual truths found in the word of God and compare them with the spiritual truths found in other places in the word of God (and thus, the principle of *comparing scripture with scripture*). And as we utilize this principle, something happens to our spiritual *eyes*, our spiritual *ears*, and our spiritual *hearts* (2:9). They are able to *see, hear* and *understand* the revelation of God's wisdom in His word (2:10).

This, my friend, is the God-ordained method the Holy Spirit uses to *reveal* His truth to us and is what constitutes the Key of Comparison.

KEY THOUGHT:

In the 1000 year period known historically as the Dark Ages (approximately 500 to 1500 AD), the Bible was overtly taken out of the hands of the common man through persecution.

What I'm about to say may be a little unsettling for some, and it may at first sound like I have an axe to grind with Roman Catholics, but let me assure you: I don't! I love Roman Catholics, and would go to the ends of the earth to see them freed from the death-grip their church holds on them. Again, I love Roman Catholics, but I must admit that I have a righteous hatred for their church (Psa

97:10; 119:104,113,128,163). I realize that some of the things I'm about to say may be hard for religious Roman Catholics to believe, but I assure you: this is anything but hate speech. The things I'm about to reference can be found in any Catholic Encyclopedia on this planet. It's all there in black and white.

What took place during the Dark Ages is that the Roman Catholic Church basically said, "Peter is the one who was given the keys to the kingdom of Heaven, and he was our first Pope, so now we're the ones with spiritual and physical authority on this planet! So, here's the deal: there's no need for you to have that Bible. From now on, we'll tell you what the Bible says. You come to us, and we'll tell you what's in there, and you won't have to worry yourselves with what it actually means, because we'll interpret it for you! So, you just be good little Catholic boys and girls—or we'll kill you!"

Now, obviously, I'm taking a 1000 year period and seeking to cut it to the chase—but again, as I said previously, that's not hate-speech, intolerance, or religious bias. It's simply the cold, hard, historical facts. In 1994, when Pope John Paul II came out with *What Catholics Believe* (which was touted as the premier clarifying document concerning modern Roman Catholic beliefs and doctrine), it reiterated the historic Roman Catholic position that the Catholic Church is the sole interpreter of scripture.

But during the Dark Ages, things weren't as civil, and there was an overt operation to make certain the common man would not have the Bible in his possession. Though even portions of Bibles were obviously scarce prior to the invention of the printing press, books such as *Foxe's Book of Martyrs* and *Martyr's Mirror* record both pagan and papal Rome's insistence upon getting the Bible out of the hands of the common man. With those in local churches and regions throughout Europe who had been entrusted with the responsibility of the stewardship of their handwritten portions of scriptures, failure to relinquish those scriptures resulted in persecution, torture, imprisonment, and even death.

What had actually taken place on the earth during the Dark Ages is that Satan had developed an antichrist religious system through which he could operate *in the name of Jesus*, as it were, in an attempt to actually defame *the name of Jesus* on the earth. It was really nothing more than a *counterfeit* church developed by Satan in an attempt to *counter* Christ's true church. Always keep in mind Satan's insidious passion to "be *like* the most high" (Isa. 14:14)! He is a master counterfeiter of our Lord Jesus Christ! And the counterfeit Christian religious system through which Satan operated during the Dark Ages (and up to this present day!) is none other than the one that goes by the name of "the universal Christianity," or the Roman Catholic Church. (Note that the word "Catholic" actually means "the universal Christianity.") Revelation 2:9 actually refers to this religious system or "church" as "the synagogue of Satan." (For a thorough explanation of the "synagogue of Satan" and Satan's role in and through the Roman Catholic Church, please avail yourself of the book entitled, <u>Church History</u>, by my fellow Living Faith Fellowship pastor and friend, Greg Axe.) And thus, the Key Thought from above:

In the 1000 year period known historically as the Dark Ages (from approximately 500 to 1500 A.D.), the Bible was <u>overtly</u> taken out of the hands of the <u>common man</u> through <u>persecution</u>.

But, the Key Thought continues...

In the last 100 years or so, we have entered into a new type of Dark Ages. The Bible is now being <u>covertly</u> taken out of the hands of the <u>common man</u> through <u>education</u>. (Mar 12:37)

Now, when I refer to it being a covert operation, I don't mean that dastardly people secretly sat around a table in a dimly lit room somewhere and with hushed tones and creepy laughter said to each other, "Hey, the common man has had the word of God back in his possession for the last several hundred years, so let's find a way to very subtly get it back out of his hands! Ah-ha-ha-ha-ha!" No, it certainly didn't come down that way—and yet, practically speaking, that's exactly what the Devil has been successful in orchestrating! Through education, the enemy has been able to find a new way to cause the world to be void of the light of the word of God, that he might keep it in darkness. And sad to say, few people have even recognized that it happened, much less how.

So, just how is it that education has been used to take the Bible out of the hands of the common man? Well, in the last hundred years or so, though the enemy has forged an all-out attack on the word of God, at the same time it has been an ever-so-subtle attack—very similar to the "Yea, hath God said?" strategy he subtly put into operation against Eve in the Garden in Genesis 3. Without most believers even realizing what has happened, many in the educated theological community have successfully led the common man to believe that the word and words of God—which the Spirit of God so carefully gave to the human authors by *inspiration*—has been *preserved* for us solely in the "original manuscripts."

Now, it's very important that we understand what is actually involved in this whole "original manuscript" discussion. Because at first glance, it would appear that what is reflected in the doctrinal statements of most churches which are viewed as conservative, evangelical, Bible-believing, and Bible-preaching is that they possess a strong belief in the authority of scripture. The way it is typically worded on their websites or official church documents is something to this effect: "We believe the Bible is God's holy and inspired word, and is therefore completely infallible and inerrant…"

Now, that statement would be great if it stopped there, but it typically doesn't. It's usually followed by a phrase that, for all practical purposes, completely nullifies everything stated before it: "…in the original manuscripts." Because you see, to say you believe the Bible is the inspired, infallible and inerrant word of God *in the original manuscripts* is to say that you don't actually believe that an authoritative Bible even exists. I know that sounds ludicrous, but the reason I say that is because there is not an original manuscript anywhere in existence. The oldest manuscript in existence is a copy that's dated at least 100 years after the date of the original writing.

Chapter 5 — The Key of Comparison

So, if the inspired, infallible, and inerrant Bible is locked up in the original manuscripts, but the original manuscripts don't actually exist, it means that there is not an authoritative Bible anywhere on this planet. There's no infallible word of God which can be held in our hands, or which we can read, study, hide in our hearts, preach from, and lead a soul to Christ!

Many conservative Bible-believing people in the last 100 years have often come to their local church with Bibles in hand, only to hear the pastor say that the verse they're looking at in their Bible isn't found in the original manuscripts, or that the English word they're looking at in their Bible is a poor translation of the word in the so-called original Greek or Hebrew, and it actually means something completely different. And because of the pastor's vast education and the degrees after his name, or the prominent place he holds within their denomination or the evangelical community, people trust what they say. But do you see what has happened? The preacher has once again usurped the place of sole interpreter of the scripture, and people have to come to them to find out what is and isn't in the Bible.

In other words, we now have a new kind of "priest class" over the common man which makes him dependent on them to give him the word of God. That's why I stated in the Key Thought that we have entered into a new type of Dark Ages. And the result has been that the common man is left without a Bible again. We must never lose sight of God's introductory description of Satan in the Bible: "Now the serpent was more subtil than any beast of the field which the Lord God had made" (Gen 3:1).

The passion behind the *Keys of Bible Study* is very simply to get the Bible back into the hands of common man where it belongs. In Jesus's ministry, it was the pious, religious, theologically educated, intelligentsia who had such a hard time with Him and who sought to discredit and silence Him. In great contrast with them, however, Mark tells us in Mark 12:37 that "the common people heard him gladly." And historically, the God-fearing, Jesus-loving, Devil-despising, sin-hating, world-renouncing, Christ-exalting, mission-minded, soul-winning foot-soldiers and sword-slingers in the body of Christ have always been the *common people* (Mar 12:37; 1Co 1:26-28). No wonder the enemy is so dead-set on getting the Bible out of their hands!

I would like to offer one final word about those precious original manuscripts with which Christianity has become so enthralled and infatuated in the last 100 years. The fact is, the Bible has never existed as a complete compilation of divinely inspired "original manuscripts"! By the constant references to them by preachers, teachers and commentators, it sounds as if there is a complete set of original manuscripts from each of the 66 books of the Bible in some library or museum somewhere, to which they have access. But there is no such thing—nor has there ever been! And like I said above, there is not even a single original manuscript to be found anywhere on this entire planet—not one!

So much for all of this hoopla about the Bible being *preserved* in the original manuscripts. Sometimes kids use their imagination to play with an imaginary friend. That's fine for kids, but if adults are asking you to come over and hang out with their imaginary friend, they likely have a serious problem! May I simply be a voice to say that many in the educational community (the scholars, the doctors of theology, the religious aristocracy, if you will) have asked us to hang with their imaginary original manuscripts long enough. It's about time we woke up and trusted the God of the word to *give* and *teach* us His word, rather than trust those who appear to champion the cause for the word of God while they are very subtly in the process of taking it out of our hands.

Yeah, I get a little passionate about this—because I believe God is! He tells us there is a holy, inspired, infallible, inerrant, preserved Bible that we can hold in our hands! (Mat 5:18, 24:35; Mar 13:31; Luk 21:33; 1Th 2:13; 2Pe 3:2) He also tells us to be careful not to let it out of our grasp (2Ti 1:13). And as we've been seeing in 1 Corinthians 2:9-13, God is careful to tell us that if we have the Spirit of God living in us and use His God-ordained method of comparing scripture with scripture, we can know the Bible because the Holy Ghost living inside of us will supernaturally reveal it to us. And again, not just the *basic things*, but *the deep things of God* (1Co 2:10). Hallelujah! I'm passionate about everybody who has the Spirit of God living in them believing they actually have a Bible, and that they can know the Bible they have!

Now, we've already talked quite a bit about the Key Principles that flow out of 1 Corinthians 2:9-13, but let's see if we can sift them down into succinct statements which, Lord willing, can serve as handles to help us carry them with us.

KEY PRINCIPLES:

Principle #1:
The Bible is both a SPIRITUAL and SUPERNATURAL book. It is, therefore, closed to the intellect and heart of a NATURAL MAN (i.e. someone who is SPIRITUALLY DEAD).

We've just spent quite a bit of time looking at 1 Corinthians 2:1-13. In the very next verse (2:14), Paul continues, "But the natural man..." Let's stop there, and make sure we understand what a *natural man* is biblically.

You'll remember from Genesis 1:26 that the Godhead (the Three-in-One) made the declaration that They were going to make man "after [their] likeness." In the historical record of God actually making the man in Genesis 2:7, we find that He fulfilled exactly what He had declared in Genesis 1:26 in giving man His likeness! God made man a three-in-one replica of Himself, as it were, giving man a **body**, a **spirit**, and a **soul**. (God the Father representing the soul or the "soulish" part of man; God the Holy Spirit representing the spirit or "spiritual" part of man; and God the Son/Word, who would be "made flesh", representing the body or "physical" part of man.) Paul also identifies this three-in-one *likeness* in 1 Thessalonians 5:23, saying, "And the very God of peace sanctify you wholly; and I pray God your whole **spirit** and **soul** and **body** be preserved blameless unto the coming of our Lord Jesus Christ."

The Keys of Bible Study

That is how man was made from the beginning: a three-part being who was very much alive in every way, and in perfect fellowship with his God and Father who had created him. But factor into this original design that when Adam chose sin, it meant he was also choosing death! God had told him that *in the day* he would make the fateful choice of sin, he would *surely die* (Gen 2:17). And die he did! As soon as the forbidden fruit touched his lips, death was set in motion. Though he would live approximately another 900 years before dying **physically**, recognize that the instant he had partaken of that fruit, he died **spiritually**. God said that Adam would die in the day that he ate the fruit. And though Adam didn't die physically, something did die that day. And that death caused Adam and the woman to run for cover when God came down to walk with them as He had done in previous days. And whatever died was something that caused that same death to be passed upon all men (Rom 5:12), requiring that all men experience a new spiritual birth (John 3:1-8), whereby we are "born of the Spirit."

It was from man's **spirit** that he fellowshipped with God in a personal love relationship. And so, because of the spiritual death that was the consequence of sin, perfect and holy relationship with God was immediately severed. That same spiritual death passed on to every one of us who have been born into this world of a human father. This means that from our very birth we are all born into this world with a **body**, which holds a **soul** that will live forever somewhere, but inside of that soul resides a **spirit** that is dead (Eph 2:5a). And that, biblically, is the definition of a *natural man:* our natural state as the offspring of Adam.

With that understanding, what Paul says about the *natural man* should be simple to comprehend. Paul says,

> But the natural man [fleshly **body**, an eternal **soul**, dead **spirit**) receiveth not the things of the Spirit of God: for they are foolishness unto him: neither can he know them, because they are spiritually discerned. (1Co 2:14)

Simply put, spiritually dead people have no capacity to comprehend

152

or apply God's spiritual and supernatural truth.

Principle #2:
God's WISDOM (1Co 2), or, in other words, God's WORD (the BIBLE) cannot be discerned or understood using MAN'S WISDOM. It must be REVEALED by God's own SPIRIT.

We saw this earlier in the explanation of 1 Corinthians 2:1-10, but I bring it up again to make a very specific point. This book is titled *Keys of Bible Study* and through it, to the best of my human ability, I'm seeking to identify the biblical tools needed to understand and know the word of God. But let me hasten to say that what this passage is telling us, is that in the end, the Holy Spirit of God is the One who teaches us the Bible—human teachers or no human teachers, and keys or no keys! How much we're able to comprehend about the Bible actually comes down to how much we depend upon the Holy Spirit of God to *reveal* it to us.

In John 14, Jesus is beginning to talk to the disciples about the fact that He would be leaving them. He says in verses 15-17:

> If ye love me, keep my commandments. And I will pray the Father, and he shall give you another Comforter, that he may abide with you for ever; Even the Spirit of truth... (Joh 14:15-17)

For three and a half years, Jesus had been their Comforter. He had walked with them, He had loved them, had always been there for them, and had taught them the truth of God. But all of that was about to change. However, before He left, Jesus desperately wanted His disciples to know that the Father was going to give them *another Comforter*—and He (that *other Comforter*) would never leave them, but would abide with them forever.

In this same discourse, Jesus says to His disciples:

> I have yet many things to say unto you, but ye cannot bear

The Keys of Bible Study

them now. Howbeit when he, the Spirit of truth, is come, he will guide you into all truth… (Joh 16:12-13)

Notice now, how much truth did Jesus say His Spirit would guide us into? All of it! And if there were any question whatsoever about just what Jesus meant when He speaks here of *truth*, He settles that in this very same discourse as well. As Jesus is praying in the very next chapter, in John 17:17, He prays to the Father saying, "Sanctify them through thy truth: thy word is truth." May we all carry away from Jesus's declaration that the Bible isn't just a true book, and it doesn't simply contain truth; rather, the Bible is truth. But to understand *the truth*, do you know what we need? Jesus tells us: we need the *Spirit of truth* to *guide* us into *all truth*.

The Apostle John talks further about this same reality in his first epistle. He says:

But the anointing which ye have received of him abideth in you, and ye need not that any man teach you: but as the same anointing teacheth you of all things, and is truth, and is no lie, and even as it hath taught you, ye shall abide in him. (1Jo 2:27)

The anointing John is referring to is the anointing of the Holy Spirit we received at salvation. John's point here isn't that the Holy Spirit doesn't use human instrumentality to teach truth, because He does! His point is that it is ultimately the Holy Spirit of God's job to teach us the truth of the word of God, because it is not a *human work*—it is a *divine work!*

In Ephesians 4:11, God lists for us the gifts and gifted men the Spirit of Christ gave the church. He goes on in verse 12 to tell us the specific purpose for which they were given: "For the perfecting of the saints, for the work of the ministry, for the edifying of the body of Christ." The Holy Spirit is always the Teacher, but He often chooses to use human instruments to faithfully declare the word of truth, utilizing God's principle of comparing scripture with scripture. But again, even though we may be reading or listening to Spirit-filled human teachers, we are ultimately dependent upon

154

the resident truth Teacher of the Holy Spirit to reveal His truth to us (1Co 2:9; 1Jo 2:27).

In Acts 8, the Ethiopian eunuch is cruising along in his chariot down a desert road, and he just happens to be reading Isaiah 53—one of the strongest and clearest Old Testament chapters detailing the crucifixion of Christ! Now, the Holy Spirit knows that this eunuch doesn't have a clue about what he's reading, so He directs Philip out onto that desert road to help that old boy! Philip sees the eunuch coming down the road, and the Spirit directs him to ask the eunuch if he was able to understand the things he was reading. Acts 8:31 says that the eunuch's response was, "How can I, except some man should guide me? And he desired Philip that he would come up and sit with him." And verse 35 says, "Then Philip opened his mouth, and began at the same scripture, and preached unto him Jesus." Now, it sure sounds like Philip is the teacher, and yet notice that throughout this entire episode, while the Holy Spirit used human instrumentality, it was actually He who was guiding the eunuch into *all truth* (Joh 16:13), and Philip was simply following the leading of the Spirit in proclaiming His truth.

As you can see, anywhere we slice the Bible, the principle is consistent: the truth of the word of God must be revealed to us by the Spirit of truth Himself (Joh 16:13).

Principle #3:
Anyone who is SPIRITUAL can understand not only the BASIC truths of God's Word, but even the DEEP things of God, without a Bible College or Seminary education.

Having a biblical understanding of what a *natural man* is, it is obvious then that a *spiritual man* is someone who has had their dead spirit brought to life, or been *born again*. And as we use his prescribed method, verse 10 tells us that "the Spirit searcheth all things, yea, the deep things of God." God is letting us know that as we employ the Key of Comparison in our Bible study, something supernatural takes place as He, by His Spirit, *reveals* His wisdom/

The Keys of Bible Study

word to us. And it's not just the simple or obvious truths, but as Paul says here, even the *deep things of God!* Those are the *wondrous things* that David prayed his eyes would be opened to see in Psalm 119:18.

And may I add that in order to possess far more than just a working knowledge of the Bible, nowhere in this passage does it mention the need for Bible college, seminary degrees, knowledge of Hebrew and Greek, or anything of the sort. Those things do have their place in the overall spiritual growth and development of God's people! I am a part of the Living Faith Fellowship, and our churches combine resources (both human and financial) to train the people in our churches in what we call the Living Faith Bible Institute, and I couldn't recommend it more highly. But my point is that, in this key passage which tells us how the Spirit of God reveals His truth to us, none of these things are listed as a requirement or prerequisite.

KEY POINT:

The best commentary on the Bible is the Bible!

People often ask me if there is a particular commentary that I recommend. My answer is always the same. I'll say something like this: "I certainly don't want to sound like a smart aleck or like I think I'm super-spiritual, but really—the best commentary on the Bible is the Bible!" I'll try to explain to them that because of 1 Corinthians 2:9-13, when you come to something in the word of God you don't understand, first believe God can and will *reveal* it to you, and then look up all the other places in the Bible where God talks about that same thing (compare scripture with scripture!) and meditate on those verses. As you do, the Spirit of God will begin to *reveal* His truth to you.

People often also ask me why I use so many cross references when I preach. Since the word of God has to be revealed to us by the Spirit of God (1Co 2:9-10), why in my preaching would I not seek

156

to utilize the Spirit-given method He said He uses to reveal it? To actually *preach the word*, as pastor-teachers have been commanded to do (2Ti 4:2-4), is simply taking people on a spiritual journey through a passage of scripture, taking them to the same scriptures the Spirit of God used to reveal His truth as the pastor was *studying* and *labouring* in the word and doctrine (1Ti 5:15,17)! Preaching is that simple... and that hard!

But we must realize that because *comparing scripture with scripture* is the Holy Spirit's chosen method for revealing His truth to us, and because of the far-reaching implications and ramifications of this principle, we must also factor into our Bible study these...

Key Warnings:

Warning #1:
Never base a doctrine on a single verse or passage that has no cross reference.

Because God said He would reveal His truth by *"comparing spiritual things with spiritual"* (1Co 2:13), this poses somewhat of a dilemma when we're seeking to understand a verse or passage in which we're unable to locate another scriptural reference with which to compare it. In those cases, though we trust the Spirit of God that lives in us to guide us into the truth of the verse or passage (John 16:13), and though we give ourselves to diligent study to come to a calculated biblical understanding of the verse or passage, we are very careful never to *force* a dogmatic conclusion of its meaning, and would certainly never base a doctrine upon it.

For example, in 1 John 5:14-16, the Apostle John says this:

> And this is the confidence that we have in him, that, if we ask any thing according to his will, he heareth us: And if we know that he hear us, whatsoever we ask, we know that we have the petitions that we desired of him. If any man see his brother sin a sin which is not unto death, he shall ask, and he shall give him life for them that sin not unto death. There is a sin unto

The Keys of Bible Study

death: I do not say that he shall pray for it. (1Jo 5:14-16)

Now, do you know all of the other places in the Bible where it specifically talks about this *sin unto death?* I don't either! To my knowledge, this concept only appears in this place in the Bible. So, how are we to interpret it devotionally, knowing that the usual path by which the Holy Spirit reveals His truth is by comparing it with other verses that refer to the same biblical concept or principle? What do we do? What should be our approach? We simply trust the Spirit of God to guide us into the truth of this passage using the other keys of Bible study, and begin stacking up things we do know about sin biblically and what the Bible says is the result of committing these sins, and attempt to make biblically-directed and scripturally-consistent calculations!

So, what would that look like in this passage? Well, we certainly know that it is not God's will for His children to sin (Rom 6:1-2; 1Jo 2:1a). But we also realize that, though sinning should never be our desire, it is a reality even for the best of us (1Jo 2:1b; Rom 7:18-23). And we know that when we sin, the Spirit of God who lives in us will begin to put up roadblocks, as it were, to keep us from continuing down that sinful path. We learn from John 16:8 that when we sin, the Spirit of God will *reprove* us of that sin. We learn from 2 Corinthians 7:1 that it is His intention that we *cleanse ourselves* of that sin, and that we *perfect holiness.* If we fail to do that, Hebrews 12:5-10 says that God will lovingly and graciously *chastise* us so *we might be partakers of his holiness.* And for those who blast through the barrier of God's conviction and chastisement, we enter the arena of Ephesians 4:30, where we then *grieve the Holy Spirit* that has sealed us in Christ. And failure to hear and heed His grieving enters us into the realm of 1 Thessalonians 5:19, where we *quench the Spirit.*

By the time a person has blasted past all of these roadblocks, it might well be that the *sin unto death* is God finally saying, "The best thing for you, and the best thing for My church, is just to take you home."

Now, though I am personally convinced from my study that this is the Spirit-guided devotional application of the truth of this passage, am I going to make what I believe to be a biblically-

Chapter 5 — The Key of Comparison

directed and scripturally-consistent interpretation of this passage a matter of fellowship with other brothers and sisters in the body of Christ? Am I going to try to establish my interpretation as a hardline doctrine? Certainly not. I believe there is safety in heeding the warning to **never base a doctrine on a single verse or passage that has no cross reference**.

Another example is this strange inference in 1 Corinthians 15:29, where Paul asks,

> Else what shall they do which are <u>baptized for the dead</u>, if the dead rise not at all? why are they then <u>baptized for the dead</u>? (1Co 15:29)

And, once again, the crazy thing about this verse is that there is no cross reference I've ever come across in the entire New Testament with which to compare it. So, unlike the Mormons (and the Latter Day "Aint's") who have developed an entire doctrine upon this verse that includes bizarre rituals involving baptizing dead people, we approach a passage like this with caution. Is the Holy Spirit capable of guiding us into the truth of this passage? Based upon John 16:13, we must believe that He is! Should we take the the the time to study this passage utilizing the other keys of Bible study to come to a Spirit-guided, biblically-directed, scripturally-consistent conclusion concerning the interpretation of this verse? For sure! But again, for safety's sake, we must **never base a doctrine upon a single verse or passage that has no cross reference**.

Which leads to another key warning...

<u>Warning #2:</u>
Never violate a clear passage when trying to interpret one that is obscure.

Students of the Bible would readily recognize that the verse we were just talking about, 1 Corinthians 15:9, is a rather obscure verse. As we saw, it is obscure in the fact that there are no other places in scripture that talk about being *baptized for the dead*. And as we saw,

159

The Keys of Bible Study

though the Spirit of God is more that capable of guiding us into the truth of this verse, we would never claim that the Spirit of God guided us to an interpretation of this passage that would violate the clear teaching concerning baptism in other church epistles. As we saw when we were discussing the Key of Context in the previous chapter, once all the transitions are made in the book of Acts, the remainder of the New Testament is very clear about what believer's baptism *is* and *isn't!* We would never, then, violate the clear teaching of scripture regarding baptism by teaching something different, based upon a verse that is at least, somewhat obscure.

Warning #3:
Don't allow yourself to be overwhelmed with what you don't understand or can't seem to understand. God will reveal it to you in His time if it is something He intends for you to know.

Earlier in this chapter, we discussed how the Spirit of God will reveal all truth to us—and by comparing scripture with scripture, yes, even the *deep* truths! So how are we to process it biblically when we've employed all of the keys of Bible study, and yet we're still unable to comprehend the meaning of a verse or passage?

Jesus said something very significant to His disciples concerning this in John 16:12: "I have yet many things to say unto you, but ye cannot bear them now." In other words, "There are many other things I want you to know and understand, but at this point, you're not ready for them. You're not at a place of maturity to be able to actually assimilate these truths right now—but it'll come!" Gleaning from Jesus' instruction in this passage, when we encounter biblical truths we just can't seem to get our heads wrapped around, we must simply recognize that it may be that God knows we're not quite ready for them—and so we press on, believing that in His time, God *will* reveal it to us if it's something He wants us to know.

A great biblical example of this principle is found in Acts 9. Saul, whose name was about to be changed to Paul, is walking along the road to Damascus when all of a sudden... BAM! The Lord reveals Himself to him in blazing, blinding light! And Saul immediately

160

asks in Acts 9:6: "Lord, what wilt thou have me to do?" Can you imagine what would have happened had the Lord actually answered his question? Because based on Paul's testimony years later in 2 Corinthians 11:24-28, our Lord's answer would have sounded something like this: "Okay, Saul, here's what I want: I want you to be severely beaten by the Romans on five separate occasions; three times I want you to be beaten within an inch of your life with rods; once I want you to be stoned and left for dead; three other times I want you to experience shipwreck—one in which you will spend an entire 24 hour period out in the sea fighting desperately for your life; I want you to go into city after city and be used, misused and abused; you're going to go hungry; you'll endure the cold; you'll go without clothes; you'll often endure fasting; you'll be laden down with all kinds of burdens; and then you'll finally have your head lopped off!"

Do you think for a second that Saul was ready for the Lord to reveal all that to him at that point in his new-found faith? Obviously not! Rather than reveal it all to him at that point, the Lord says to Saul, in essence, "Don't concern yourself right now with what you don't know. Just let Me reveal the answer to your question in my time. You simply focus on doing the next right thing, and I will guide you by My Spirit as you go along." And it is with that same mentality and attitude with which we are to approach our Bible Study. Sure, we seek to be *workmen* who *study* to know and learn *the word of truth* (2Ti 2:15)—but we must not allow ourselves to become frustrated or disenchanted with the things the Spirit of God is not quite ready to reveal to us.

In this next section, let's take a few passages of scripture, and see how the "Comparison Key" can be used of God to unlock treasures in His word.

Key Examples:

Example #1:
The Virtuous Woman (Proverbs 31:10–31)

The Keys of Bible Study

Usually when we talk about the virtuous woman from Proverbs 31, she's the theme either on Mother's Day or at a women's conference or Bible study. And well she should be! She epitomizes what God intends every woman in any generation to both be and do. However, by utilizing the Key of Comparison, we find that the virtuous woman has far greater reach and impact.

Notice in Proverbs 31:10, that Solomon begins by asking us a question: "Who can find a virtuous woman?" And sure, in a historical sense, Solomon is asking the question because he is suggesting that his son (and men in general) would be wise to find this kind of a woman to marry.

But wait just a second. What would happen if we believed that our Lord Jesus Christ, "the son of David, king of Israel" (Pro. 1:1), was the One asking this question, and we believed that He wanted us to go to His book and see if we could *find a virtuous woman* in the pages of scripture?

If we were to do that, do you know what we would find? That of all of the 188 women listed by name in the Bible, there is actually only **one** that is referred to as a *virtuous woman!*

That's certainly not to say that there weren't other women who could be classified biblically as a *virtuous woman,* but it becomes evident that God was specifically reserving that title for one very special woman, whose story just happens to paint an incredible spiritual masterpiece! Do you know who that one woman is? Her name is Ruth, and her story is found in the book of the Bible that bares her name. In Ruth 3:11, a man by the name of Boaz is speaking, and he says to Ruth, "...all the city of my people doth know that thou art a **virtuous woman**." And there is our key cross reference! By comparing scripture with scripture, we have successfully and biblically been able to *find a virtuous woman!* And so with that vital piece of information, we start to look deeper into the four short chapters of the book of Ruth to find out more about her. And we find that her story is quite fascinating! In a nutshell, it unfolds like this...

162

Chapter 5 — The Key of Comparison

Ruth was a Gentile from a cursed race, a Moabitess. If you go back to the book of Genesis, it lets us know that the Moabites were a cursed people. And this Gentile from a cursed race finds herself living during a famine. And in the midst of this famine, she receives good news from a far land that the Lord had visited His people in Bethlehem in giving them bread. Upon hearing that good news, she leaves her father and mother and all she held dear, making a beeline to Bethlehem to partake of that bread. When she got there, she just happened to go to work in a harvest field of a man who just happened to be her Jewish kinsman-redeemer! When he sees her, he immediately falls head-over-heels in love with her. He then takes her out of his harvest field, makes her his bride, takes her to his home, and they lived happily ever after.

Nice story, huh?

But allow me to take another minute to tell you *our* story!

We, too, are Gentiles from a cursed race... we call it the human race! And we also found ourselves living in the midst of a famine, one in our souls. But one day, we heard good news from a far land that the Lord had visited His people in giving them Bread in Bethlehem. And upon hearing that good news, we left our father and mother and all we held dear, and made a beeline to partake of the Bread of Life. And now we are laboring in the field of our Jewish Kinsman-Redeemer from the city of Bethlehem, and do you know what we're anxiously awaiting? For Him to take us out of His harvest field to make us His bride, taking us to His home where we will forever live happily ever after with Him!

Now listen, either I'm one whale of a good storyteller, or God is! And my bet is on the latter! All I've done is connect the biblical dots by comparing scripture with scripture.

Only one woman in the Bible received the title of being a *virtuous woman*, and she just happens to be one of the clearest and greatest pictures, or types, of the church in the entire Old Testament! Once we're able to see, by comparing scripture with scripture, that the *virtuous woman* doubles as a picture of the Bride of Christ... wow! When we come back to Proverbs 31, we suddenly see that while this passage does have direct (and important!) application for women of God, it is also one of the greatest passages in the entire Bible which expresses what our Lord Jesus Christ expects His bride to be and do.

Would you look with me at Proverbs 31:10? Solomon (*the son of David, the king of Israel*—an obvious picture of Christ!) asks: "Who can find a virtuous woman?" And we did! We found her in the book of Ruth, and we learned that *she* is *us*—the church!

And notice, verse 10 goes on to say, "For her price is far above rubies." He draws our attention to *her price*; this should remind us of 1 Corinthians 6:19-20, which tells those of us who comprise the bride of Christ that we have been *bought with a price!* And 1 Peter 1:18-19 lets us know that the price that the Lord Jesus Christ paid for us, was, indeed, far above rubies. He bought us with a substance that is red, like rubies, and yet was extremely more precious and valuable and rare—because he bought us with His own precious blood!

The next verse, Proverbs 31:11, tells us, "The heart of her husband doth safely trust in her, so that he shall have no need of spoil." In 2 Corinthians 11:2 we see that as the church, the Bride of Christ, we have been espoused to the Lord Jesus Christ as our *one husband*. And you know what He expects of us, as His bride? He expects to be able to trust us to be faithful to Him! Men, can you imagine being married to a woman you couldn't trust? A woman who was constantly out committing adultery? Yet James 4:4 says that when we allow ourselves to be a *friend of the world,* our Husband views it as spiritual adultery! He wants to be able to trust us to be in the world, and not love it! (1Jo 2:15) And as James says here, not even to be *a friend* of it.

Watch what he says in verse 12: "She will do him good and not evil all the days of her life." I've been in the ministry for over four decades now, and it has been my observation that there are many

Chapter 5 — The Key of Comparison

who start the Christian life well, but there are few who actually finish well. It's hard to find people who don't look back. It's hard to find people who don't waver. It's hard to find people who don't compromise. It's hard to find people who are responsible enough and love Jesus enough to do Him good and not evil all the days of their life.

Look with me at verse 16: "She considereth a field, and buyeth it..." Do you remember what Jesus said in Matthew 13:38? Jesus said, "The field is the world." And, as the Bride of Christ, we must recognize that we have a responsibility to the world! In Mark 16:15, Jesus said, "Go ye into all the world, and preach the gospel to every creature." And the idea from Proverbs 31:16 is that each of us is to *consider* the responsibility we have to get the gospel to the whole world—but part of our *consideration* of it is determining where it is on this planet He wants us to labor, and buy that field! In other words, selling ourselves out to that field and doing whatever is necessary to *buy it*—even if it costs us, like it did Jesus, our own blood.

Look at verse 20: "She stretcheth out her hand to the poor; yea, she reacheth forth her hands to the needy." Something else we find that Jesus expects of His bride is that she will be moved, like He is, with compassion for the poor and the needy. Paul said in Galatians 2:10 that as the church, "we should remember the poor." And Proverbs 31:20 says, "she reacheth forth her hands" to them. But just like Jesus, the *virtuous woman* knows that the greatest need people have is not in their stomachs, but in their souls (Luk 4:18). And so, just like Philippians 2:16 says, along with stretching forth our hands with food, we are also *holding forth the word of life*.

And then, look at what it says in Proverbs 31:21: "She is not afraid of the snow for her household: for all her household are clothed with scarlet." When we do a word study on *snow* in the Bible, we find that it's a picture of the righteous judgment of God that will one day cover the earth, like snow. But verse 21 says that the *virtuous woman* isn't afraid of the snow. In other words, she isn't afraid for that day when God pours out His righteous judgment upon the earth, because everyone in her household is clothed with scarlet... the scarlet blood of Jesus Christ! Romans 5:9 says, "...Being now justified by His blood, we shall be saved from wrath through him."

Look at verse 23: "Her husband is known in the gates, when he sitteth among the elders of the land." One of these days, our Husband, the Lord Jesus Christ, is going to sit down on His throne at the East Gate in Jerusalem, and according to Matthew 19:28, He "shall sit in the throne of his glory" and His twelve disciples shall also sit with Him "upon twelve thrones." Revelation 4:10 refers to them as *elders,* just as it says here in Proverbs 31:23. And the *virtuous woman,* the bride of Christ, longs for that day when He sits on His throne in His kingdom, finally receiving the glory that is due His name! And that's why 2 Timothy 4:8 says she loves his appearing. She lives for that day when her Husband is seated on that throne in the midst of the gates!

But the *virtuous woman* also knows there is a day of honor coming for her as well. Proverbs 31:25 says, "Strength and honour are her clothing; and she shall rejoice in time to come." You see, she isn't living for this life or this temporal world. She's living for the world to come, because she knows her day of rejoicing is then! She understands what Paul said in 2 Corinthians 4:18: "While we look not at the things which are seen, but at the things which are not seen: for the things which are seen are temporal; but the things which are not seen are eternal."

And look at verse 28: "Her children arise up and call her blessed." If we invest our life like the *virtuous woman,* there is coming a day at the rapture of the church when all of our spiritual *children,* both those we have personally won to Christ as well as those we spiritually adopted, as it were, by seeking their growth and development through discipleship, are going to *arise up* (1 Th 4:17; 1 Co 15:51–52). I can only imagine that following the rapture and the subsequent Judgment Seat of Christ, our spiritual children will seek to express their thanksgiving by calling us *blessed.* Perhaps that blessing might sound something like this: "Bless you! Bless you, because I was in that field that you 'bought' with your life! Bless you for 'considering that field,' and 'holding forth the word of life' to a 'poor' and 'needy' sinner like me! Bless you for making that spiritual investment in me!"

And then, look at the last part of verse 28: "Her husband also [blesses her], and He praiseth her." And do you know what those words of praise will be? Matthew 25:21 tells us: "Well done, thou good and faithful servant." Can you imagine your Husband, the Lord Jesus Christ, looking at you from His Judgment Seat, counting you a virtuous woman and saying, "Well done, thou good and faithful servant?"

And verse 31 says, "Give her of the fruit of her hands, and let her own works praise her in the gates." In other words, let the reward for her works on earth be her praise when she enters into Christ's kingdom. Peter put it this way: "For so an entrance shall be ministered unto you abundantly into the everlasting kingdom of our Lord and Saviour Jesus Christ" (2Pe 1:11).

Isn't it amazing how God reveals His wisdom/word, simply by comparing scripture with scripture? By utilizing the Key of Comparison, the Lord has revealed to us one of the greatest passages in the entire Bible concerning what we, as the bride of Christ, are to be and do!

Example #2:
Leviathan (Job 41:1-34)

Let me take you to Job 41 to give you another example of how the key of comparing scripture with scripture opens the treasure chest of the word of God. In Job 41:1, we're introduced to some kind of weird and ferocious creature God calls *leviathan*. The tribulation Job had been experiencing, compiled with the subsequent interrogation he received from his three friends, had finally worn Job down, and he had begun to question God's sovereignty in allowing all of the calamity in his life to befall him. God responded with a series of about 75 rapid-fire questions for which Job had no answer! That's the context as we come into Job 41.

The Keys of Bible Study

Here, God begins to ask Job specific questions regarding leviathan. In verses 1-3, God asks,

> Canst thou draw out leviathan with an hook? or his tongue with a cord which thou lettest down? Canst thou put an hook into his nose? or bore his jaw through with a thorn? Will he make many supplications unto thee? will he speak soft words unto thee? (Job 41:1-3)

In other words, "Job, do you actually think you're going to go fishing for leviathan? And if you caught him, do you think you're going to hook him on a little string and hang him over the edge of your tiny boat?" God is actually being somewhat sarcastic with His questions to Job about leviathan. But we could miss that, because most of us common people aren't even sure we know what a leviathan is! So, what are we to do? How are we come to a biblical understanding of what leviathan is?

Well, sadly, it's usually at this point we look to Bible scholars and commentators or a lexicon to help us poor common people to understand *the deep things of God,* rather than trust the Holy Spirit to *reveal* them to us by comparing scripture with scripture.

Now, in my case, I don't even have to exert a whole lot of effort to get the scholars' input, because the Bible I typically use is a study Bible, which means that the publisher hired Bible scholars to help readers like you and me understand certain words, and to direct us to key cross references for various verses by including notes in the center column. So, when I get to the word *leviathan* in my Bible, there is a small number after it that's intended to direct me to the coinciding number in the center column for explanation. And what these Bible scholars let me know is that *leviathan* is, and I quote: "a whale or whirlpool." Now, I realize I'm not always the sharpest knife in the drawer, but I must confess, I fail to see the connection! I mean, there sure seems to be a major difference between a *whale* and a *whirlpool.*

But, hey, let's go with it! Let's see if their scholarly insight helps to

Chapter 5 — The Key of Comparison

unlock this passage. As we saw in verse 3, God asks Job concerning leviathan: "Will he make many supplications unto thee? will he speak soft words unto thee?" I mean, if leviathan is a whale, let me ask you: have you ever been out in the ocean and had a whale come over to your boat, gently nudging it to get your attention, and then start riddling you with questions using hushed tones? Or have you ever been walking by one of the aquariums at SeaWorld and had the infamous Shamu the whale slowly swim to the surface of the water, whispering softly, "Pssst! Hey you! Come here a second. I wanna ask you a few questions." That doesn't seem to fit.

So, what about their other suggestion about leviathan being a whirlpool? Let's give that deep insight a try. Have you ever been chillin' out in a jacuzzi, minding your own business, when all of a sudden you heard it whisper, "Hey, human! Man, am I glad you're here! There's some things I've been wanting to ask one of y'all! Get in a little deeper, 'cause I don't wanna say this too loudly." That's a little far-fetched, wouldn't you say? Now, of course I know that the editors of my study Bible aren't saying that Leviathan is a hot tub, but rather an oceanic maelstrom. But given all the characteristics and descriptions we'll soon read, I don't see how Leviathan could be a mere aquatic phenomenon, either.

As I've talked with other people who have a study Bible about what their Bible says under the note concerning leviathan, most say that it is anything from a crocodile to a hippopotamus to a large sea creature. And though, as we're about to see, Leviathan is most definitely aquatic as well reptilian, serpentine, and amphibious, he is no mere crocodile or hippopotamus! Some scholars are at least honest enough to say, "exact identity unknown." But one thing is for sure: we definitely don't come away from the Bible scholar's comments with any certainty as to leviathan's identity. So most people will come back into the passage and continue reading, with the idea that they'll probably never really know what leviathan is, or what Job 41 is actually trying to get Job and us to see. But let me assure you: that's *exactly* the way the Devil wants it!

So, how about this? Rather than trusting the word of scholars, we

The Keys of Bible Study

will simply trust the word of God and look to the Holy Spirit to reveal leviathan's identity, by comparing scripture with scripture. If we set out to do that, what would that actually look like? I mean, where would we even begin?

Well, what if we just began by seeing if the word *leviathan* shows up any where else in scripture? And if it does, let's see what God tells us about it in these other places and see if the Spirit of God can lead us to any biblical conclusions. So, we take a very basic concordance, we look up the word *leviathan*, and we find that the Bible does, indeed, talk about him in several different other places! Hallelujah! And so the process begins.

We turn to Psalm 74:14, the next mention of the word *leviathan*, and find that the psalmist declares of God,

> Thou brakest the heads of leviathan in pieces, and gavest him to be meat to the people inhabiting the wilderness. (Psa 74:14)

Now, that doesn't exactly reveal his identity to us, does it? And the truth is, as we compare scripture with scripture, we won't always initially see how every cross reference applies. But we can't allow that to discourage us or to deter us. Because, as in the case of Psalm 74:14, though the verse may not reveal *who* or *what* leviathan is, we do pick up a very pertinent piece of information about him. Do you already know what it is? Whoever or whatever he is, he has more than one head! That's pretty unique... and bizarre!

Another place he shows up is Isaiah 27:1, where Isaiah tells us:

> In that day the Lord with his sore and great and strong sword shall punish leviathan the piercing serpent, even leviathan that crooked serpent; and he shall slay the dragon that is in the sea. (Isa 27:1)

Now, in this verse, we pick up quite a few significant details about leviathan! First of all, as we discussed in great detail in chapter two when we were discussing the Key of Theme, Isaiah begins with the phrase *in that day*. You'll remember that anytime we find

170

Chapter 5 — The Key of Comparison

that phrase in the Bible, it always sets the context for us, pointing us to the second coming of Christ, or, the *day of the Lord*. So, we learn from Isaiah 27:1 that something major is going to happen to leviathan at the second coming of Christ! Then, Isaiah talks about the Lord punishing leviathan, which, of course, would cause us to wonder just why it is that the Lord felt that leviathan deserved to be punished. And then, notice that Isaiah also refers to this creature as a *serpent*, and not just any old serpent, but a *piercing* and *crooked serpent*, that is also known as a *dragon!*

And as we read that, if we have a general background concerning biblical truth, all kinds of bells and whistles start going off in our minds, because we immediately begin to think about something God revealed to the Apostle John:

> And there appeared another wonder in heaven; and behold a great red dragon, having seven heads and ten horns, and seven crowns upon his heads. (Rev 12:3)

Wow! Do you see that? A dragon with more than one head! As we keep reading, we find down in this same chapter that John adds,

> And there was war in heaven: Michael and his angels fought against the dragon; and the dragon fought and his angels, And prevailed not; neither was their place found any more in heaven. And the great dragon was cast out, that old serpent, called the Devil, and Satan, which deceiveth the whole world: he was cast out into the earth, and his angels were cast out with him. (Rev 12:7-9)

Are you seeing what the Holy Spirit is revealing to us here as we simply employ His method of revealing truth to us? I mean, how hard could this possibly be? Because here is **a dragon** who has **more than one head** (seven of them, in fact!), who is identified as **that old serpent,** who is getting his behind whipped (**punished**) at the second coming of Christ!

So, let's go back to Job 41. Do you think leviathan is a whale,

171

whirlpool, crocodile, hippopotamus, unknown sea creature, or something we'll never really identify with biblical certainty? Or do you think he might just happen to be, as Revelation 12:9 says, none other than Satan himself? Now do you see why the Devil would want us to throw our hands up in the air when we come to the identity of leviathan in Job 41? Because the reality is, folks, Job 41 just happens to be a description of Satan the way *God* sees him, and just happens to be *the* most comprehensive place in the entire Bible revealing the person of Satan and how he operates in this world.

God says in Job 41:12, "I will not conceal his parts, nor his power, nor his comely proportion." And God clearly lets us know here that He doesn't intend for Satan to remain concealed—but rather, that He fully intends to reveal him! And, of course, how did 1 Corinthians 2:9-13 say God reveals His wisdom/truth to us? As we compare scripture with scripture!

And so God asks us in Job 41:13, "Who can discover the face of his garment?" And then in verse 14, "Who can open the doors of his face?"

Now, to grasp what God is actually asking here when He refers to *the face of his garment* and *the doors of his face,* you'll remember as recently as the days of Shakespeare, a theatrical performance would actually be executed utilizing a very limited cast. The characters would be portrayed by actors holding a mask that was held up in front of their face on a stick about two feet in length, wearing clothes to match that character. When the scene called for a different character, the actors would simply go behind the stage to change their clothes, and re-enter holding another mask to cover their face. It was the same actor; he was simply portraying a different character by changing his clothes and his mask.

And what Satan has found is that he can keep himself concealed in the unfolding of history, by doing the same thing: by simply changing his mask and his clothes! So if the situation at a particular

Chapter 5 — The Key of Comparison

time in history calls for a religious leader, you know what he does? He puts on religious clothes and wears a religious mask and performs in a religious manner. If at another time the situation calls a political leader, he simply puts on political clothes and mask, and conducts himself accordingly—whether it be as a smooth diplomat or as a ruthless dictator. So, what God is asking in verses 13 and 14 is, "Who will be biblically discerning enough to look past the different clothes Satan wears, and past the various masks he uses to cover his face, and be able to identify him in the affairs on the earth?" And perhaps it should be stated that we'll never be able to find Satan in history if we can't even find him in Job 41!

In the next verses, God tells us,

> His scales are his pride, shut up together as with a close seal. One is so near to another, that no air can come between them. They are joined one to another, they stick together, that they cannot be sundered. (Job 41:15-17)

What God is letting us know in these verses is that Satan is completely shrouded in pride. His pride is so vast and so extensive that it covers him like scales which cannot be penetrated or separated from who he is. In other words, he is the very epitome of pride! And with what we know about the pride that generated his infamous five "I will" statements that caused him to become Satan in the first place (Isa 14:13-14; Eze 28:17), you would think that God's description of leviathan's pride in Job 41:15-17 would cause people to readily identify him as Satan! And if we somehow missed that telltale sign, surely we would figure it out when God just flat-out tells us down in Job 41:34: "He is a king over all the children of pride!" Ephesians 2:2 calls those children of pride the "children of disobedience," who walk "according to the prince of the power of the air," which, of course, is none other than Satan.

Notice also in verse 33 that God tells us about leviathan, "Upon earth there is not his like..." In other words, in all of God's creation,

173

The Keys of Bible Study

there is absolutely *none* like Satan. There is no being that wields the kind of power he wields! Something rather interesting about Job 41:33 is that it made its way into one of the stanzas of one of the great hymns of the faith. In Martin Luther's great hymn "A Mighty Fortress Is Our God," the first stanza says:

A mighty fortress is our God, a bulwark never failing;
Our helper He, amid the flood of mortal ills prevailing;
For still our ancient foe doth seek to work us woe;
His craft and power are great, and armed with cruel hate;
On earth is not his equal.

Though few in the 21st century recognize Job 41 as a description of Satan, Martin Luther had nailed it way back in the year 1530, almost 400 years ago! Finding Satan in Job 41 isn't some new truth or discovery. It's just so old, it's new!

In Job 41:10, God says, "None is so fierce that dare stir him up; who then is able to stand before me?" And, basically, God is telling Job (and us!), "There's nobody other than me who is awesome enough to mess with Satan." Do you remember what Jude 9 tells us about Michael, the archangel? That even he wouldn't bring a railing accusation against the devil, but said, "The Lord rebuke thee!" That's just how powerful Satan actually is. But the point God wanted Job (and us!) to see in the second half of Job 41:10 is that if you wouldn't do anything to *stir up* Satan, a created being, what would give you the audacity to even *think* about stirring up the very Creator Himself by questioning him?

And you'll remember, that's actually the context of Job 41. Job was questioning God because he couldn't understand why he had been forced to deal with such horrific tribulation. And something quite interesting about Job's questioning of God is that most people think that God never did reveal to Job the reason for his tribulation and suffering. With our biblical understanding of Job 41, however, we recognize that He actually did! It was Satan (leviathan), who

174

was actually the cause of Job's suffering and tribulation (Job 1:12).

That, my friend, is the incredible value of the Key of Comparison. And God has promised to reveal the wisdom of His word to us by His Holy Spirit as we employ this God-given method!

THE KEY OF APPLICATION

As a student of the word of God, it will be impossible to fully comprehend and appreciate both the depth and the beauty of the word of God apart from utilizing this next key of Bible study.

The fifth key of Bible study:
RECOGNIZE THE THREE LAYERS OF APPLICATION

The fact that the Bible actually has three layers of application may be a new biblical reality for you, so allow me to introduce this to you by laying some groundwork. Let's first of all, establish the biblical basis for this key by looking at some...

KEY VERSES: John 5:39

"Search the scriptures; for in them ye think ye have eternal life: and they are they which testify of me."

The context of this verse is that Jesus has just healed a man on the Sabbath day. The religious leaders, the Pharisees, of course, are tripped out of their minds that this "new religious leader" had the

The Keys of Bible Study

audacity to do something like that—and they've certainly let Jesus know about it! So, Jesus begins this discourse to let them know who He actually is. And the reality is that while they're all freaked out about Him healing somebody on the Sabbath, He is the very Lord of the Sabbath Himself! So Jesus says to them in John 5:39: "Search the Scriptures; for in them ye think that ye have eternal life." In other words, "You Pharisees have based your whole religious system on the premise that you're going to gain eternal life because of your vast knowledge of the scriptures. What I'd love for you to do is go back and dig into those scriptures that you think you know so well—because if you really do, you'll find that they're all actually pointing to Me!"

Now, obviously, we know that the *scriptures* to which He's referring at this time in history are none other than the Old Testament. And, of course, we know there are certain places in the Old Testament that were written specifically referring to Christ. Places like Isaiah 53 for example, or the serpent on the pole in Numbers 21:9 (Joh 3:14), or the Rock Moses struck in the wilderness in Exodus 17:6 (1Co 10:4). Sure, we all certainly know about these Old Testament references to Christ—but what Jesus seems to be saying here is that the *entire* Old Testament is testifying of Him. Ponder that for a moment! What is Jesus actually saying?

John 5:46 For had ye believed Moses, ye would have believed me: for he wrote of me.

And this verse, of course, is the same exact context as the previous key verse. But here, Jesus seeks to get the undivided attention of these religious leaders who prided themselves in their unmitigated belief in and vast knowledge of the Old Testament, that their real issue wasn't that they didn't believe *Him*—but that they really didn't believe *Moses*. And let me tell you: *that* certainly would have perked up their ears! Because in their minds, Moses was the man! What our Lord means by this reference to *Moses* is, of course, the Pentateuch (the first five books of the Old Testament), which God spoke through Moses as he was inspired of the Holy Ghost. So Jesus says, "For had ye believed Moses, ye would have believed me:

Chapter 6 — The Key of Application

for he wrote of me." Listen, that's quite a statement! I mean, was Jesus actually saying that the Old Testament books of Genesis, Exodus, Leviticus, Numbers and Deuteronomy were all about Him? Yes, that's exactly what he's saying! How can these things be?

John 1:45 Philip findeth Nathanael, and saith unto him, We have found him, of whom Moses in the law, and the prophets, did write, Jesus of Nazareth, the son of Joseph.

In this passage, not only do we learn that the first five books of the Old Testament written by Moses are indeed all about Jesus, but so are all the books written by the prophets! What? Are you kidding me? Where? How?

Luke 24:27 And beginning at Moses and all the prophets, he expounded unto them in all the scriptures the things concerning himself.

The context of this verse is that this is the very day of Christ's resurrection. Early that Sunday morning, the two Marys (Mary Magdalene and Mary, the mother of James) and Joanna had been to the sepulcher where Christ had been buried. When they arrived, they found the stone had been rolled away, and Christ's body was nowhere to be found. Two angels then appeared to them declaring the fact that Christ had risen from the dead, so the three ladies quickly made their way to inform the eleven apostles.

Upon hearing the testimony of these ladies, the apostles didn't believe them and simply passed off their words as idle. Later that day, as two of the apostles were traveling upon the road to Emmaus, talking about all of the monumental events that had taken place in recent days, almost out of nowhere, Jesus Himself appeared to them and asked them about the things they had been talking about, and why it was that they were so sad. At that point, they didn't even realize they were talking to the Lord!

The Keys of Bible Study

But it was in this ensuing dialogue that Jesus gave these men a jet tour through the books of the Old Testament written by Moses (Genesis through Deuteronomy) along with all of the Old Testament books written by the Prophets, showing them Himself in each one. I love the way they worded what had happened to them on that day at the end of verse 32. They said: "...he opened us to the scriptures." Oh, that that would happen for you and me!

The next Key Verse is found a little later in this same chapter...

Luke 24:44 These are the words which I spake unto you, while I was yet with you, that all things must be fulfilled, which were written in the <u>law of Moses</u>, and in the <u>prophets</u>, and in the <u>psalms</u>, <u>concerning me</u>.

After the two apostles had their eye-opening experience with Christ on the road to Emmaus, they immediately made their way back to Jerusalem to inform the other apostles, who were already gathered together in one place. While the two apostles were in the midst of recounting their encounter and conversation with the risen Christ, Jesus appeared in the very room where they were assembled. And it was in this gathering with all eleven of the apostles that, once again, Christ began taking these men on a journey through the law of Moses (the first five books of the Old Testament), the prophets, and the Psalms, revealing where He was throughout the whole Old Testament.

Though many Christians have never recognized this teaching concerning the Old Testament, as you can see, the principle is anything but hidden! The key verses we just looked at all let us know that there is another tremendously exciting and supernatural quality to the word of God that most people have never seen!

<u>KEY THOUGHT</u>:

The Old Testament is actually the picture book of New Testament truth.

180

Chapter 6 — The Key of Application

When we're teaching children to talk, we don't grab a big dictionary, sit them in our lap, and start looking up words like ball, tree, kite, and car and read lengthy definitions of the words. There will be a time for that, but in their earliest years of development, we have learned that children are able to make key associations in their little brains simply through the use of picture books. We simply point to the picture on the page while clearly annunciating the word, and in a relatively short period of time that word is indelibly lodged into their minds for the rest of their lives.

Interestingly enough, do you know how our Heavenly Father teaches His children? Through the use of a picture book! We call that picture book the Old Testament.

KEY EXPLANATION:

God has taken New Testament concepts and precepts that are sometimes difficult to understand and has very graphically and masterfully painted incredible pictures of them so they can be clearly seen and understood through the carefully recorded events of history given to the Old Testament human authors by inspiration (2Ti 3:16).

Do you remember what Peter said in 2 Peter 3:16 as he was talking about the writings of Paul? Even the great Apostle Peter said of the scriptures that there "are some things hard to be understood." And this is one of the wonderful things about how God lovingly guides us as His children! He knew that some of the New Testament concepts and precepts we need for our spiritual growth and development would sometimes be difficult for us to get our little spiritual brains wrapped around. So, He masterminded the recording of the events in the history of the Old Testament so that they *picture* New Testament truth. Now He can simply point to those pictures, as it were, and help us make associations that cause His word to be indelibly lodged into our hearts and minds for a lifetime. For New Testament believers, this is one of the most important reasons we need to both read, study, and become

181

completely familiar with the Old Testament!

KEY QUOTE:

We will never really understand the New Testament without understanding the Old Testament—and we will never really understand the Old Testament without understanding the New Testament.

In other words, we must become very familiar with the concepts of the New Testament in order to recognize how they're being pictured in the Old Testament—but we must also become very familiar with the pictures in the Old Testament in order to recognize the concepts in the New Testament. Again, this is why we must make reading the word of God a daily priority! Because do you realize what is actually happening to us as we do? God is giving to us the biblical and spiritual capacity to make associations and connections that will allow us to actually *see* the truth of the word of God that we so desperately need to know.

KEY PRINCIPLE: The Three Layers of Application in the Bible

As we are reading and studying the word of God, we must recognize there are three layers of application...

1. The Historical Application

First of all, with everything we read in the word of God, we must recognize that it actually took place at some point in history. It really happened to real people at a real point in time. With the historical application, we are simply equipping ourselves by becoming completely familiar with and believing that the events about which we are reading really happened exactly the way God chose to record them.

For example, if we're reading in the Old Testament about Joshua and the battle of Jericho, we approach it believing not only that it

Chapter 6 — The Key of Application

was a real event in history, but that the event unfolded exactly the way God said it did. So the question we first ask ourselves is: **What is happening at this time and through this event in history?** Very simply, we seek to make sure we understand everything that is going on in this historical event recorded in the passage.

Or, let's say we're reading in the New Testament book of 1 Corinthians, for example, and we come upon the doctrinal instruction concerning divorce, remarriage and singleness found in 1 Corinthians 7. Obviously, the Holy Spirit inspired Paul to write these truths specifically to the church in Corinth, based on circumstances that were taking place historically in that specific church in the first century. And yet, we recognize that this was the Holy Spirit's method to present New Testament church doctrine He intended to be applied in the life of every individual believer, as well as every individual church throughout the church age. To understand the actual teaching of the passage, however, before determining how the teaching applies to us personally or to our own individual local church, it is important to become so acquainted with the text that we are able to understand the historical circumstances that precipitated the instruction. These are the things involved in determining the Historical Application.

2. The Doctrinal or Prophetic Application

This is the layer of application we're going to spend the bulk of our time talking about, because this is the one with which most believers are least acquainted. Yet it is this application that actually brings the Bible to life! This is the layer of application that some have referred to as the spark plug of the Bible—meaning that it is what ignites the engine of the Bible, getting it running and working. May I also add that it is this application of scripture which ignites in us a passion to dig even deeper and more carefully into God's word. As we do, it won't be long before we find ourselves falling in love with the word of God, which means it won't be long before we notice that our Lord Jesus Christ has laid something on our shoulder—and do you remember from chapter one what it will be? The Key of David!

183

Do you remember how David prayed in Psalm 119:118? He cried out to the Lord saying: "Open thou mine eyes, that I may behold wondrous things out of thy law." Just what do you think David was asking God to open his eyes to be able to see? In effect, what David was actually saying to the Lord was: "Oh God, I know that this is a supernatural book, and that it's literally all about You! So, O Lord, will You please open my eyes, that I may behold wondrous things in this book, because I know I won't be able to see them without You opening my spiritual eyes."

In Ephesians 1:17, Paul was praying for the Ephesians (and I believe he was also praying for us!) when he said, "That the God of our Lord Jesus Christ, the Father of glory, may give unto you the spirit of wisdom and revelation in the knowledge of him." And again I ask you, what do you think Paul was praying we would be able to see and understand in God's word? Certainly not just the natural history of what happened in the Old Testament, right? No, he was praying that we would be able to see the supernatural, wondrous things found in God's written record of history. He was praying God would reveal to us Jesus in the Bible, as well as the other countless and mind-blowing pictures in the Old Testament— knowing that something has to happen to our spiritual eyes, ears, hearts and minds to be able to do so! We must have what Paul calls here *the spirit of wisdom and revelation in the knowledge of him.* That's what the Doctrinal Application is about.

When we refer to it as the Doctrinal Application, recognize that the word *doctrine* simply means *teaching.* When we refer to it as the Prophetic Application, recognize that *prophecy* has to do with future events. So what we're asking in this layer of application is: **What is the actual teaching of this passage, what is this teaching pointing to from a prophetic standpoint?** Since Jesus taught us that the whole Old Testament was actually about Him, what was written was pointing to something yet in the future. That's why we refer to this layer as both the Doctrinal and Prophetic Application. And so the final question we ask in determining this application of Old Testament scriptures is: **What is this <u>doctrinal</u> teaching actually pointing to <u>prophetically</u>?** Be sure to recognize, however,

Chapter 6 — The Key of Application

that the Doctrinal or Prophetic Application has primarily to do with the Old Testament. In the letters of the New Testament written to the church (Romans through Philemon), the clear truths that are written actually are the doctrinal teaching of the passage.

3. The Devotional or Inspirational Application

In my formal training for ministry, I was taught what is known in hermeneutics (the process of biblical interpretation) as the historical-grammatical method of interpretation. As the name suggests, this method emphasizes being careful to have a proper understanding of the history surrounding the events and time period of the passage, as well as giving careful attention to examine the usage and meaning of the particular words in the passage. Once an understanding of the history and grammar has been established, this method teaches that the Bible student or teacher is then able to make biblical and practical application of the passage to our lives today. That sounds well and good; however, if we go straight from historical to devotional and skip the middle layer of application (the Doctrinal/Prophetic Application), we will often miss the actual point of most Old Testament passages, and thus miss the major emphasis of the passage to our lives inspirationally, devotionally, and practically! From an inspirational standpoint, it's like trying to start a car without a spark plug.

In the Devotional or Inspirational Application, the question we ask is: **How do the truths in this passage apply to my life?** With both the Historical and Doctrinal Applications fully set in place, we will stand amazed at the great truths the Spirit of God by *the spirit of wisdom and revelation* has allowed us to see and know. We must then ask ourselves: what do these truths practically mean for our lives moving forward? How do we apply these truths in real, day-to-day life situations, recognizing that they weren't intended to simply provide us with *information,* but to produce in us *transformation?*

So, as we're studying the Bible, these are the **three layers of application** we must be sure to understand, observe, and utilize. But again, because the first and third applications are commonly

185

known and easily understood, we will spend the remainder of our time focusing on gaining a biblical understanding of that middle layer of application which is not as commonly known or understood, by looking at two key examples of how these three layers of application actually work together in our study of the Bible.

KEY EXAMPLES:

EXAMPLE #1:
The Book of Proverbs

A. The HISTORICAL Application

As we seek to lay out the Historical Application of the book of Proverbs and this character of the Old Testament by the name of Solomon, let's consider, first of all...

- The WRITER of the Book of Proverbs.

And, of course, we learn from the first 11 words of the book of Proverbs, that the writer is none other than Solomon. Proverbs 1:1 says: *"The proverbs of Solomon the son of David, king of Israel."* But, also notice next...

- The RECIPIENTS of the Book of Proverbs.

As we learned when studying the Key of Context in chapter four, to fully understand a given passage, it is crucial to identify the audience receiving specific instruction. As we examine the recipients of the specific instruction of the book of Proverbs, we find that Solomon was actually writing to his *sons*. We find this constantly being repeated throughout the book...

Proverbs 1:8   "My SON, hear the instruction of thy father..."
Proverbs 1:10   "My SON, if sinners entice you..."
Proverbs 2:1   "My SON, if thou wilt receive my words..."
Proverbs 3:1   "My SON, forget not my law..."

186

Chapter 6 — The Key of Application

Proverbs 3:11   "My SON, despise not the chastening of the Lord…"
Proverbs 3:21   "My SON, let not them depart from thine eyes…"
Proverbs 4:20   "My SON, attend to my words…"
Provers 5:1   "My SON, attend unto my wisdom…"
Proverbs 6:1   "My SON, if thou be surety for thy friend…"
Proverbs 6:20   "My SON, keep thy father's commandment…"
Proverbs 7:1   "My SON, keep my words…"

I think you get the idea! If you ever sat down to study the book of Proverbs, you couldn't miss that if you tried. The book of Proverbs was written to all of Solomon's sons, though you'll notice that he does so from a very individual standpoint, so that each one of them would receive the instruction very individually and personally. Perhaps I could illustrate it this way: if I preached in your church on a Sunday morning and asked your local body of believers to pray for me, you would probably receive my request very differently than if I called you up on Sunday afternoon and asked you individually and very specifically and personally to pray for me. That's why the instruction is directed to Solomon's *son* rather than to his *sons*.

The CONTENT of the Book of Proverbs.

As we glean from what we now know about the writer and the recipients of the book of Proverbs, we find that this book is what Solomon, the wisest man who ever lived (other than Christ Himself), wrote as he was seeking to instill wisdom into his sons.

B. The DOCTRINAL (PROPHETIC) Application

Let's go back now and look at some of the details we observed in the Historical Application. As was noted, the writer of this book, is Solomon. But did you notice the words given by inspiration from the Holy Ghost that Solomon actually used to describe himself? He calls himself *the son of David, king of Israel*. We already touched on this in the last chapter! Just like Solomon was, Jesus is the Son of David, King of Israel, which we know from comparing scripture with scripture. Once we recognize this similarity, we should find out if there are other similarities between these two sons of David.

187

The Keys of Bible Study

WHO ACTUALLY IS SOLOMON?

- HIS INCREDIBLE NAMES

The name *Solomon* actually means *peace* or *peaceable*. And since Solomon was the son of King David, we could say, then, that Solomon was a **prince of peace.**

The name given to Solomon by the prophet Nathan is *Jedidiah* (2Sa 12:25). Not only did his father name him, but for some reason, so did the prophet Nathan—and for some reason, God wanted to make sure it got recorded. The name *Jedidiah* just happens to mean *beloved of Jehovah.* So, not only is Solomon the **prince of peace,** but he is also the **beloved of Jehovah**—or the beloved of God the Father. Wow! Those are some pretty incredible names!

And then, as we continue to compare scripture with scripture, we also begin to notice some things about...

- HIS POWERFUL TITLES

The first title we are struck with is that Solomon is the **son of David,** as we see in Proverbs 1:1. And yet, be that as it may, in 1 Chronicles 28:6, God says to David: "...Solomon thy son, he shall build my house and my courts: for I have chosen him to be my son, and I will be his Father." So check that out! Not only was Solomon the **son of David,** but at the very same time he was also the **son of Jehovah.**

Then, in 1 Chronicles 22:9, David tells Solomon that the Lord had spoken to him, saying: "Behold, a son shall be born to thee, who shall be a man of rest..." Which is the next significant and powerful title given to Solomon. Biblically, Solomon is also the **man of rest.**

All we're really doing is looking up the word *Solomon* and the passages that refer to him and taking note of our observations. And as we continue, we begin to notice some things the scripture has to say about...

188

Chapter 6 — The Key of Application

Paul talks about the rest of Christ, and says that Christ is the only one who gives "rest to the people of God."

Revelation 3:21 tells us that our Lord Jesus Christ will sit on **the very throne of God His Father** in an **everlasting kingdom**! Isaiah 9:7 tells us that when the Lord Jesus Christ takes up His throne at His second coming, that throne will be "established from henceforth even for ever." Luke 1:33 says: "...and of his kingdom there shall be no end."

Back in Isaiah 9:7, it also tells us that Christ's kingdom will be **a kingdom of peace**. Isaiah said: "Of the increase of his government and peace there shall be no end..." And, of course, one of the reasons for such peace is the fact that when Christ's kingdom comes, it will be **a kingdom with no adversary present**. And do you know why? It's because Revelation 20:2-3 says that when Christ returns, He's going to lay "hold on the dragon, that old serpent, which is the Devil, and Satan [which means *adversary*!]," bind him with a chain, cast him into the bottomless pit, shut his sorry behind up, and set a seal upon him for the entire duration of His millennial (1000 year) reign!

And just like it was in Solomon's reign, when all the kings of the earth were coming to Jerusalem seeking audience with Israel's king, Revelation 21:24 says concerning Christ's reign, "...**the kings of the earth do bring their glory and honour into it.**" And when they come, they will all bow their knee before the **Son of God**... the **Son of David**... the **beloved of the Father**... the **Prince of Peace**... the **eternal king**... in the **eternal kingdom of peace and rest**... because he has finally **dealt with the adversary** through the ages! Hallelujah!

Listen, *that's* who wrote the book of Proverbs from a Doctrinal perspective! You can't make this stuff up! Everything we looked at in the Old Testament describing Solomon has its equivalent in the true Son of David... the true King of Israel... the Lord Jesus Christ.

And when we realize just what the book of Proverbs is—and

191

The Keys of Bible Study

just how much wisdom is in it—the book of Proverbs becomes a completely different book to us. We'll read it in a totally different way, especially when we add in the Doctrinal or Prophetic Application of who the book of Proverbs is actually written *to!*

From a historical perspective, we saw that it was written to Solomon's sons. But the moment we receive the Lord Jesus Christ as our personal Savior, we receive one of the most significant titles in all of Scripture. That title is **son of God**! Don't miss that this title is inclusive of every lady who believes on the Lord Jesus Christ and calls upon His name, because the title **son of God** isn't gender specific. Biblically, this title takes us back to a time in the original creation (Gen. 1:1) when Lucifer had a throne in Eden (Isa 14:12-13; Eze 28:13) and led a race of beings that were called the **sons of God** (Job 38:7) to love, worship Him, honor, and glorify the Lord.

What was actually happening on the earth at that time is that all the earth was worshipping the Lord Jesus Christ, singing unto His name (Psa 66:4), and our Lord was receiving the glory due His name (Psa 29:2; 96:8). But there came a day when Lucifer no longer wanted to direct the worship of the *sons of God* toward Christ, but to his own sorry self (Isa 14:13-13; Eze 28:15), and he led an angelic rebellion. The point I want you to see is that God's plan has always been for this planet to be inhabited by a race of beings called the *sons of God* who would love, worship, and praise Him, and give to Him the glory due His name. As you'll remember, that's really what all of history is about!

That's why, as soon as we believe on Christ and call upon His name to save us, we really did become new creatures in Christ—because we became the **sons of God**. The first chapter of the Gospel of John says concerning Christ,

> He came unto his own [the Jews], and his own received him not. But as many as received him, to them gave he power to become <u>the sons of God</u>, even to them that believe on his name. (Joh 1:11-12)

Chapter 6 — The Key of Application

And this isn't just some random occurrence of this usage. Romans 8:19 says: "For the earnest expectation of the creature waiteth for the manifestation of **the sons of God.**"

And the end of Romans 8:23 says that *the earnest expectation* that the **sons of God** are waiting to *manifest* is when we have received the redemption of our bodies and receive what Philippians 3:21 calls a body "like unto [Christ's] glorious body." This is another way of explaining the theme of the Bible: everything on this earth is coming back to the way God intended. That includes a race of beings called **the sons of God** inhabiting the earth in glorified bodies, singing in worship to give unto the Lord the glory that is due His name.

By the time the Apostle John had become an old man, the reality of God's glorious plan had come crashing in on him. He says in 1 John 3:1: "Behold, what manner of love the Father hath bestowed upon us, that we should be called **the sons of God...**" John got it, y'all! It was overwhelming to him that God's plan for those who have received Christ was that glorious and intricate.

The point I'm wanting you to see is that from the Doctrinal/ Prophetic Application, the book of Proverbs was written *by* the Son of David, the king of Israel, the Lord Jesus Christ—and it was written *to* those of us He has made His *sons*. Wow! When we understand who actually wrote the book of Proverbs, and we understand that it was actually written to us, nobody has to coerce us to read Proverbs daily! And do you remember how in the Historical Application, though Solomon was writing to His *sons* (plural), he addressed it to them individually, personally, and specifically through the singular usage of the phrase *my son*. That's how personally the Lord wants each of us to receive these truths!

Do you recognize how we were able to make all of these tremendous biblical connections? We were simply tipped in that direction when we heard the words of Proverbs 1:1: "The proverbs of Solomon the son of David, king of Israel." And all we did was start poking around biblically, comparing scripture with scripture, looking at all

193

The Keys of Bible Study

the places the Bible gave other descriptions of Solomon, and the Spirit of God began to reveal to us the kinds of things I believe our Lord Jesus Christ was revealing to the fellas about the Old Testament during that 40-day period after His resurrection (Luk 24:44-45). I believe it was this Doctrinal or Prophetic Application of scripture He was opening their eyes to see!

C. The DEVOTIONAL (INSPIRATIONAL) Application.

From Solomon's instruction to his sons, we find great inspiration to learn God's wisdom that should govern our lives as we seek to live a quiet and peaceable life marked with His blessing. The wisdom our Lord is imparting to us in this book is the wisdom by which our Lord Jesus Christ will rule in His millennial Kingdom, and he wants each of his sons to know this wisdom intimately.

With the book of Proverbs, we actually hold in our hands a manual for kingdom living. This allows us to live in these physical bodies *now* with the same wisdom with which we'll live on this earth in our glorified bodies *then!* And because there are 31 chapters in the book, which coincides with the number of days in most months, by simply reading a chapter a day we could read through God's wisdom manual 12 times every year. If we live what the Bible suggests is the average lifespan of seventy years (Psa 90:10), we could actually read through the book of Proverbs over 600 times in adulthood! And well we should! There's a lot of wisdom to be gleaned from this incredible book.

EXAMPLE #2:
The STRANGE WOMAN of the Book of Proverbs.

There are two key women in the book of Proverbs. In the previous chapter, we looked at the first one: the *virtuous woman* (Pro 31:10-31). And you'll remember that in Proverbs 31:10, God asks a question. He asks: "Who can find a virtuous woman?" And we found her, didn't we? We found that Ruth is one of the greatest pictures of the church in the entire Old Testament. By comparing scripture with

194

scripture, we learned that in the Doctrinal/Prophetic Application, the *virtuous woman* in Proverbs is a picture of the church. But this *virtuous woman* is also presented in direct contrast with another woman in the book of Proverbs: the *strange woman*. From the very outset, recognize that these two women are diametrically opposed to each other. Other than both of them being of the female gender, there is absolutely no similarity whatsoever!

The *strange woman* shows up in various places throughout the book of Proverbs, but just as Proverbs 31 is the key chapter dealing with the *virtuous woman*, Proverbs 7 is the key chapter dealing with the *strange woman*. Just to begin to give you an idea of what a *strange woman* actually is, she is a seductive woman who is seeking to get somebody into her bed. Anywhere you find her in scripture, that's what she's ultimately seeking to do!

A. The HISTORICAL Application.

Notice in Proverbs 7:1, Solomon says: "My son, keep my words, and lay up my commandments with thee." So, from a historical perspective, here is this wise father Solomon writing to his son, with what is about to be a stern warning for him to stay away and guard himself against being seduced by strange (foreign) women. And since this wise father just happened to be the king of Israel, once this was written it would have been a warning to all young men in the nation of Israel for them to not allow themselves to be seduced by foreign, or strange, women.

Notice, Solomon says...

1 My son, keep my words, and lay up my commandments with thee.
The way we might say that today is, "Son, now I want you to listen to me, and I want you to listen to me good!"

2 Keep my commandments, and live; and my law as the apple of thine eye.
In other words, "If you'll do what I'm about to tell you and make

The Keys of Bible Study

these things a priority in your life, you'll be able to hold onto the things that life is really about."

3 Bind them upon thy fingers, write them upon the table of thine heart.
"Take these truths, and keep them right at your fingertips, etched into the very fabric of everything that you are."

4 Say unto wisdom, Thou art my sister; and call understanding thy kinswoman:
"You need to become so related to and intertwined with wisdom and understanding that they've become like your sister and cousin."

5 That they may keep thee from the strange woman, from the stranger which flattereth with her words.
"If you'll do what I'm telling you, you won't fall prey to the woman of the night who is out there seeking to flatter you with her words to seduce you into her bed."

6 For at the window of my house I looked through my casement,
"You don't even have to go on a search to see this happening. I can see it happening just by looking out of the window of my house!'"

7 And beheld among the simple ones, I discerned among the youths, a young man void of understanding,
"I look out of my window, and I can pick the guy out of the crowd who is gonna go down for the count."

8 Passing through the street near her corner; and he went the way to her house,
"He's the one who gets as close to the fire as he can get, thinking he won't get burnt..."

9 In the twilight, in the evening, in the black and dark night:
"And he puts himself in the midst of this temptation at the time of day when the seduction is at its peak..."

10 And, behold, there met him a woman with the attire of an

196

Chapter 6 — The Key of Application

harlot, and subtil of heart.

"And before he even knew what happened, there she was, standing right in front of him, scantily dressed, and with nothing but evil intentions in her heart."

**11 (She is loud and stubborn; her feet abide not in her house:
12 Now is she without, now in the streets, and lieth in wait at every corner.)**

"She's constantly running her mouth, constantly working to get what she wants. And once you find yourself in her neighborhood, it's like there's no escaping her. She is literally at every turn!"

**13 So she caught him, and kissed him, and with an impudent face said unto him,
14 I have peace offerings with me; this day have I payed my vows.
15 Therefore came I forth to meet thee, diligently to seek thy face, and I have found thee.**

"She pounces on her prey by kissing him, wearing a shamelessly seductive face, and making him think that she's simply been out taking care of all kinds of wholesome responsibilities, when all of a sudden she found him, the man she always wanted."

**16 I have decked my bed with coverings of tapestry, with carved works, with fine linen of Egypt.
17 I have perfumed my bed with myrrh, aloes, and cinnamon.
18 Come, let us take our fill of love until the morning: let us solace ourselves with loves.
19 For the goodman is not at home, he is gone a long journey:
20 He hath taken a bag of money with him, and will come home at the day appointed.**

"And, oh how convenient, my bedroom just happens to be so romantic right now! It looks just right, it feels just right, it smells just right. So let's not waste any time! Let's go express our love for each other until the morning light! We don't have anything to worry about, because the man of the house is on a business trip, and won't be home for several days."

21 With her much fair speech she caused him to yield, with the

flattering of her lips she forced him.

"And she got him! With all of her seductive words, he just couldn't resist."

22 He goeth after her straightway, as an ox goeth to the slaughter, or as a fool to the correction of the stocks;

"Just like one ox follows behind the ox in front of him straight into the slaughter house, he followed her straight into her bedroom."

23 Till a dart strike through his liver; as a bird hasteth to the snare, and knoweth not that it is for his life.

"He thinks this is going to give him what he really wanted, but he doesn't realize that in getting what he wanted, he was going to lose what he had. Life as he once knew it is over."

24 Hearken unto me now therefore, O ye children, and attend to the words of my mouth.

"Oh my dear children, please hear what I'm saying, and heed what you hear."

25 Let not thine heart decline to her ways, go not astray in her paths.

"Don't let your heart go down into her ways, because your feet will surely follow."

26 For she hath cast down many wounded: yea, many strong men have been slain by her.

"Because let me assure ya, you won't be the first life she's destroyed. She's chewed up and spit out all kinds of men who should have known better."

27 Her house is the way to hell, going down to the chambers of death.

"She will take your life and make it a living hell. She will bring death to everything you really care about: your marriage, your relationship with your kids... maybe even your very life, through sexually transmitted disease."

Chapter 6 — The Key of Application

That's the very simple and basic Historical Application, which is very easy to see, understand, and recognize. And yet, also recognize that there is a completely different layer of application that the Holy Spirit of God is seeking to impart to *us* through this wisdom Solomon was imparting to his sons!

B. The PROPHETIC/DOCTRINAL Application

As we just saw in the Historical Application, the *strange woman* is a real *physical* woman that we need to take every precaution imaginable to avoid. And yet we also need to understand that in the Doctrinal/Prophetic Application, she is also just as real, a *spiritual* woman. The strange woman in the book of Proverbs and throughout scripture is a picture of the false religious system of Satan. And again, this is consistent throughout the Bible.

For example, in Revelation 2:20, as Jesus is writing a letter to the church of Thyatira, He talks about how this church had crawled into bed with "that woman, Jezebel" to commit fornication with her. Now, do you think for a minute that old Jezebel somehow got resuscitated, came to the church at Thyatira, and started having sexual relationships with its members? Not on your life! Jesus is talking about something that had happened as people crawled into bed with this *strange woman* **spiritually**.

Another great example is found in Revelation 17, where we read about "the **great whore** that sitteth upon many waters." But do you know who the *great whore* actually is? She is a *strange woman* who is sitting on and riding on the back of a scarlet-colored beast. The beast, of course, is none other than the very Antichrist himself, who in 2 Thessalonians 2:8 is called "that Wicked" (i.e. *wickedness* personified in a man... or, Satan in a human body). Interestingly enough, the *wicked man* in scripture happens to be the counterpart to the *strange woman* in the book of Proverbs.

There is a Historical and Devotional Application of the *wicked man* described in the book of Proverbs, and the biblical injunction is that we are to avoid him and avoid becoming like him. But

199

The Keys of Bible Study

in the Doctrinal Application, the *wicked man* always points to a very particular man—the Antichrist. Likewise, the *strange woman* always points to the false religious systems of this world that are under the power of Satan. And in Revelation 17, the *strange woman* and the *wicked man* have finally found each other and have made their unholy alliance not just to deceive the world, but to rule the world during the tribulation period. And once we see who the *strange woman* actually is, we are able to come back to the in-depth description of her in Proverbs 7 and see how Satan uses the false religious systems of the world to seduce mankind, just like he did with the church in Thyatira, to commit spiritual fornication with her.

Notice in Proverbs 7:7 that God says this unholy connection with the *strange woman* happens to the *simple,* or to those who are *void of understanding.* I say to you my brothers and sisters, though most of Christianity right now has no clue whatsoever about how the *strange woman* is lurking "in the twilight... in the black and dark night" of these last days (Pro 7:9), we can learn an unbelievable amount from Proverbs 7 about what Satan is doing and how he is operating through the false systems of religion in this nighttime of Christianity that we call the Church Age (Rom 13:12; 1Th 5:5).

Satan is operating at this very moment through false doctrine, false teachers, and the false systems of religion—and just like in the red light districts of every major city in the world, in these last days there is a *strange woman* on every corner (Pro 7:12). Be assured that Satan knows exactly how to dress those false systems (Pro 7:10) so that they are seductive and enticing (Pro 7:13). He knows exactly how to lead his *strange woman* to use her fair speech (Pro. 7:21) to make his system seem irresistible. Those who are not void of understanding, however, recognize that God clearly states in Romans 16:17-18 how Satan works through false doctrine to "deceive the hearts of the simple," and that he's successful in doing so, "by good words and fair speeches." Proverbs 7:21 goes on to say that "with the FLATTERING of her lips she forced him." That's one of the things that make the false religious systems so alluring and enticing to the undiscerning—the fact that they flatter

200

Chapter 6 — The Key of Application

us. They appeal to our base nature that always wants to think that we have what it takes, or that there's something we can do to earn our salvation. True Bible Christianity on the other hand, is very clear that "we are all as an unclean thing" (Isa 64:6), and there is absolutely nothing we have to offer God (Rom 3:12). Whereas as Satan's false system will flatter us, God's truth will flatten us.

And notice, Proverbs 7:26 says: "For she hath cast down many wounded..." Have you ever noticed that when people get wounded by the trials and difficulties of life, they often look to religion to help bring them out of their pain? And rather than finding the bride of Christ to love and minister the healing balm of the word of God to them to lead them to Christ, they most usually end up committing spiritual fornication in the bed of Satan's *strange woman* (a false system of religion). Verse 26 goes on to say: "... yea, many strong men have been slain by her." Notice, it's not just troubled, wounded people whom she seduces. Many people whom our culture would view as successful or strong are also lured into her bed through her flattery. We'll often hear cultural icons talk about how they have become a "spiritual person." That's just the way Satan operates. Even people society thinks have it all together are vulnerable to the advances of the *strange woman*.

C. The INSPIRATIONAL/DEVOTIONAL Application.

Once we understand the Historical Application and the Doctrinal/ prophetic Application of Proverbs 7, we are now ready to see how this chapter applies to us from a very practical standpoint. Though there are many ways this chapter applies to our lives, one of the key truths this chapter certainly teaches us is that in the same way men get flattered into illicit sex by an alluring *physical* woman, mankind is very easily flattered into illicit religion by an alluring *spiritual* woman. And don't miss Satan's ultimate agenda through this *strange woman!* Verse 27 says: "Her house is the way to hell." Yes, getting connected to a *strange woman* physically will make life hell on earth—but listen, getting connected to her spiritually is even worse, because it lands people in a *literal hell*. Sadly, there are a lot of religious people who would never even think about allowing

201

themselves to be *physically* connected with a strange woman, and yet without even realizing it have allowed themselves to be connected to her *spiritually* through their connection with their false system of religion.

Recognizing that there are three layers of application in our study of the scripture is absolutely paramount! Sure, most Christians believe the Bible is a supernatural book, but understanding how to see biblically into the Doctrinal/Prophetic Application of the Old Testament is what allows us to personally experience the Bible's supernatural quality. And as the Lord begins to reveal to us the supernatural aspect of His word, we begin to find that we are developing those two key ingredients for which the Lord Jesus Christ is looking for us to possess before entrusting to us the key of David: a *reverential attitude* and *passionate love* for the word of God. Oh, may we continuously cry out with David: "Open thou mine eyes, that I may behold wondrous things out of thy law" (Psa 119:18). May we join Paul in fervently praying: "That the God of our Lord Jesus Christ, the Father of glory, may give unto [us] the spirit of wisdom and revelation in the knowledge of him: The eyes of [our] understanding being enlightened; that [we] may know what is the hope of his calling, and what the riches of the glory of his inheritance in the saints."

THE KEY OF WORDS

As with most of the keys of Bible study, though they can be stated very simply and succinctly, the ramifications of the principle are unbelievably deep and far-reaching. Such is the case with the Key of WORDS.

The sixth key of Bible study:
REALIZE THAT THE KEY TO THE *WORD* OF GOD—IS THE *WORDS* OF GOD.

KEY THOUGHT:

The Bible doesn't claim to communicate just God's thoughts, ideas, concepts, principles, or precepts, but His very words!

Now, if the only thing the Bible promised to communicate to us was God's thoughts, ideas, concepts, principles and precepts... hey, it's God's book, and He can do anything He jolly well wants to do with it. And again, if that's all He intended—praise God! That's certainly His prerogative! But God's promise to us in His word is *more* than that... and *better* than that! Because what He tells us

The Keys of Bible Study

is that His book contains His very **words**! Recognizing that, my friend, is a game-changer when it comes to Bible Study.

As we begin this discussion concerning the **words** of God, to fully appreciate and comprehend the significance of this key, please allow me to provide a bit of significant history.

At the end of the 1800s, as the world was preparing to enter the 20th century, a lot of craziness had been going on in Europe as far as Christianity is concerned. Darwin had proposed his atheistic answer to the origin of life through evolution. Existentialism was running rampant, as was both rationalism and humanism. And all of these teachings and philosophies are what were playing into a great divide that had formed in Christianity between those who were conservative and those who were liberal. It was a time of mass confusion in history, and particularly in Christianity, when it was hard to tell what was what and who was who, precipitating a tremendous need for clarity to be brought to the issues at hand.

The conservatives rallied their troops, and published a set of five volumes that were called *The Fundamentals*. Everybody who adhered to these "fundamentals of the the faith" presented in the publication became known, as you might guess, as *Fundamentalists*. That was a descriptive word that was widely used throughout the 20th century, and though most people today don't know the origin of the term, it is a descriptive word that is still used in Christian circles today.

But the way it shook out in Christian circles in the early days of the 20th century is that you were either a fundamentalist or you were a liberal. And one of the key areas of debate had to do with whether or not the Bible was the word of God. The Fundamentalists said, in no uncertain terms, that the Bible *is* the word of God. In fact, they said the Bible is not just the *word* of God, but the very *inspired* word of God—and as such, it is *infallible,* it is *inerrant,* it has been *preserved* for us, and it is *authoritative* in our lives. And Fundamentalists were unbelievably strong in their belief and conviction about these truths.

204

Chapter 7 — The Key of Words

The Liberals, of course, were the polar opposite extreme of that. They said, in effect, "Sure, the Bible is certainly a great book, and it no doubt has historical and literary value, but as far as it being 'supernatural' or it actually being the 'word of God', well, it certainly isn't that!"

So, at the turn of the 20th century, those were the two basic schools of thought within the Christian ranks in regards to the Bible.

And yet, in just a matter of time, another group began to surface—a sort of "middle-of-the-road" group, if you will. What they believed was that both the conservative and liberal positions were way too extreme. So, they more or less said that both positions were right, and yet at the same time that both positions were wrong. They believed there was a need for balance between the two popular yet extreme positions. In other words, they didn't want to be too *hot*, and they didn't want to be too *cold*. They wanted to land in a very comfortable, shall we say, *lukewarm* position. And, of course, we know what Jesus wrote to the church of the Laodiceans about that. (Rev 3:15-16)

The position this middle-of-the-road group was propagating was essentially this: "We believe the Bible *contains* the word of God, but we certainly don't believe it is inspired—nor do we believe it is inerrant and infallible. Though it *isn't* the word of God, we believe that as a person reads it, it *becomes* the word of God to them." They said that it's important to read the Bible, because even though the actual words may be flawed, God is still able to get His *message* across as we read it. This position was held by those who referred to themselves as "Neo-Orthodox" (i.e. "a new type of orthodox").

So, to provide a simple summary:

- The Fundamentalists said **the Bible *is* the word of God**.
- The Liberals said **the Bible *isn't* the word of God**.
- The Neo-Orthodox said **the Bible *contains* the word of God** and it *becomes* the word of God to you as you read it.

205

The Keys of Bible Study

The Neo-Orthodox position never got much traction in that time period, so it didn't survive very long. The reason many of us probably never knew that the Neo-Orthodox position even existed is because it was such an outlandish and whack position.

And yet, here's the crazy thing! Though many of us have never heard of this Neo-Orthodox position in scripture, it is most definitely alive and well in the 21st century! We just don't call it Neo-Orthodoxy anymore. Do you know what we now call the people who believe what Neo-Orthodoxy was teaching at the first part of the 20th century? We now call them Fundamentalists! Through the course of the last 100 years or so, the Neo-Orthodox position has become the position of people who refer to themselves as Fundamentalists. Because now, people who claim to be "fundamental" and "conservative" are going to tell you that when it comes to the Bible, the real issue isn't so much the *words* of God—the important thing is that we get the *idea* or *message* God was trying to get across. If you are discerning as you listen to most preaching today, that is the essence of their preaching: that God has chosen to simply communicate His *thoughts,* rather than His actual *words.*

Now, I went into all of that historical background information so we might understand that there is actually quite a bit of weight behind the aforementioned Key Thought in this principle of Bible Study. Allow me to state it again: **The Bible doesn't claim to communicate just God's thoughts, ideas, concepts, principles or precepts, but His very words.** And I want to show you that by taking you to some very...

KEY VERSES:

Psalm 119:140 Thy word is very pure: therefore thy servant loveth it.

Notice a few significant things concerning this verse: First, notice that the psalmist doesn't simply say that the word of God is pure. That would be a powerful and wonderful reality in itself—and yet the psalmist is careful to emphasize the fact that God's word isn't just *pure;* it is *very pure!*

Chapter 7 — The Key of Words

And secondly, notice the connection in this verse between believing in the absolute *purity* of the Bible and *loving* it! You'll remember that where we started in the *Keys of Bible Study* in chapter one was with me telling you that the most important Key of Bible Study is a key that I can't give you. It is the Key of David—and as we saw biblically, it is entrusted to people who have the same heart attitude toward God's word that David had. And we saw how that on 11 separate occasions in Psalm 119, David expressed his great love for the word of God. But I want you notice here in Psalm 119:140 that David said that the reason he loved the word of God was *because* of his unwavering belief in its absolute purity!

Now, someone might ask, "Well, just how pure is 'very pure'?" That is certainly a legitimate question—and one to which there is a definite biblical answer! The answer is found in the next key verse...

Proverbs 30:5 Every word of God is pure...

Just how pure is it? The Spirit of God tells us through Solomon that every single last word of it is pure. And you know how we might describe that? Probably the same way David did in Psalm 119:140! That it isn't just *pure*—but *very pure*. It's so pure, that, after stating that *every word of God is pure* in verse 5, the Spirit of God continues in verse 6, saying: "Add thou not unto his words." In other words, they're so pure that God doesn't need or want us messing with 'em! And after clearly commanding us to keep our grubby little hands off of His words, verse 6 goes on to say: "...lest he reprove thee, and thou be found a liar." Wow, that's strong. But that's how pure the *word of God* is—and that's how pure the *individual words of God* actually are! Just think with me about this tremendous reality for a second: we can know with absolute biblical certainty that every **thought** of God expressed in His word is pure. We can know with absolute biblical certainty that every **idea** of God found in His word is pure. We can know with absolute biblical certainty that every **principle** of God delineated in His word is pure... along with every **concept**! But glory be to God, on the authority of God's word, we can also know with absolute biblical certainty that **every word** of God recorded in His word is pure. Hallelujah! Which

207

The Keys of Bible Study

leads to the next key verse...

Psalm 12:6-7 The words of the Lord are pure words: as silver tried in a furnace of earth, purified seven times. Thou shalt keep them, O Lord, thou shalt preserve them from this generation for ever.

Did you know that the words of God actually *have* to be pure? Do you know why they *have* to be pure? It's because Jesus *is* the Word!

> In the beginning was the <u>Word</u> and the <u>Word</u> was with God and the <u>Word</u> was God....And the <u>Word</u> was made flesh, and dwelt among us, (and we beheld his glory, the glory as of the only begotten of the Father,) full of grace and truth. (Joh 1:1, 13-14)

> (Note: When a particular verse in the Bible is referring to the incarnate Word, the Lord Jesus Christ Himself, the King James translators chose to use an uppercase *W*. When it is referring to the written word, the Bible, they chose to use a lowercase *w*.)

Jesus (*the Word*) is the actual embodiment of the written word! Do you understand just how supremely holy, impeccable, and pure our Lord Jesus Christ is? Well, that's exactly how pure the written *words of the Lord* in the Bible are! They are just as holy, impeccable, and pure as Jesus Himself.

Notice the illustration David uses in Psalm 12:6 to further help us grasp just how supremely pure the individual words of God are. He uses the illustration of the refining process that silver went through in biblical times to make it as pure as it could possibly be. David says that the pure words of the Lord are "as silver tried in a furnace of earth, purified seven times." And, of course, we've talked several times about the fact that the number seven in the Bible is the number of *perfection* and *completion*. What God is revealing to us here is that the very **words** of God that comprise the very **word** of God are nothing short of *perfectly* and *completely pure*.

Verse 7 continues, *"Thou shalt keep them..."* And let's just stop there

208

Chapter 7 — The Key of Words

for a second. The pronoun *them* here in verse 7 takes us back to the noun in verse 6, which is *the **words** of the Lord*. David is letting us know that the Lord knows exactly what those words are and that He fully intends to *keep* (or guard) them. In other words, those individual words of the Lord are not going to get out of His grasp. David continues, "Lord, thou hast preserved them [those "pure words"] from this generation for ever."

God is letting us know that He is going to take the *pure words* that were inspired by the Holy Ghost to become part of the canon of scripture and *preserve* them throughout the entire annals of history. Why did God choose to do that? It's because of the key of Bible study to which this chapter is referring: **the key to the *word* of God is the *words* of God.** And if He has not *preserved* His words, we're all in a lurch, folks! Because **the <u>power</u> of the *word* of God is the *words* of God.** Let's take a look at some New Testament passages which confirm this.

Jesus said,

> It is the spirit that quickeneth; the flesh profiteth nothing: the <u>words</u> that I speak unto you, they are spirit, and they are life. (Joh 6:63)

If we don't have Jesus's preserved *words*, the word of God is void of both *spirit* and *life*.

A couple chapters later, Jesus said in John 8:47, "He that is of God heareth God's **words**." And the reality is, those of us who are *of God* wouldn't be able to hear God's **words** unless those **words** are actually recorded somewhere for us to be able to *hear* them.

Peter wrote,

> This second epistle, beloved, I now write unto you; in both which I stir up your pure minds by way of remembrance: That ye may be mindful of the <u>words</u> which were spoken before by the holy prophets, and of the commandment of us the apostles

209

The Keys of Bible Study

of the Lord and Saviour. (2Pe 3:1-2)

And again, how could we possibly be *mindful* of the **words** of the Old Testament *prophets* and New Testament *apostles* unless it was possible for us to access them?

Jude wrote,

> But, beloved, remember ye the words which were spoken before of the apostles of our Lord Jesus Christ. (Jud 1:17)

By now I'm sure you're picking up on the line of reasoning; there would be no way for us to *remember* the **words** of our Lord's apostles unless we have access to those very **words**.

As the Spirit of God concluded His final written revelation to man in The Revelation of Jesus Christ in the final book in our Bible, He says,

> For I testify unto every man that heareth the words of the prophecy of this book, If any man shall add unto these things, God shall add unto him the plagues that are written in this book: And if any man shall take away from the words of the book of this prophecy, God shall take away his part out of the book of life, and out of the holy city, and from the things which are written in this book. (Rev 22:18-19)

And once again, it is more than apparent, that the issue concerning the *word of God* is the *words of God!* So much so that God ends His revelation to man with a very stern warning not to add to or take away from the very **words** contained in His **word**.

That's the significance of the preservation of the very **words** of the **word** of God! And be it known, that if God has gone to those lengths both to *inspire* and *preserve*, not only His **word** but His very **words**, then you can rest assured that the devil is going to do anything and everything within his power to come against the *word of God* by seeking to come against the *words of God*.

Chapter 7 — The Key of Words

KEY PRINCIPLES:

The first recorded words of Satan in the Bible come in the form of a question, and the question had to do with God's *words*.

In Genesis 3:1, the Spirit of God records through Moses,

> Now the serpent [who is clearly identified for us in Rev 12:9 as Satan] was more subtil than any beast of the field which the Lord God had made. And he said unto the woman, <u>Yea, hath God said</u>, Ye shall not eat of every tree of the garden? (Gen 3:1)

Satan was trying to find a way to get the first woman to *question* whether or not she really knew what God had actually *said* to the first man, Adam. When God gave His clear **words** to Adam regarding the trees of the garden in Genesis 2:16-17, it was actually prior to God fashioning the woman from one of his ribs. This means that when God gave the proclamation concerning Adam's freedom to eat of every tree in the garden (2:16) and the prohibition concerning not eating of the tree of the knowledge of good and evil (2:17), the woman hadn't yet been made. So, obviously, everything she knew about God's instruction concerning the trees of the garden, she learned directly from Adam, *not* directly from God. And since all she had actually received was a *translation*, as it were, of God's *original* words to Adam, Satan saw this as a key position from which to leverage his attack. In other words, since she wasn't aware of God's *original* words, he thought that maybe he could get her to *question* the **words** God had given to man.

Lest we spend time identifying the details of this passage and miss its application to our time, please recognize up front that for approximately the last one and a half centuries, all Satan has done in his attack upon the word of God is borrow from his playbook here in Genesis 3! He has sought to come against the word of God (just like he did with the woman) by intimidating people into thinking that since we don't have the original manuscripts, and since the common man doesn't have knowledge of the original languages in

211

which the human authors penned the original manuscripts, maybe we don't really know or have access to the actual **words** of God that comprise the **word** of God. And maybe we need someone "in the know" (like him!) to tell us what *is* and *isn't* the word of God and *interpret* it for us.

Back to the passage, Satan says to the woman, "Yea, hath God said?" In other words, "Did God really say what you *think* he said? Or did God say what Adam *told you* He said? Did God really say and mean, 'Ye shall not eat of every tree of the garden?'" And this was key, because as this passage goes on to reveal, once Satan got her to question what God had said, he knew that he could then lie to her about what God said. Which is exactly what he did! Verse 4 says, "And the serpent said unto the woman, **Ye shall not surely die**." Notice that he tells her the exact opposite of what God had actually said ("in the day that thou eatest thereof **thou shalt surely die**" [Gen 2:17]).

What's shaking out here in Genesis 3 is exactly how Satan operates in our time. It's methodical, folks! His strategy is to first get us to *question* the word of God so that he can flat-out *lie* to us about the word of God, and then step in and tell us what God meant by what he said, or why it was that he said what He said in the first place. In verse 5, he poses as a spokesman for God, saying: "For God doth know that in the day ye eat thereof, then your eyes shall be opened, and ye shall be as gods, knowing good and evil." And what's so crazy about that statement is that everything that Satan said, in its strictest sense, was true! God did most definitely *know*... and if they ate of the tree, their eyes would most definitely *be opened* (which isn't always a good thing, Gen 3:5)... and they would most definitely be *as gods,* in that they they would know experientially both *good and evil*. Again, in the strictest sense, everything Satan said to her in verse 5 was true! But the way he communicated these things to her, he was implying that God had told them not to eat from the forbidden tree because He wanted to *restrict* them, rather than wanting to *protect* them, which definitely *wasn't* true. The way Satan twisted what God had told Adam, he made it sound as if God's ultimate motive in His prohibition was so He could keep

Chapter 7 — The Key of Words

them limited in their capacity as mere humans.

By getting Eve to *question* the word of God, and then getting her to entertain a direct *lie* about the word of God, as a spokesman for God, Satan successfully "changed the truth of God into a lie" (Rom 1:25). By the time it was all over, in verse 6, Eve succumbed to the very three things 1 John 2:16 says comprise the world's system of evil over which Satan is the head: the lust of the flesh, the lust of the eyes, and the pride of life.

And when the woman saw that the tree was good for food [the lust of the flesh], and that it was pleasant to the eyes [the lust of the eyes], and a tree to be desired to make one wise [the pride of life], she took of the fruit thereof, and did eat, and gave also unto her husband with her; and he did eat. (Gen 3:6)

Satan successfully got the first man and woman to do the one and only thing their loving God and Father had forbidden them to do. And please don't miss—and please don't ever forget—that it all began with a *question* about the **word** and **words** of God!

The second **key principle** that is crucial to see concerning the **words** of God, is that...

God chooses His words very carefully and for a specific purpose.

One of the key places God teaches us this principle is in the Gospel of John. As John was bringing his Gospel to a close, the Spirit of God who was inspiring him lets us know something significant. In the next-to-last chapter, John writes,

And many other signs truly did Jesus in the presence of his disciples, which are not written in this book: But these are written, that ye might believe that Jesus is the Christ, the Son of God; and that believing ye might have life through his name. (Joh 20:30)

What John is basically saying here is, "To take everything that Jesus did and accomplished in His ministry and try to get it into one book—oh my!—there's no way in the world that would have even been possible. But as the Holy Spirit was inspiring me, He used a sifter, as it were. He only wanted me to record the things that would cause people in every generation to believe that Jesus is the Christ—so people might believe, and thereby have life through His name."

And then, in the final verse of the final chapter, the Spirit of God inspires John to reemphasize just how careful He was being concerning what actually made its way into this incredible book of the Bible:

> And there are also many other things which Jesus did, the which, if they should be written every one, I suppose that even the world itself could not contain the books that should be written. Amen. (Joh 21:25)

Once again, God is revealing to us the key principle He employed concerning the process of determining what would and would not be included in all of His inspired and preserved word, and that is that there is absolutely no filler, no fluff, and no superfluous details. The Holy Spirit of God specifically chose every word that got included, and every word was included for a specific purpose. One of those purposes is so we would be able to pick up the cross references we need for the Spirit of God to reveal His wisdom and truth to us as we employ the Key of Comparison by comparing scripture with scripture (1Co 2:9–13). And, of course, we're able to pick up those cross references by simply tracing the words of the Bible, because of the sovereign selection of those words by the Holy Spirit of God Himself!

Which leads us to a...

Chapter 7 — The Key of Words

KEY OBSERVATION

The first time key words, concepts, or principles appear in the word of God, we can expect them to foreshadow the key truth regarding them that will unfold and be revealed throughout the rest of the Bible.

This is what many have referred to through the years as **the law of first mention**. It is a principle of Bible study that, in my estimation, is just one other uncanny way God reveals that He has supernaturally and sovereignly inspired and preserved, not only His **word**, but His very **words**.

KEY EXAMPLES

The first mention/usage of the word the word love

The first mention of *love* is in Genesis 22:2, when God tells Abraham: "Take now thy son, thine only son Isaac, whom thou **lovest,** and get thee into the land of Moriah; and offer him there for a burnt offering upon one of the mountains which I will tell thee of."

And notice, first of all, the incredible fact that a *loving father* is faced in this passage with *offering his only son* as a *sacrifice for sin*. Can you already hear John 3:16?

And notice in the next verse, Genesis 22:3, Abraham steps forward in obedience to carry out the plan. And then, Genesis 22:6 says, "And Abraham took the wood of the burnt offering, and laid it upon Isaac his son; and he took the fire in his hand, and a knife; and they went both of them together." This *only son* is *carrying the wood* up the mountain that would be used for his own execution. John 19:17 lets us know that when our Savior had been delivered to be crucified, he carried his own wooden cross to the place of his execution.

Then, Genesis 22:7 says that Isaac asked concerning the whereabouts

215

The Keys of Bible Study

of the sacrifice, and notice Abraham's response in verse 8: "And Abraham said, My son, **God will provide himself a lamb** for a burnt offering!" Did you catch that? Notice that Abraham didn't say, "God will provide a lamb for himself." No! He specifically said, "**God will provide <u>himself</u> a lamb!**" You can't make this stuff up, folks!

Then, the loving father proceeds to offer his son. But just as Abraham was about to sacrifice his son, verses 11 and 12 say: "And the angel of the Lord called unto him out of heaven, and said, Abraham, Abraham: and he said, Here am I. And he said, Lay not thine hand upon the lad, neither do thou any thing unto him: for now I know that thou fearest God, seeing thou hast not withheld thy son, thine only son from me." And then, immediately in verse 13, it says: "And Abraham lifted up his eyes, and looked, and behold behind him **a ram caught in a thicket by his horns**: and Abraham went and took the ram, **and offered him up for a burnt offering** in the stead of his son." When we look at verses 8 and 13 together, we gather that God provided **a male lamb wearing a crown of thorns!** And that spotless lamb, wearing a crown of thorns, becomes the offering and sacrifice for sin.

In this example, it's easy to see how the first mention of the word *love* gives us an example of how love will be manifested throughout the rest of the Bible: by sacrifice.

The first mention/usage of the word the word *worship*

The word *worship* appears for the first time in scripture in this same account of Abraham and Isaac in Genesis 22. Verse 5 says that, before Abraham and Isaac had gone up the mountain, "Abraham said unto his young men, Abide ye here with the ass; and I and the lad will go yonder and **worship**, and come again to you."

Worship in 21st-century Christian culture has become some sort of a crazy, overused buzz word. In recent years, "worship" music has actually even become a multi-million dollar industry. Sadly,

Chapter 7 — The Key of Words

there are a myriad of things that get tucked up under the heading of worship today that quite honestly have no biblical precedence whatsoever.

Jesus taught us in John 4:23 that worship is tremendously important to His Father. In fact, Jesus said that the Father was actually *seeking* worship from worshippers on the earth! But don't miss the fact that what Jesus actually teaches us in this passage is that the Father is seeking a *certain kind* of worship from a *certain kind* of worshipper. Jesus called it **true** *worship* that arises from **true** *worshippers*. This lets us know that there is such a thing as **false** *worship* that is offered by **false** *worshippers*. Since the first mention of a word or concept contains its fundamental biblical components and its future scope throughout the Bible and throughout time, we would do well to observe what God reveals to us about what **true** *worship* is in its first usage here in Genesis 22.

Perhaps it should be noted from the outset that in this account of *true worship* in Genesis 22, nobody played any musical instruments, and nobody sang any songs. Sure, playing music and singing songs can certainly be expressions of *true worship*—but with "worship" in our day, by and large, being relegated to music and a certain vibe or ambiance, we should see what God actually establishes and foreshadows concerning worship from its first account in the Bible.

As we consider Abraham's worship in Genesis 22:1-19, we are actually able to observe at least four key elements of true biblical worship, along with four key characteristics of it, that should be used to help us evaluate any experience that goes under the heading of "worship".

1. **Obedience**: True worship involves a **choice**

Notice in verse 1 that when God calls him by name, Abraham doesn't respond with a question regarding what it was that God was about to ask of him. Rather, he responds with the declaration of his readiness to obey whatever God was about to put before him, saying, "Here I am."

The Keys of Bible Study

In verse 2, as God detailed His will for Abraham to take Isaac unto an undisclosed location in the land of Moriah for the purpose of offering him as a sacrifice, verse 3 reveals Abraham's **choice** to **obey** God unequivocally. Without hesitation, reservation, or deliberation, verse 3 says, "And Abraham rose up early in the morning…and went unto the place of which God told him."

As was mentioned previously, Jesus informs us of the Father's will in seeking our worship—so, like Abraham, we too are faced with whether or not we will exercise the choice of unequivocal obedience to worship Him individually on a daily basis (and corporately on a weekly basis).

2. **Sacrifice**: True worship involves a **cost**

God was obviously well aware of the **sacrifice** He was calling on Abraham to make and the incredible **cost** it would require for Abraham to offer his son as a sacrifice of worship to the Lord. Notice that when God was detailing His will concerning Abraham's sacrifice of Isaac, God doesn't simply refer to Isaac as Abraham's son, but his *only son Isaac* (22:2)—and He acknowledges His awareness of the intimate relationship Abraham had with Isaac, even referring to him as *"thine only son Isaac, **whom thou lovest**"*.

Biblically, as Jesus goes on to reveal in Mark 12:41-44 and Paul goes on to reveal in 2 Corinthians 8:1-5, worship always involves **sacrifice**. God intends for it to **cost** us something. David made a classic statement regarding this principle in 2 Samuel 24:24: "… neither will I offer burnt offerings unto the Lord my God of that which doth <u>cost me nothing</u>."

3. **Encounter**: True worship involves a **connection**

As Abraham made the choice to step out in obedience to sacrifice Isaac (22:9-10) and was in the midst of carrying out this supreme act of worship, it led to an incredible **encounter** with God, in which Abraham **connected** with God in a way he had not previously experienced (22:11-18). It was in the **connection** of this **encounter**

218

Chapter 7 — The Key of Words

that Abraham received the infamous Abrahamic Covenant (22:16-18).

And here we learn that worship is not simply in emotional experience, or even a solely spiritual experience! It is an **encounter** we have with God in which we **connect** with Him as our Jehovahjireh (22:14)—the Lord, our Provider.

4. **Redirection**: True worship involves a **change**

Verse 19 lets us know that this incredible encounter Abraham had with God led to a **change of direction** in Abraham's life. Prior to God speaking to Abraham about going into the land of Moriah (22:1-2), Genesis 21:34 tells us: "Abraham sojourned in the Philistine's land many days." But the connection Abraham made with God in this encounter in the land of Moriah resulted in a **change of direction**. Abraham simply couldn't go back to life as usual. Rather than returning to the land of the Philistines, he makes his way to Beersheba.

So often in the 21st century, we hear people talk about experiencing "killer worship" where the presence of the Lord was "thick" or "heavy." The crazy thing, however, is that in this supposed encounter with God—during which this awesome connection with Him was supposedly made—it somehow didn't lead them to choose obedience in the areas of disobedience in their lives. They were no more willing to offer the sacrifice of anything that actually cost them something than before they experienced this incredible "encounter". And when it was all said and done, they went back to life as usual the next day, with no notable change in the direction of their lives.

As was noted previously, much can be gleaned about worship from its first mention!

The first mention/usage of the word *life*

The first time the word *life* appears in scripture is in Genesis 1:20,

The Keys of Bible Study

where it says: "And God said, Let the waters bring forth abundantly the moving creature that hath **life**..." It's important that we pay close attention to what the context reveals to us about *when* that actually was! The previous verse (verse 19) lets us know that it just happened to be after *"the fourth day."*

And since the power of the word of God is the words of God, and since every word was specifically chosen by God for a particular purpose and set within the context of God's own choosing, notice some things that are specifically connected to the first usage of the word **life**. After the *fourth day* in verse 19, God says in verse 20: "Let the **waters** bring forth **abundantly** the moving creature that hath **life**."

Is it not incredibly interesting that, in Jesus's encounter with the woman at the well in John 4, He referred to Himself as *living water?* (Joh 4:10) He goes on to tell her that if a person drinks of this **water**, they will have **life**! Keep in mind that in John 10:10, that's why Jesus said He had come: to give us **life**, and that we might have it more **abundantly**. Can you see that this is why the **individual words of God** are so important? God preserved His actual **words** because they lead us to the right cross references.

Additionally, have you ever thought about when it actually was that Jesus, who *is* life and who came to *give* life, actually came? Biblically, He just happened to **come** after the **fourth day**!

You might say, "What do you mean?" Well, remember in chapter two when we were seeking to get our minds wrapped around the Key of Theme? We talked about how God was very careful throughout Genesis 1 to repeat on six different occasions the exact words He wanted us to have to make the point that "the evening and the morning were the first day... second day... third day... fourth day... fifth day... sixth day." Then, in Genesis chapter 2, when God recorded for us the details concerning the seventh day, we noted that though God blessed, sanctified, and rested on the seventh day, He very purposely and purposefully broke the pattern that He, Himself, had established in the first six days, in that the seventh

220

Chapter 7 — The Key of Words

day was the only day that had no record of *the evening and morning.*

As we've seen in previous chapters, the *seventh day* in the creation account pictures the coming seventh 1000-year day we call the Millennium, where Jesus Christ will rule on earth for a period of 1000 years (Rev 20:1-3). With that, we also saw that the first six days of the creation account, while being literal 24-hour days, also represent the 6000 years of human history prior to the Millennium. (Refer to 2Pe 3:8 and Chapter 2 for a refresher.)

So with the biblical equation of the days in mind (a day representative of a thousand years), just when was it that Jesus came to give to man the **water** that was Himself, so that man could not only have **life**, but have it more **abundantly?** It was after the *fourth day,* or after four thousand years of human history. In other words, four thousand years after Adam's creation, Jesus was born in Bethlehem. And once again, please note the individual words the Spirit of God used to describe what actually happened after the fourth day. Genesis 1:20 says: "Let the **waters** bring forth **abundantly** the **moving creature** that hath **life.**" And don't miss that the One who was born in Bethlehem after the *fourth day* is the **water of life** (Joh 4:14; Rev 21:6), and all who drink of that **water** receive **life** (John 4:14) and become new **creatures** in Christ (2Co 5:17), in whom we **live** and **move** and have our being (Act 17:28). Like I said before... you can't make this stuff up!

I hope that by now, the Spirit of God is beginning to flood you with an excitement about the word of God, along with the confidence that you really can know and understand it (Pro 1:23). And I hope that the Spirit of God is also reminding you of the fact that just as Satan "beguiled Eve through his subtilty," Satan's desire is now that "[our] minds should be corrupted from the simplicity that is in Christ" (2Co 11:3). There is no doubt, folks: Satan wants to move us away from the fact that God made His word very simple by not only giving us His thoughts, ideas, concepts, principles and precepts, but His very words. It is through those inspired and preserved words that God provides the path to allow us to compare scripture with scripture, which is the biblically-ordained method the Holy

221

The Keys of Bible Study

Spirit uses to reveal His word to us (1Co 2:9-13). As He does, we begin to get more and more excited about the word of God.

That excitement becomes a passion inside of us to know the word of God, and before long we find that we've actually fallen in love with it! And because of our love for the word of God, we wake up one day to realize that our Lord Jesus Christ has entrusted to us the Key of David, the key that opens the doors to the treasures in the *word* of God and the treasure in the *work* of God. And all of a sudden, we find that we're seeing things in the word of God we never saw before, and we find that we're being used in the work of God like we've never been used before.

The entrance of thy words giveth light; it give the understanding unto the simple. (Psa 119:130)

Chapter 7 — The Key of Words

KEY WORDS

JESUS CHRIST

- Innocent blood
- Jesus Christ– (earthly to heavenly)
- Christ Jesus– (heavenly to earthly)
- Without a cause
- Son of Man (earthly)
- Son of God (spiritual)
- Light (Word of God)
- Bread (Word of God)
- Gold (deity)
- Silver (redemption)
- Bridegroom
- Right hand (counterfeited)
- Right arm (counterfeited)
- Lion (counterfeited)
- Image (of God)
- Passover

HOLY SPIRIT

- Dove
- Oil
- Holy Spirit– 3rd person of Trinity
- Holy Ghost– indwelling work

WORD OF GOD

- Sword
- Truth
- Light
- Hammer
- Rain (blessings)

• ISRAEL

- Virgin daughter
- Thy people
- Precious stones (OT)
- Wife (relation to God)
- Remnant (in tribulation)
- Women in travail (in tribulation)
- Barren (women)

223

The Keys of Bible Study

- Olive leaf/tree
- Sign
- Father(s)
- Fig leaf/tree

CHURCH, CHRISTIAN, CHURCH AGE

- Night – church age
- Virgin – church
- Pearl – church
- Precious stones – church (NT)
- Bride – church (relation to Christ)
- Last days – church age and millennium
- Son of God – Christian
- Body – body of Christ

MAN

- Clay (flesh)
- Grass (flesh)
- Flower of grass (glory of man)
- Vessel (human body)
- Chaff (unsaved man)
- Waters (masses of people)
- Ass (unsaved man)
- Flesh
- Body
- Flesh and Blood

SATAN AND HIS IMPS
- Iron (giants)
- Principalities and powers
- Beast (Antichrist)
- Adversary
- Enemy
- Leviathan
- Dragon
- Serpent
- Leopard
- Bear
- Lion
- Young Lions
- Man of Sin
- Son of perdition
- Sons of God (fallen angel)
- Gods

- Confusion
- Mark
- False witnesses
- Spot

JUDGMENT OF GOD

- Brimstone
- Fire
- Hell
- Vengeance
- Deep
- Rain
- Wrath
- Small and great (white throne)
- Threshing (method)
- Threshingfloor (place)
- Winepress (2nd Coming)
- Punish

RAPTURE

- Wings of the morning
- Come up hither
- Sickle
- Harvest
- Day of Christ (church)
- Thunder (God's voice)
- Firstfruits
- Gleanings

TRIBULATION

- Trouble (time of)
- Those days
- Wilderness
- Shadow of death
- Former rain or early rain (mid-tribulation)
- Man child
- Remnant (Israel)
- Virgins (144,000)
- Endure

END OF TRIBULATION INTO SECOND ADVENT

- Turn the captivity
- Darkness, thick darkness
- Women in travail (Israel)
- Latter rain
- Gloominess
- Wasteness
- Distress
- Desolation, desolate
- Destruction
- The End

SECOND ADVENT OF JESUS CHRIST

- The day of the Lord
- That day
- The day
- Brightness
- Cloud
- Whirlwind
- Morning
- Winepress (Battle of Armageddon)
- Day of Wrath
- Fire (God's judgment)

MILLENNIUM

- Selah
- Rest
- Day of the Lord (Second Advent)
- Last Days (includes church age)
- Seventh day
- Reign
- Sabbath
- Eighth day (end of millennium)
- Throne
- Kingdom of heaven

DEATH

- Sleep
- Billows and waves
- Deep
- The floods

MISCELLANEOUS

- Last days – end of a dispensation or the last 3,000 years of human history
- Field – the world
- Sea – top of universe
- Council – against Jesus Christ (except Mat. 5:22)
- Third day – power of resurrection
- Strangers – Gentiles
- Ears – Spiritual hearing and understanding
- Eyes – Spiritual seeing and understanding
- Waters – the sea or the deep at top of universe
- Stars – angels

THE KEY OF CONSISTENCY

By now you may be asking yourself, "So, which is the *most important* key of Bible Study?" The answer is simple: they're *all* the most important! Or, perhaps we could say it this way: the most important key of Bible Study is whichever one we happen to be talking about at any given time. In this chapter, we will be talking about another of "the most important" keys of Bible study:

The seventh key of Bible study:
INTERPRET SCRIPTURE IN LIGHT OF GOD'S CONSISTENCY

We must constantly keep in mind that God is God. And as such, God can do anything He jolly-well wants to do, whenever He jolly-well wants to do it, and He doesn't have to check in with me, you, or anybody else to do it.

But based on what God has revealed about Himself in His word, we know that the God of the Bible is extremely consistent. No, we can never limit God or try to put Him in our own little theological box and tell Him what He can and cannot do. But it is more than biblically apparent that the one true God is very ordered, structured and patterned. He is the one thing in this universe that is stable.

He doesn't have ups and downs. He doesn't have highs and lows. He doesn't have bad hair days. He is always totally and completely consistent.

KEY THOUGHT:

God <u>does</u> what He <u>does</u> and <u>says</u> what He <u>says</u> because He <u>is</u> who He <u>is</u>.

Which is to say, that God doesn't just randomly and indiscriminately *do* or *say* things. What He *does* and what He *says* is predicated upon and dictated by *who He is*.

Because God is totally consistent in His PERSON, we can, likewise, expect Him to be totally consistent when it comes to His WORD.

We know that to be true because in John 1:1, God lets us know that there is a key connection between His *person* and His *word*— they are actually one and the same! Now, there are certainly many implications, ramifications, and applications of this incredible truth, but one of the key truths we can glean from this verse is the fact that whatever is true of God's *person* will also be true of His *word*.

KEY PRINCIPLE:

God is immutable...

The word *immutable* isn't a word we use very often, but it is a Bible word—and as a student of the Bible, it is a word we must get into our spiritual vocabulary. It simply means that *God never changes*, that God cannot and will not change. So with that definition, let's continue on with the **Key Principle**...

God is immutable. His nature, His attributes, and His counsels have always been the same and will always be the same.

230

Chapter 8 — The Key of Consistency

`In fact, in order for God to actually be God, **immutability** must be one of His attributes. And here's why...

KEY QUOTE:

"All change must be for the better or for the worse. If God is perfect, He could not change for the better. You cannot improve on perfection. And if He is perfect, He cannot change for the worse for the same reason. If God ever changed or could ever change, we could never be sure of anything. God cannot change because His very nature is unchanging. Therefore, He can never be wiser, more holy, more just, more merciful, more truthful; nor less. Nor do His plans and purposes change. He is the same yesterday, today, and forever." —Max Anders

Now, it's one thing for Max Anders to say that, and I quote him here because I think he makes the point very succinctly and quite eloquently. But even more importantly than how Anders says it is how *God* says it in His holy and immutable word.

KEY VERSES:

Malachi 3:6 For I am the Lord, I change not...

It doesn't get any simpler or clearer that that! God Himself tells us that it is impossible for Him to change.

Numbers 23:19 God is not a man, that he should lie; neither the son of man, that he should repent: hath he said, and shall he not do it? or hath he spoken, and shall he not make it good?

We see this incredible connection between *who God is* in His *person* and what He *says* in His *word*. Because of who He is, we can take it to the bank: He's never going to change! If He could change, as

231

The Keys of Bible Study

God Himself tells us in these verses, He just flat-out *could not* and *would not* be God. And since He is one and the same with His word, the same could be said for the Bible: if it changes, then it's not the Bible!

The Spirit of God reiterates this same principle of God's *immutability* in the New Testament...

Hebrews 13:8 Jesus Christ the same yesterday, and to day, and for ever.

Note here that this is in reference to Christ's *person*. We can always be certain beyond any shadow of a doubt that Christ's *nature*, *character*, and *attributes* will never and could never change! We must recognize, however, that how He works with people in different time periods (dispensations) *does*, in fact, change. For example, He worked differently with the Nation of Israel in the Old Testament (Lev 1:1-13) than He does with the Church in the New Testament (Heb 10:1-14). He worked in the Church differently prior to the completion of His word (Heb 2:3-4) than He does now that we have the complete revelation of God (1Co 13:10). Likewise, He will work differently with people during the tribulation period (Mat 24:13) than how He is presently working with us right now in the Church Age (Rom 10:13). But though his methods change depending on the time and people he is dealing with, his character never changes.

James 1:17 Every good gift and every perfect gift is from above, and cometh down from the Father of lights, with whom is no variableness, neither shadow of turning.

Now, there are certainly a lot of good and perfect gifts that have come down from *the Father of lights* to people in every generation, for all of which we are grateful. But may I humbly, and yet dogmatically, say that apart from the Holy Spirit taking up residence inside of those who call upon the name of the Lord Jesus Christ for salvation, the best and most perfect gift anyone on this

Chapter 8 — The Key of Consistency

planet has ever received is the preserved word of God in our own language that we can hold in our hands! And James says that "good and perfect" book has come down to us "from the Father of lights, with whom is no variableness, neither shadow of turning." James is basically saying, "Forget the possibility of God turning from who he is. Our Heavenly Father is so full of light, there's not even the possibility that there could be a *shadow of turning* from who He is!"

Hebrews 6:17 Wherein God, willing more abundantly to shew unto the heirs of promise the immutability of his counsel, confirmed it by an oath.

God wanted "the heirs of promise" to be so confident in His counsel (the word of God) that He *confirmed it by an oath.* That's how sure God wanted us to be, both of His *person* and in His *word.* Because God knew that if He and His word were not immutable, we could never be sure of anything.

Can you even begin to imagine what life would be if we had to wonder and worry about God somehow changing midstream? Do you understand the devastating implications of that? I mean, He might say one thing, and yet do another! Even if He loved us today, there would be no guarantee He would love us tomorrow. And we could go on and on with the disastrous ramifications if God weren't immutable. But the fact that God *is* immutable lets us know that we can count on Him to be consistent. And because He *is* the Word of God (Joh 1:1), it lets us know that we can approach the Bible believing it will likewise possess a supernatural unity and consistency.

KEY HISTORY:

The supernatural quality of the Bible's unity and consistency is amazing when you see how it was actually achieved.

It's one thing for us to talk about how the Bible is God's book, and is, therefore, totally consistent and will never change. But when

The Keys of Bible Study

we consider all the moving parts that all had to come together to achieve this unity and consistency, we discover that it is beyond amazing! It is completely supernatural! And these supernatural qualities can be observed through...

• The incredible LENGTH of TIME in its writing.

- The Bible was written over a period of almost 1600 years, or over 60 generations.

Just to be sure we're understanding the significance of that length of time, do you realize that if we were to go back 1600 years (or 60 generations) from where we are right now, we would find ourselves in the 400s? Do you realize the incredible changes that have taken place in the world and in the thinking of the world over that period of time? And yet, amazingly, the Bible was written over that same length of time, and is totally and completely consistent in every minute detail.

Not only was this consistency achieved despite the incredible length of time in it's writing, but consider also...

• The WRITERS themselves.

- **There were over 40 different human writers of the Bible**.

That's a whole lot of personalities for the Holy Spirit to juggle, not to mention a lot of quirks and idiosyncrasies, especially when the goal is one unified and consistent book! See also...

• The many different BACKGROUNDS of the writers.

- Moses was an Egyptian prince
- Joshua was a soldier
- Samuel was a priest
- David was a king

Chapter 8 — The Key of Consistency

- Job was a rich farmer
- Amos was a poor farmer
- Ezra was a scribe
- Nehemiah was a cup bearer
- Isaiah was a prophet
- Daniel was a prime minister
- Matthew was a tax collector
- Mark was an evangelist
- Luke was a physician
- John was a wealthy fisherman
- Peter was a poor fisherman
- Paul was a scholar

And the Bible's consistency becomes even more astounding when we consider...

• The many different PLACES from which they wrote.

• The Bible was written from three different continents.

If you've been able to travel the world, you recognize what a significant reality this actually is. Especially when going from one continent to another! People not only *talk* and *act* differently—they actually even *think* differently! The implications of culture upon communication simply cannot be overestimated. And be it known, the human authors of scripture weren't just writing from three different *countries* within a particular region. That would have been astounding enough! My goodness, there are cultural differences that affect communication between different *states* within our own country! The writers of scripture wrote from *three different continents!* And from those continents...

• The Bible was written from all kinds of different PLACES.

235

The Keys of Bible Study

From the desert (Exodus 17)
On Mount Sinai (Exodus 20)
In Palestine (Most books)
In Egypt (Jeremiah)
On the Isle of Patmos (Revelation)
In Babylon (Daniel)
In Persia (Esther)
In Corinth (1 and 2 Thessalonians)
In Ephesus (Galatians)
In Rome (Colossians, 2 Timothy)

But then, take into consideration, not only take the different continents and places from which the writers of scripture wrote, but...

• The different LANGUAGES in which they wrote.

- The Bible was written in three different languages.

- The Old Testament was written in Hebrew, and the New Testament was written in Greek and Aramaic.

One would think that the differences of languages alone would strongly affect, if not negate, the Bible's consistency! But then, add to that...

• The different TIMES in which they wrote.

- Some writers wrote in times of peace, while others wrote in times of war.

Historically, these considerations have greatly affected literature! But add to that...

• The different MOODS in which they wrote.

- Some wrote in the heights of joy, while others wrote in the depths of sorrow.

236

Chapter 8 — The Key of Consistency

• The different SUBJECTS on which they wrote.

- They wrote on hundreds of controversial subjects.

Do you have any idea how hard it is to get people to agree about anything, much less a controversial subject? I'm a part of a fellowship of churches that identifies itself as the Living Faith Fellowship (LFF). The fellowship exists because we are a very biblically likeminded group of pastors and churches who network together for encouragement, enrichment, and the equipping of the members of our churches to carry out the mission. We all have a faith-based view of the Bible (i.e. we believe we have the preserved word and words of God in the Bible we hold in our hands, as was discussed in the previous chapter); we believe in expository preaching; we believe that every believer is to have an active role in making disciples; we believe in global missions; we believe in Christlike holiness; we believe the only way the Bible can be properly understood and taught is from a dispensational standpoint; and we believe that everything we do is to be done for the glory of God. That is quite a list of things for a group of pastors and churches to agree upon!

However, if we were to get the word out to our Living Faith Fellowship churches that we were going to publish a book on the subject of abortion, for example, and we wanted every member of all of our churches to write a chapter in the book that we would then compile them together and title, *What the Living Faith Fellowship Believes About Abortion*—Oh my! Do you realize what a literary monstrosity that would be? It would be the most conflicting, contradictory, and whacked out piece of literature imaginable! And that's what it would be if it were written by people who are very biblically likeminded!

So what's the point?

Though the Bible was written over a period of almost 1600 years, over 60 generations; with over 40 different writers who came from all kinds of different backgrounds; who wrote from three different continents, in three different languages, and in all kinds of different times, places, and moods; and wrote on hundreds of controversial subjects—from Genesis to Revelation, the Bible is consistent and reads as if it were written by one author. And, of course, it was… by God!

EXAMPLE #1: The Book of GENESIS and the Book of REVELATION

Obviously, when we're talking about Genesis and Revelation, we're talking about the Alpha and the Omega of the Bible: the first and the last books.

In the United States, the country I'm from, we tend to think linearly. That is, we tend to think in a straight line. We move from A to B to C, and we work our way down the line all the way to Z. When it comes to the Bible, we tend to think the same way. We have Genesis here, and then next in line is Exodus, and then Leviticus, Numbers, Deuteronomy, Joshua and Judges… and again, we work our way down the line, until we finally get to Revelation.

What's interesting, however, is that in other parts of the world, as in Asia for example, people don't tend to think in a line—they think in a circle. And this difference in thinking isn't a matter of right or wrong—it's simply a cultural difference—but it is definitely one that, for the sake of unity, needs to be recognized! What I have had to come to grips with, however, is that the Bible isn't an American or Western book. The Bible is actually laid out more in a circle than it is a line. In that respect, it is more Asian in its revelation than it is Western (which makes sense, since most of it was written on the Asian continent). If we were going to illustrate how the Bible is actually laid out, rather than Genesis beginning at one particular point and Revelation being way down at the end of the line or

Chapter 8 — The Key of Consistency

list, the more proper layout would be in a circle—so that if it were a clock, Genesis would take the position at 12:00, and the other books would follow that same pattern clockwise around the clock, until Revelation would take the position at 11:00.

According to this layout, we are able to see how the first and the last books of the Bible cause all of the teaching of the rest of the Bible to dovetail into a supernatural unity that can only be explained as it being *God's book* that reflects *God's nature, God's attributes,* and *God's person.* Let me show you what I mean.

In **Genesis** we read: "In the beginning God created the heaven and the earth." (1:1)
In **Revelation** we read: "I saw a new heaven and a new earth." (21:1)

In **Genesis** we find the first Adam with his first wife Eve in the Garden of Eden, reigning over all the earth. (1:26–28)
In **Revelation** we find the last Adam (1Co 15:45), Christ, with His wife, the Church, in the city of God reigning over the entire universe. (21:9–23)

In **Genesis** we are told; "And the gathering of the waters called he seas." (1:10)
In **Revelation** we are told: "And there was no more sea." (21:1)

In **Genesis** God created the sun, the moon, and the day and the night. (1:5,16)
In **Revelation** we see that "there shall be no night" (22:5) and "the city had no need of the sun, neither the moon, to shine in it: for the glory of God did lighten it, and the Lamb is the light thereof." (21:23)

In **Genesis** the Tree of Life is denied to sinful man. (3:22)
In **Revelation** the Tree of Life "yielded her fruit every month: and the leaves of the tree were for the healing of the nations." (22:2)

In **Genesis** man hears God say: "Cursed is the ground for thy sake." (3:17)

239

The Keys of Bible Study

In **Revelation** man will hear God say: "And there shall be no more curse." (22:3)

In **Genesis** Satan appears to torment man. (3:1)
In **Revelation** Satan "shall be tormented forever and ever." (20:10)

In **Genesis** man's first home was beside a river. (2:10)
In **Revelation** man's eternal home will be beside a river. "And he showed me a pure river of water of life clear as crystal, proceeding out of the throne of God and of the Lamb." (Rev. 22:1)

Genesis ends with a believer in Egypt, lying in a coffin. (50:1–3)
Revelation ends with all believers reigning forever in eternity where there shall be no more death. (21:4)[1]

Do you see what God has done in His word? He comes "full circle," as it were. The Bible *ends* exactly the way it *begins*, because the Bible is consistent from Genesis to Revelation.

EXAMPLE #2: The Book of ISAIAH

When we allow ourselves to step back from the book of Isaiah, it becomes obvious that this book is actually a microcosm of the Bible. In other words, it is a small representation of the whole. For example, we could say that New York City is a microcosm of the world. If you don't have time to see all the people groups of the world, just go to New York City and start traveling the blocks. You'll find the entire world right there on a 15mi x 15mi parcel of land! Another example of a microcosm is the capstone of a pyramid: the finishing stone that completes the structure which is actually just a small representation of the whole of the pyramid. In other words, the capstone is simply a miniature version of the entire pyramid.

---

[1] H.L. Wilmington, *That Manuscript from Outer Space*, (Nashville, Thomas Nelson Inc., Publishers, 1974), 83–84.

Chapter 8 — The Key of Consistency

In that same way, we could say that the book of Isaiah is a microcosm of the Bible. The Bible is comprised of 66 different books; the book of Isaiah is comprised of 66 chapters. The Bible is divided into two different sections that we call the Old Testament and the New Testament—the Old Testament containing 39 books, and the New Testament 27. Interestingly enough, the first chapter in the book of Isaiah has a strikingly similar connection to the first book of the Bible. In Isaiah 1:1-2, it talks about the heavens and the earth, just like Genesis begins, "In the beginning God created the heavens and the earth" (Gen 1:1).

As we go through the first 39 chapters in Isaiah, we then make our way into the 40th chapter, which, of course, would coincide with the 40th book of the Bible, the Gospel of Matthew—the beginning of the New Testament. And do you know how the Gospel of Matthew begins? Matthew 3:3 says: "The voice of one crying in the wilderness, prepare ye the way of the Lord..." And do you know what Isaiah 40:3 says? "The voice of him that crieth in the wilderness, Prepare ye the way of the Lord..."

From there, if we continue on through the next 27 chapters in Isaiah to the last chapter of the book, chapter 66, which coincides with the 66th book of the Bible (Revelation), take a wild guess at what's going on here. Isaiah 66:15 says: "For behold the Lord will come with fire, and with his chariots like a whirlwind, to render his anger with fury, and his rebuke with flames of fire."

He is, of course, describing the second coming of Christ! In verse 18 of this same 66th chapter, Isaiah continues talking about that event, saying, "...I will gather all nations and tongues; and they shall come, and see my glory." He continues in verse 22 talking about "the new heavens and the new earth." And when we come to the 66th book of the Bible, the book of Revelation, do you remember how it ends? Revelation 19 talks about the second coming of Christ, when He comes in flaming fire (19:12), exercising His judgment upon the nations (19:15) as He stands revealed in all of His glory (19:16). In Revelation 21–22, it records the establishment of "a new heaven and a new earth."

241

The Keys of Bible Study

Could all of this just be mere coincidence? I think not. There's only one explanation. Because the Word (Christ—John 1:1) is consistent, His word (the Bible) is consistent!

EXAMPLE #3: The Book of PROVERBS

Take a minute to look at the layout of the Old Testament books below.

Proverbs

```
              Psalms Ecclesiastes
            Job    Song of Solomon
          Esther           Isaiah
        Nehemiah          Jeremiah
       Ezra           Lamentations
    2 Chronicles           Ezekiel
    1 Chronicles          Daniel
      2 Kings             Hosea
    1 Kings               Joel
    2 Samuel              Amos
    1 Samuel            Obadiah
      Ruth               Jonah
     Judges              Micah
    Joshua              Nahum
  Deuteronomy          Habakkuk
    Numbers           Zephaniah
   Leviticus             Haggai
    Exodus            Zechariah
   Genesis              Malachi
```

What we see here is that since there are 39 books in the Old Testament, the book of Proverbs is the middle book. There are 19 books before it, and there are 19 books after it. I've chosen to lay it out in this fashion to show *graphically* what happens *compositionally* through the content of the first 19 books that lead up to, what we're about to see, is the pinnacle of the Old Testament—the book of Proverbs.

As we simply tell the story of each of these books in the order in which we find them in our Old Testament, we discover that God has found a masterful way not only to provide for us the overarching message of the entire Bible, but the complete unfolding of the entire history of mankind upon the earth! Once again, it reveals to us *God's* consistency and the consistency of His *supernatural book!*

Chapter 8 — The Key of Consistency

The Book of GENESIS

Genesis means *beginning*, and Genesis is the "book of beginnings." It records the beginning of everything! The beginning of the universe... the beginning of man... the beginning of woman... the beginning of family... the beginning of government—but most importantly, it details for us the beginning of sin and death. The book of beginnings ends with a man in a coffin in Egypt (Egypt, in the Bible, is consistently a picture of the world and sin). And in the book of Genesis, from chapter 3 all the way to the end of the book, man is a slave to the world and sin.

And ever since Genesis chapter 3, our beginning is just like that; we are born into this world spiritually dead, alienated from God, and, therefore, a slave to sin.

The Book of EXODUS

Exodus means "brought out." At the beginning of Exodus, God's people were slaves in Egypt. Egypt was the world power at that time, and they were being held captive there by Pharaoh, Egypt's wicked ruler. Day after day, God's people labored under the taskmaster's whip, longing for a deliverer. Finally, God delivered them (or, brought them out—and thus, the name of the book!) through the blood of the Passover Lamb.

Interestingly enough, the Bible teaches that we, too, were slaves in Egypt (again, Egypt being a picture of the world and sin), and we were being held captive there by Satan, the wicked ruler of this world (2Co 4:4 calls him "the god of this world"). And day after day in our lost condition, we labored under the taskmaster of sin, until God delivered us (or "brought us out") through the blood of the Passover Lamb, the Lord Jesus Christ (1Co 5:7).

The Book of LEVITICUS

The book of Leviticus derives its name from the priestly tribe of Levi. The name *Levi* actually means "joined to." The purpose of

243

The Keys of Bible Study

Israel's exodus wasn't just to deliver them from their bondage to Pharaoh. It wasn't just to deliver them from the torment of their taskmaster. Their deliverance and freedom from their oppression and oppressor was to allow them to be "joined to" a whole new kind of existence in a whole new land. On numerous occasions God told them that he brought them out not as an end to itself, but to a specific place and purpose (Deu 6:23; Exo 3:8; Lev 25:38).

And, oh my, don't miss this: the purpose of *our* exodus wasn't just so we could be brought out of our bondage to Satan. We were brought out of our bondage to Satan so we could be joined to God! The purpose of our exodus wasn't just so we could be brought out of our sin; He brought us out of our sin so we could be joined to God's righteousness. The purpose of our exodus wasn't just so we could be brought out of the power of darkness in this world's system; He brought us out of its power so we could be joined to His kingdom of light.

The Book of NUMBERS

The book of Numbers gets its name because of two "numberings" of God's people that take place in the book. One of the numberings takes place at the beginning of the book, and one takes place at the end. What's amazing is that the two numberings reveal that over a 40 year period, there was basically no growth in the nation of Israel. Do you remember what God's people were doing in that 40 year period? They were wandering in the wilderness of unbelief. The land of Canaan God had promised them was only an 11-day journey from where they had been delivered out of Egypt (Deu 1:2), but for 40 years they failed to believe God—or shall we say, they failed to take God at His word.

Through the children of Israel's negative example, God is trying to get us to see that it is possible to be brought out of our sin and death and be joined to God, and yet never really grow because we fail to believe God… or we fail to take Him at His word! We could trust Him with our eternal destiny, but never really trust Him day by day—and because of that, never really get where God wants to

244

Chapter 8 — The Key of Consistency

take us. We just spend 10, 20, 30 and even 40 years in our Christian life, wandering in the wilderness of unbelief—never really fulfilling God's purpose in bringing us out.

The Book of DEUTERONOMY

Deuteronomy means "second Law." God gave the Law the first time in the book of Exodus, and it was pretty much like this: "Obey Me because I'm God, and because I said!" It was connected to duty. But in the book of Deuteronomy, when God gives the Law the second time, it's connected to a different word. This time it's connected to love! And for the first time, God talks about His love for His people and the desire in His heart for His people to love Him! God lets us know that, yes, He wants us to obey Him—but He wants us to do it not out of obligation or duty, not out of fear, and not because of the consequences if we don't—He wants us to obey because of our love for Him. He wants us to fulfill the Law of love! (2Co 5:14-15)

The Book of JOSHUA

The first five books of the Bible are called the "books of the Law." They were written by and connected to Moses. But as good of a man as Moses was, and as hard as he tried to get God's people into Canaan (the land they were promised), he just wasn't able to do it.

But then comes the book of Joshua, and this is how it begins: "Now after the death of Moses the servant of the Lord, it came to pass, that the Lord spake unto Joshua..." (Jos 1:1) Do you know what the name *Joshua* means? It means "Jehovah is salvation." And do you know what the name *Jesus* means? It, too, means "Jehovah is salvation." It's actually the same name! *Joshua* is simply the Hebrew rendering, while *Jesus* is the Greek. In fact, Acts 7:45 even refers to the Old Testament Joshua as Jesus!

The point is this: the Law is a good thing, but it can never bring us into the abundant life that God intended for us. Only Joshua (Jesus!) can do that!

245

The Keys of Bible Study

The book of Joshua is all about Joshua leading God's people into battle with a sword, defeating the enemies in the land, and taking possession of the inheritance God had promised them. And, of course, he pictures for us how the Lord Jesus Christ, with the sword of the word of God, defeats the enemies we face on a daily basis—the world, the flesh and the devil—and allows us to possess the fullness of our inheritance in Christ!

The Book of JUDGES

There is a phrase that is repeated four times in the book of Judges: "And there was no king in Israel: every man did that which was right in his own eyes."

This book shows us what happens in the life of a believer when we refuse to let our king, the Lord Jesus Christ, rule in us. What happens over and over in this book is this: God blesses His children, and in the midst of His blessing, they become complacent, and their complacency leads them into sin. Their sin, then, causes God to chasten them, so they repent—and because they repent, God blesses them. And in the midst of God's blessing, they become complacent, and their complacency leads them into sin... and here we go through the same cycle all over again!

The story of Judges is actually the story of most Christians in the 21st century. I'm not quite sure how many times that sin cycle is repeated in our lifetimes—but I do know that this sin cycle is repeated seven times in the book of Judges! And interestingly enough, those seven cycles of sin just happen to line up perfectly with the seven periods of church history that are represented in the seven letters Jesus wrote to the seven churches in Revelation 2 and 3.

The Book of RUTH

Ruth is a lady in the Old Testament with whom we must make sure we are very familiar, because her story is extremely important to us! You should remember it from our discussion of the Key of

246

Chapter 8 — The Key of Consistency

Comparison. As a refresher, her story unfolds like this: Ruth is a Gentile from a cursed race. She is a Moabitess, so she is separated from God and His promises. Ruth lives in a time of famine. But one day she hears good news from a far land that God had visited His people in Bethlehem in giving them bread. Upon hearing this good news, she turns from her people, her land, her gods, and everything she held dear and goes to Bethlehem to partake of that bread. When she arrives there, she immediately goes to work in the field of a man who, without her realizing it, was her Jewish kinsman-redeemer. He takes one look at her in his field, falls head-over-heels in love with her, takes her out of his harvest field to become his bride, and then takes her to his father's house for their marriage!

Like Ruth, we are from a cursed race: the human race. We, too, were totally separated from God and His promises, leaving our souls completely famished. But one day, like Ruth, we heard good news from a far land that God had visited His people as the "bread of life" in the city of Bethlehem. And upon hearing that good news (gospel = good news), do you know what happened to us? We turned from our people, our land, the gods we served, and everything we held dear so we could partake of the Bread of Bethlehem. Right now, we are working in the harvest field of our Jewish Kinsman-Redeemer, as we await His coming to take us out of the harvest field to be His bride, and then to His Father's house for our marriage!

And do you know what happens once we're raptured out of His harvest field? The same thing that happens in the next two books of the Bible!

The Books of 1 and 2 SAMUEL

First, Israel allows the wrong king to be crowned. Historically, that was Saul. But after a short period of time, he is revealed for the person he really is, and then God's choice for Israel's king comes to the throne. That, of course, was David.

But, if you're familiar with how God reveals the events of the last days, you recognize that after the bride of Christ has been removed from the harvest field of this world, Israel will once again allow the wrong king to be crowned. This time, of course, it will be the Antichrist. But then, after a short period of time, he'll be revealed for who he really is, and then God's choice for Israel's King, the Lord Jesus Christ, will come to the throne—and He will sit on the throne of David!

The Books of 1 and 2 KINGS and 1 and 2 CHRONICLES

What's interesting in these two sets of books is that God covers the same ground twice. Basically, these books cover the downward spiral of the nation of Israel morally and spiritually—which finally culminated with the destruction of the Temple and the people being taken into captivity. Again, for some strange reason, God records that for us twice! And it's interesting that in history, the destruction of Israel's Temple happened not just once, but twice! Once in the days of Nebuchadnezzar, and once in 70 AD under Titus.

The Book of EZRA

The book of Ezra tells of the remnant of Jews coming back into the land following the declaration of a pagan king by the name of Cyrus, who just happens to be a king who boasted that his kingdom spanned the entire earth.

And it's interesting that a remnant of Jews started heading back to the land of Israel at another time in history—and coincidentally enough, they, too, were able to do it because a pagan king, who just happened to boast that "the sun never sets on the British empire", pronounced an edict called the Balfour Declaration which permitted the Jews to return to their homeland at the end of World War I.

Chapter 8 — The Key of Consistency

The Book of NEHEMIAH

As we just talked about, some of the Jews returned to the homeland in the days of Cyrus in the book of Ezra. But it's in the book of Nehemiah where the walls of the city of Jerusalem where established. In ancient times it was said that a city without walls is not a city at all. And here was the city of Jerusalem with no walls, completely exposed to the world. Under Nehemiah's leadership, the walls were constructed once again, giving them a border and protection from their enemies.

Once again, it's rather interesting that following the Balfour declaration and the return of a remnant of the Jews into the homeland, in 1948 the borders of modern day Israel were established, and Israel took its place among the nations once again. Jesus told us to keep our eye on the fig tree (biblically, a term used to refer to the nation of Israel) because when it blossoms, the generation that witnessed it would not pass away until all of the events of the last days unfold (the rapture, the tribulation period, and the second coming of Christ).

The Book of ESTHER

Do you know what happens at the beginning of the book of Esther? Please read carefully! The sovereign king who ruled the world "in those days" invites his princes and his servants into his palace to partake of a feast that lasts for seven days. During this time, he replaces his incredibly beautiful Gentile bride with a Jewish bride, and he pours out his grace and his favor upon her. And yet, while he does that, the villain in the story, a man referred to in the book as "this wicked" seeks to destroy the entire Jewish race. On the very day that his devious plot was to be enacted, the tables were turned, his head was crushed, and the book of Esther ends with absolute jubilation and victory in the kingdom.

It would be near impossible to tell the story of what will happen once the borders of the nation of Israel were established (represented in the book of Nehemiah) better than that! Because "in those days"—a

249

phrase found 75 times in the Bible, and always points to "those days" of tribulation—the Sovereign King of the world is going to call His princes and his servants that comprise the church to His palace for a feast that we call the Marriage Supper of the Lamb and which will last for seven days (or a "week of years"). During this time, on earth, the Sovereign King will replace His beautiful Gentile bride (the church), with a Jewish Queen (the Nation of Israel) and He will pour out His grace and His favor upon her, fulfilling all of His promises to her!

And while God is moving to do that, the Antichrist—the one that 2 Thessalonians 2:8 refers to as "that wicked"—will be seeking to destroy the Nation of Israel. And on the very day that his devious plot is about to be enacted at that final battle, the Battle of Armageddon, the Lord Jesus Christ will step in and turn the tables, the Antichrist's head will be crushed, and it will end just like the book of Esther ends—with jubilation and victory in the kingdom!

The Book of JOB

Much like Esther, Job is a man who sits in tribulation on the earth for seven days. Throughout the whole ordeal he has no idea that the tribulation he is enduring is being brought on him by none other than Satan himself. Though Job didn't understand it, God actually did identify the source of his tribulation by talking about a beast that rises out of the sea—a beast that was actually a dragon with seven heads. This just happens to be the same exact beast John saw in Revelation 13, having seven heads, that arose out of the sea as Israel sits in tribulation for seven days (or week of years).

Do you know where Job is during this time of tribulation? He's in the land of Uz. Uz is where Edom is. And Edom is where Petra is. Do you know the biblical significance of Petra? It is the exact place that God is going to preserve the Jewish remnant in the last 3 ½ years, or 42 months, of the tribulation period (Rev 12:14), referred to biblically as the Great Tribulation. And all of this just happens to take place in a book that just happens to have 42 chapters in it!

250

The Book of PSALMS

Then, the book that follows the tribulation of Job for seven days is the book of Psalms, or songs, where the king is established on his throne in his kingdom, and all the earth is singing. Psalm 66:4, speaking of Christ in His millennial kingdom says, "All the earth shall worship thee, and sing unto thee; they shall sing to thy name. Selah" (rest!). That's why we have a book of songs in our Bible: because when the King of kings takes up His throne, all the earth will finally have something to sing about!

The Book of PROVERBS

And then, here it is! The pinnacle of the Old Testament! And do you remember who wrote the book of Proverbs? It was Solomon, right? And do you remember that tenfold description we collected concerning him back in Chapter 5 by simply employing the Comparison Key?

We found that as we took the time to compare scripture with scripture, Solomon is described biblically as the prince of peace... the beloved of the father... the son of David, and yet the son of God... the man of rest... who will sit on the throne of the Lord... in an everlasting kingdom... a kingdom that will be characterized by peace and rest... because his adversary is vanquished... and in that kingdom, all the kings of the earth will come and bow before his presence. Obviously, from a historical standpoint, Solomon wrote the Proverbs, but just as obvious is the fact that he is really just a picture of the real Author of the book of Proverbs—the Lord Jesus Christ, Himself!

And having established that, do you know what it is that the book of Proverbs actually reveals? It reveals to us the wisdom by which our Lord Jesus Christ will rule in His millennial kingdom!

God and His word are consistent, my brothers and sisters! And we must interpret scripture in light of God's consistency!

THE KEY OF ASSOCIATION

The eighth key of Bible Study:
ALLOW GOD TO TEACH YOU BY ASSOCIATION.

Key Principle #1

God uses His physical creation to teach us spiritual truth.

Obviously, the Scripture teaches us that God is the Creator of all things. Colossians 1:16-17 synthesizes almost the entirety of biblical teaching on this subject, saying,

> For by him were all things created, that are in heaven, and that are in earth, visible and invisible, whether they be thrones, or dominions, or principalities, or powers: all things were created by him, and for him: And he is before all things, and by him all things consist. (Col 1:16-17)

But as we begin to dig into the details of scripture concerning the creation, God reveals to us an incredible biblical reality: as God was creating everything we see in the physical universe, there was

The Keys of Bible Study

absolutely nothing haphazard or random about anything He was doing! With every single thing He was creating, He purposely designed it in a fashion so that it would illustrate spiritual truths He wanted us to learn and know. This is why we refer to this key of Bible study as the Key of Association.

Every good teacher knows that one of the key ways people learn is by taking something we don't quite understand and showing how it relates to something we do understand. As a preacher and teacher of the word of God, I will often take a biblical concept or principle I think is somewhat difficult to comprehend and try to relate it to some event in history or from my life that will serve as an illustration so the listeners are able to see and understand the biblical point. Again, that's just part of how humans teach and learn. And we learned to do that, of course, from the Master Teacher—none other than God Himself!

However, there is still a major difference between how God teaches and how humans teach. Throughout my years of preaching, on those weeks when I knew that the passage I'd be dealing with presented a difficult principle or concept, as I'd going through my week I'd see, hear, or remember something and think to myself, "That'll be a perfect illustration of that point!" But that isn't how God operates! That's not what the Key of Association actually is. Because it wasn't that God created everything in existence, and then through the course of time, thought to Himself, "Hey! You know what I just realized? All of this stuff I created and made would make for some great illustrations of My truth." No; with God, it was the exact opposite. As God was in the midst of creating everything in existence, He very purposely and calculatedly did so in such a way that by its very design it would perfectly illustrate the truth He knew He wanted us to be able to clearly see and understand. Again, *God created everything in His physical creation to teach us spiritual truth.*

KEY VERSE:

Romans 1:20 For the invisible things of him from

254

the creation of the world are clearly seen, being understood by the things that are made, even his eternal power and Godhead; so that they are without excuse.

This is a monumental verse. It teaches us that the *invisible things of him*—or, the truths about God that we're unable to see with our physical eyes—we're actually able to see very clearly by the things He made in His physical creation.

KEY TEACHING:

Romans 1:20 teaches us that God purposely created the things that we see in the physical world to teach us about Him. The pattern God used to create the physical world was Himself! In fact, God says that we can even understand His eternal power and Godhead (the Trinity...the 3 in 1!) by what we see in creation.

Are you hearing that? And be it known, God isn't exaggerating the point here! (Not that He ever does!) He's teaching us something very significant about the created world that we see around us. There are things in creation that our Creator specifically created to teach us about Himself.

KEY OBSERVATION:

Because God is a Trinity, it is interesting to note that everything physical in creation will always break down in to a system of threes.

KEY EXAMPLES:

- **Man**: Body, Soul, Spirit
- **Environment**: Land, Sea, Air
- **Kingdoms**: Animal, Vegetable, Mineral

The Keys of Bible Study

- **Dimensions**: Height, Width, Depth
- **Colors**: Red, Yellow, Blue
- **Matter**: Solid, Liquid, Gas
- **Atoms**: Protons, Neutrons, Electrons
- **Charges**: Positive, Negative, Neutral
- **Galaxies**: Spiral, Irregular, Elliptical
- **Flowers**: Annual, Biennial, Perennial
- **Angles**: Acute, Obtuse, Right
- **Averages**: Mean, Mode, Median
- **Natural Laws**: Physics, Chemistry, Biology
- **Physics**: Speed, Distance, Time
- **Time**: Past, Present, Future

These are just a few examples of how everything in the physical world ultimately breaks down into a system or an arrangement of threes. Regardless of what it is, somehow, someway, it is always going to come down to a system of threes, because the triune God used the pattern of Himself to create it.

<u>MORE KEY VERSES:</u>

Not only does God tell us that He is going to use His physical creation to teach us spiritual truth in Romans 1:20, He also repeats this principle throughout the Bible!

Psalm 19:1-4 The heavens declare the glory of God; and the firmament sheweth his handywork. Day unto day uttereth speech, and night unto night sheweth knowledge. There is no speech nor language, where their voice is not heard. Their line is gone out through all the earth, and their words to the end of the world.

In these verses, God tells that we can look up into the sky and gaze

256

Chapter 9 — The Key of Association

out into space, and the things we witness through the handiwork of His creation will declare to us the glory that is due His name! The things we witness in the daytime *utter speech*, and the the things we witness in the nighttime *shew knowledge*. In other words, His creation is constantly speaking to and teaching us—His creation is the universal language! Verse 3 says: "There is no speech nor language, where their voice is not heard." Regardless of a person's nationality or culture, God's creation speaks their language! Verse 4 continues: "Their line is gone out through all the earth, and their words to the end of the world." God is letting us know that through the things in the physical creation, He has dropped us a line, as it were, and is speaking words to us if we will only look and listen! Creation has a voice, and everything in it is constantly preaching, teaching, declaring, showing, and communicating things to the people of this planet, from one end of the earth to the the other.

Job 12:7-9 But ask now the beasts, and they shall teach thee; and the fowls of the air, and they shall tell thee: Or speak to the earth, and it shall teach thee: and the fishes of the sea shall declare unto thee. Who knoweth not in all these that the hand of the Lord hath wrought this?

Once again, God reiterates to us how creation was purposely designed to speak to us and teach us. He tells us that if we'll take the time to observe the animals on the earth, the birds in the air, and the fish in the sea, they will all speak volumes to us about God. This principle is so clear that He even asks in verse 9, "Who knoweth not in all these that the hand of the Lord hath wrought this?" In other words, "Who can look at creation and not know that there is a God who created it?" And quite honestly, the answer to that question in the 21st century is: a lot of people! Lost people are willfully blinded to it, and saved people are ignorantly blinded to it—not realizing that God is actually using His creation to scream a message to us about Himself.

The Keys of Bible Study

MORE KEY EXAMPLES:

The SUN

The fact is, there are a lot of suns and moons in the universe—definitely too many to count! But in terms of our world and what we can see with the naked eye, we speak, as God does in Genesis 1, in very general terms about the fact that "God made two great lights; the greater light to rule the day, and the lesser light to rule the night" (Gen 1:16). And these lights, God says in Genesis 1:14, were to be "…for signs, and for seasons, and for days, and years" and, verse 15 adds, "…for lights in the firmament of the heaven to give light upon the earth." But in light of the verses we've been looking at about how God uses His creation to preach His truth to us (Rom 1:20; Psa 19:1-2), we would have to ask ourselves: was God simply wanting to use the sun and the moon to provide light for our world, and was all He was really wanting to teach us through them is how to calculate days, years, and seasons on our calendars?

As we begin to compare scripture with scripture, we find that the Spirit of God revealed something rather monumental in John 1:9. As we just saw from Genesis 1:14, the sun and moon are what give light to the people of the world. But then John 1:9 comes along and says, speaking of Jesus: "[Christ] was the **true Light**, which lighteth every man that cometh into the world." So the question is: if Jesus is the *true Light* who lights every man that comes into the world, what was the light of the sun in Genesis 1:14-19? False light? Obviously not! What the Spirit of God is letting us know through John is that Jesus is the *true Light*—or the *spiritual reality*—and the light we see in the sky with our physical eyes is simply the *picture!* We often get that reversed! We look up into the sky and see the physical sun and tend to think that the sun is the reality, and that Christ is a picture of it. No! The sun is a biblical picture of our Lord Jesus Christ.

Jesus Himself reiterated this same truth in John 8:12 when He said, "I am the light of the world: he that followeth me shall not walk in darkness, but shall have the light of life."

Chapter 9 — The Key of Association

As parents and grandparents, part of our responsibility is to teach our kids and grandkids about God. Deuteronomy 6:6-7 tells us that parents are to "talk of [the words of God] when thou sittest in thine house, and when thou walkest by the way, and when thou liest down, and when thou risest up." But just how did God intend for us to do that? Did He really intend for us to preach sermons to our kids morning, noon, and night? Certainly not. One of the most practical ways to fulfill the spirit of this passage is to simply relate the truth of God's word to how He pictured them in creation as we're in the midst of doing life with our kids. And one of the clearest and best ways to teach them what God is like is through the picture of the sun.

Do you remember some of the seemingly worthless information we learned about the sun in elementary school? And I say "worthless" because how many of us actually went on to be astronomers? How have all those facts we learned about the sun played into anything that has benefited us practically, vocationally, materially or otherwise? Well, this may be an incredible way to way to take what has so far been a bunch of worthless information and begin allowing God to use it for His own divine purposes!

For example, do you remember learning that the sun passes three main types of rays onto the earth?

First of all, there are *ultraviolet rays*, which are invisible to the human eye. We can't *see* or *feel* them. And if the sun is a picture of the sun, which person of the Godhead, the three-in-one, do you think these rays picture? God the Father, of course! Colossians 1:15 and 1 Timothy 1:17 both refer to the first person of the trinity, God the Father, as the *invisible God*. He is the Person of the Godhead that at this present time cannot be seen or felt. Jesus taught us in John 4:24 that *God is a Spirit* and goes on in the same verse to let us know that's why we *"must worship him in spirit and in truth."*

The second are *visible light rays*. These are, clearly, the *visible* part of the sun. They, of course, are a picture of the Lord Jesus Christ. Colossians 1:15 says Christ is "the **image** of the **invisible God**." In

259

The Keys of Bible Study

other words, Christ is the *visible* expression of the *invisible* God. In John 14:8-9, when Philip asked Jesus to show he and the other disciples the Father, do you remember what Jesus said? He says, "...he that hath seen me hath seen the Father." In the same way visible light rays are the visible part of the sun, Jesus is the visible manifestation of the Godhead.

The third kind of rays the sun possess are infrared (or heat) rays. These are rays that can't be *seen*, but can be *felt!* In John 14:17, when Jesus was explaining to His disciples the coming of the Holy Spirit, He refers to Him as "the Spirit of truth; whom the world cannot receive, **because it seeth him not**, neither knoweth him." No, we can't *see* the Holy Spirit, but buddy, when He carries out His ministry, we sure can *feel* Him! In John 16:8, Jesus characterized the ministry of the Holy Spirit three ways, saying, "He will reprove the world of sin, and of righteousness, and of judgment." For all of us who have been the recipient of the Spirit reproving us in any of those three ways, we may not have been able to *see* Him, but we could testify that we certainly did *feel* Him!

So, first of all, we learn a whole lot of biblical truth about our triune God through how He is pictured in these three main rays of the sun.

But do you remember something else we learned in elementary school? We learned that the sun travels from the east to the west. As it does, it moves against the rotation of the earth. Of course, this illustrates for us, that, just like the world goes against the sun, the world (as in, the world's system of evil) also goes against the Son, the Lord Jesus Christ. Jesus said in John 7:7, "The world cannot hate you; but me it hateth, because I testify of it, that the works thereof are evil." The world isn't actually against us, but against Jesus. So, one of the facts we learn in creation simply from the direction the sun travels is that none of us as believers can remain neutral in this world; if we're going in the direction of the Son, we're going against the world. And if we're going in the direction of the world, we're going against the Son.

The MOON

In John 9:5, our Lord continues to reiterate the fact that the sun is a picture of Him. He says: "As long as I am in the world (and He was physically "in the world" for about 33 ½ years), I am the light of the world." Then, in Acts 1:9, after Christ had died on the cross, was risen from the dead, and had spent 40 days speaking to His disciples "of things pertaining to the kingdom of God" (Act 1:3), He pulled His disciples together, commissioned them to be His witnesses in every part of the world (Act 1:8), and then ascended out of this world back to His rightful place at the Father's right hand (Act 1:9; Heb 10:12).

But keep in mind the monumental statement Jesus made in John 9:5. He said, "As long as I am in the world, I am the light of the world." In Acts 1:9, the light of the world was no longer in the world. And it was at this point that we entered into a biblical nighttime, if you will. That's why Romans 13:12 says, "The night is far spent, the day is at hand." In 1 Thessalonians 5:5, Paul adds, "Ye are all the children of light, and the children of the day: we are not of the night, nor of darkness." In other words, we live in the midst of a spiritual nighttime because the Light of the world isn't here. But though we live in the night, we are not of the night! And though we live in the darkness, we are not of darkness! That's why Philippians 2:15 tells us that as "the sons of God...in the midst of a crooked and perverse nation," God's intention for us is that we "shine as lights in the world." But notice the way the Holy Spirit of God prompted the Apostle Paul to communicate the truth concerning our shining this light. He very calculatedly said that we "shine *as* lights." And you know why he was careful to word it that way? It's because we *aren't* the true light of the world—for we actually have no light of our own! Any light we provide to this dark world is what we reflect from the *true light*, the Lord Jesus Christ!

Now, what is it in creation that shines in the night, but actually has no light of its own? The moon! It's really just a dead rock, and yet it shines in the midst of the darkness of the night by reflecting the light of the sun. So if the sun is a picture of Christ, that makes the

The Keys of Bible Study

moon a picture of believers!

And once we make that connection, God's creation of the moon can begin to *utter speech* to us and show us *knowledge* (Psa 19:2). For example, do you know what a *lunar eclipse* is? In perhaps the simplest terms, it is when the earth comes between the sun and the moon, casting a shadow of the earth on the moon, drastically diminishing its light. And with that simple understanding, perhaps we could say that many, if not most, believers in the Laodicean Church Period (Rev 3:14-22) are living in a spiritual lunar eclipse. The world has come between us and the Lord Jesus Christ, casting the shadow of the world upon us, drastically diminishing the light of Christ that we were intended to reflect.

Sometimes in creation we experience what is called a *total lunar eclipse*. This happens when the earth completely blocks the light of the sun from shining on and reflecting from the moon. There are, likewise, times when believers have so allowed the world to come between them and their relationship with Christ, they reflect none of His light. Their life is complete darkness. This is why Paul warned us in Ephesians 5:11 to "have no fellowship with the unfruitful works of darkness, but rather reprove them." It's why he warned us in 1 Thessalonians 5:19 to "quench not the Spirit."

Peter describes this type of spiritual lunar eclipse by laying out for us in 2 Peter 1:5-7 the divine strategy for our spiritual growth and development after coming to faith in Christ, and warns us that failure to follow this biblical pattern will result in us coming to the place spiritually that we have actually forgotten that we were purged from our sins. In other words, we are living in total darkness, like we did when we were still in our lost condition. My, my, my... the things God made in creation really do have some things to say to us, don't they?

Sometimes the sun and the moon are visible in the same sky, picturing a time on this planet when the Lord Jesus Christ will rule and reign in all of His glory—and we will rule and reign with Him! (Rev 20:6) The Bible calls it *the day of the Lord*. We often refer

262

Chapter 9 — The Key of Association

to it as the Millennium (Rev 20:1–5).

Just like Paul said in Romans 1:20, God has so designed the universe that everything He made illustrates the intangible truths about who God is and what He's going to do. In fact, God even told us that the sun and the moon are there for *times and seasons.* Now, that's certainly true in a physical sense as far as the universe is concerned, but it's also true in a spiritual sense. We can look at the sun and the moon and find that they picture for us what God is going to do in the future. In Matthew 24:29, Jesus says that as the day of the Lord is ushered in, "the sun shall be darkened, and the moon shall not give her light."

Now, that is literally and physically going to happen. But it's also a picture! At the rapture, what's going to happen to the church? The "moon" is going to be taken out of the world. That's why God said in Amos 5:18 that "the day of the Lord will begin in darkness, and not light." Christ, the *true light*, will be gone, and those who were here to reflect His light will be gone as well. The earth will be in total spiritual darkness. But as we saw in Genesis 1, to God and his non-Gentile mind, each day begins in darkness—and then becomes light. And so shall it be with *the day of the Lord.* It is a day that will begin with darkness, and then will become light. Malachi says of that day:

> For, behold, the day cometh, that shall burn as an oven; and all the proud, yea, and all that do wickedly, shall be stubble: and the day that cometh shall burn them up, saith the Lord of hosts, that it shall leave them neither root nor branch. (Mal 4:1)

Malachi continues in verse 2, contrasting the destruction described in verse 1, saying, "But unto you that fear my name shall the Sun of righteousness arise with healing in his wings." And would you note how the Holy Spirit both inspired and preserved the reference to the Lord Jesus Christ in this verse? This is awesome! It doesn't refer to the One who is the *true light* of the world as the *Son* of righteousness as we might expect. It refers to Him as the *Sun* of righteousness! We find God reiterating the fact that *the day of the*

263

Lord will begin in darkness, but just like the sun rises in the east and burns away the overnight fog and dew, the *Sun of righteousness,* the Lord Jesus Christ, is going to arise from the east and burn up all of the proud and those who have done wickedly during the night.

LAND ANIMALS (Beasts)

In Job 12:7, Job says, "But ask now **the beasts**, and they shall teach thee…" What Job is referring to here is this same point that everything in creation was created with the intention of teaching us. Have you ever noticed as you've worked your way through the Bible the associations God makes through animals?

In John 10:14 and 10:28, Jesus likens Christians to sheep.

In 2 Peter 2:22, lost people (which we all were at one time), are likened to the two dirtiest animals on earth: dogs and pigs.

In 1 Corinthians 9:9-10, Paul likens pastors to oxen.

We see in 2 Peter 2:22 that false prophets are likened to dogs, and Matthew 7:15 likens their leaders to wolves.

In Matthew 23:33, Jesus likens self-righteous religionists to snakes, and says they give birth to vipers.

BIRDS (Fowls)

In the verse we just looked at in Job 12:7, after Job tells us about the things we can learn biblically from the land animals (beasts), he continues on, saying, "…and **the fowls of the air**, and they shall tell thee."

We find in Matthew 6:26 that Jesus likens people to **birds**.

In Revelation 18:2, John likens the unclean spirits that fly above our heads to unclean and hateful **birds**, and in Matthew 13:19,

264

Chapter 9 — The Key of Association

Jesus likened Satan to a **bird** that swoops in and "catcheth away" the seed of the word of God that is sown in the heart of a lost man.

Genesis 8:7, cross referenced with Job 1:7 and Leviticus 11:15, likens a **raven** to an unclean spirit.

Matthew 3:16 likens the Holy Spirit to a **dove**.

Song of Solomon 5:12 tells us that Christ's eyes are like those of a **dove**.

Isaiah 40:31 tells us that those who *"wait upon the Lord"* are like **eagles**.

FISH

In this same passage, Job says in verse 8: "...and **the fishes of the sea** shall declare unto thee." Do you remember the invitation our Lord Jesus Christ extended to Peter and Andrew, two brothers who, by trade, just happened to be fishermen? (Mat 4:18) Matthew 4:19 says: "And he saith unto them, Follow me, and I will make you fishers of men." Have you ever stopped to think about how much we can learn about reaching people with the gospel through the association Jesus makes through fishing?

TREES

Trees in the Bible are pictures of men. When we're talking about a man's ancestry, we refer to it as his family *tree*. Just as different trees need different types of care, some men require more looking after and tending to, while others literally grow wild! Some men grow taller than others. Some mature faster than others. Some bear fruit, while others don't. Some fall. Some change their colors. All of them die.

According to Psalm 1:1-3, the person who chooses not to conform to the ungodly is blessed, and is "**like a tree planted by the rivers of water**, that bringeth forth his fruit in his season; his leaf also shall

265

The Keys of Bible Study

not wither; and whatsoever he doeth shall prosper" (Mat 21:19; 3Jo 2).

We also observe that "a tree planted by the rivers of water" develops a deep and vast root system (Eph 3:17; Col 2:7). It's not affected by external temperature (Isa 49:10), and it's not dependent on the rain to fall from the sky for its water source (Jam 5:17-18).

Key Principle #2:

Two of the most important words in the Bible are "like" and "as"

I'm so glad that I can say that, because I'm a simple man. I'm glad that the two most important words in the Bible aren't something like supralapsarianism and infralapsarianism, because I'd be sunk!

KEY VERSE

Hosea 12:10 I have also spoken by the prophets, and I have multiplied visions, and used similitudes, by the ministry of the prophets.

The Bible we hold in our hands is, by and large, the result of what Hosea 12:10 says was "spoken by the prophets." As a student of scripture, make a mental note that 2 Peter 1:21 lets us know that in the process of the transmission of scripture, "the prophecy came not in old time by the will of man: but holy men of God **spake** as they were moved by the Holy Ghost." In other words, the human authors didn't typically write the words of their divinely inspired prophecy—they spoke it, and it was then recorded by a secretary of sorts, often referred to as an amanuensis. And as God used these prophets, as Hosea aptly points out in this verse, they often *used similitudes.* That is, they spoke using figures of speech in which two things are explicitly compared, so that we are able to make the biblical connection. (This is why we refer to this key of Bible study as the Key of Association; you could also call it the Key of Similitudes.) Biblically, these *similitudes* are often clearly

266

Chapter 9 — The Key of Association

recognizable by the Holy Spirit's usage of the words **like** or **as**. As in, "this is *like* that," or "that is *as* this."

KEY TEACHING

God takes the things He knows we might have difficulty understanding and/or applying and associates them with what He knows we do understand by the strategic usage of the words "like" and "as".

KEY EXAMPLES

A Husband's LOVE

In Ephesians 5:25, God gives a very simple and clear command to husbands, saying: "Husbands, love your wives, even **as** Christ also loved the church, and gave himself for it." Now, I can tell you, that after over four decades of ministry, I have never seen a man stand at an altar and take that bride to be his lawful wedded wife who didn't at least *think* he was head-over-heels in love with her. And if the command of Ephesians 5:25 was simply to "love your wife," every husband, at least initially, would pass the test with flying colors!

But a closer examination of the actual command for husbands to love their wives shows that there is a particular *way* husbands are to love their wives. God raises the bar into the stratosphere concerning the type of love husbands are to afford their wives by the use of a carefully placed similitude, identified through the usage of the simple word *as*. Husbands aren't just supposed to "love their wives." Husbands are to love their wives, "even *as* Christ also loved the church."

So, with that little qualifying statement, what are we forced to do? We're forced to ask ourselves, "Just how did Christ love the church?" Because that's the standard! And not only is it the *standard*—it is the actual *command* of Ephesians 5:25. Husbands are to love their wives with the same kind of love that Christ demonstrated through

267

His love for the church. And because God knows that we men can often be just a little dense, He even reminds us in the remainder of the verse that in Christ's love for the church, "he **gave** himself for it." That is, Christ laid His own life down in total sacrifice for us, because of His great love for us.

Most men I've encountered through the years—even men who profess to be "sold out" and "all in"—will claim to love their wife, and will demonstrate that, as long as she *returns* it... and as long as he thinks she *deserves* it... and as long as it doesn't *cost him too much* to give it. And from a human standpoint, all of those little qualifiers might even be classified as reasonable. But if the standard is Christ's sacrificial love for the church, and if we actually took the time to see biblically just how it was that Christ loved the church, we'd find that...

Christ loved us when we *didn't return it*. In fact, Christ loved us when we were *incapable of returning it!*

That's why 1 John 4:19 says, "We love him, because he **first** loved us!" So, If a husband is going to love his wife *as* Christ loved the church, he has the responsibility of loving her whether she returns it or not.

Secondly, we find that...

Christ loved us when we *didn't deserve it*. In fact, Christ loved us when we were *the least deserving of it!*

In Romans 5:8, the scriptures reveal to us that "God commendeth his love toward us, in that, while we were yet sinners, Christ died for us." Verse 10 goes on to let us know that in being sinners, we were actually the enemies of God. Christ wasn't waiting for us to deserve His love before He demonstrated His love for us; He demonstrated His love for us when we had made ourselves His enemies. Or, when we were *the least deserving of it!*

And then thirdly, we find that...

Christ loved us when it *cost Him something to give it*. In fact, Christ loved us when it *cost Him everything to give it!*

Philippians 2 is another incredible chapter that reveals to us just how it was that Christ loved the church. Like Ephesians 5:25 tells husbands that they are to love their wives *as* Christ did, Philippians 2:1-2 speaks to those of us who comprise Christ's church about the love we are to demonstrate to one another. In verse 5, Paul tells how it is that we can actually demonstrate that love. He says, "Let this mind be in you, which was also in Christ Jesus." In other words, we are to do it with the same mindset Christ had. And what was that mindset? Verse 8 says, "And being found in fashion as a man, he humbled himself, and became obedient unto death, even the death of the cross."

If Christians are going to love each other the way Christ loves—and if husbands are going to love their wives the way that Christ loves—then like Christ, we too are going to need to humble ourselves, become obedient to what God has command us in His word, take up our cross, and die on it. That's how Christ loved the church, and gave Himself for it.

And yet, with these scriptures staring us directly in our faces, I have had countless men through the years come to my office trying to justify why they no longer love their wives. And you know why? Because, first of all, they've never seen that little word *as* that comes with the command to love their wives; and secondly, because they've never taken the time to identify biblically just how it was that Christ loved us.

A Wife's SUBMISSION

It has been my experience that most wives find the biblical command to be submissive to their husbands an extremely difficult command to obey—particularly if they have a husband who is not loving them the way Christ loved the church. Which is certainly understandable! We must recognize, however, that God knows what he's doing, and His commands concerning a wife's submission

269

The Keys of Bible Study

to her husband actually point us back to God's beautiful original design for marriage prior to sin entering into the world.

To completely understand the New Testament teaching on the subject, it is imperative to understand some of the key things that were happening in the garden in Genesis 3 when sin entered into the world.

Prior to the man and woman violating the one prohibition God had given them by eating the forbidden fruit in Genesis 3:6, they enjoyed the beauty of being completely united in a beautiful and blessed harmonious oneness. As God provides His commentary concerning this original design for marriage in 1 Corinthians 11:3,8-9, He very clearly lets us know that the roles of headship and followship were clearly established from the beginning. But in the beginning (prior to sin), these roles were so beautifully and sovereignly designed by God, that, in fulfilling their roles, their oneness was so perfect that the distinction between the roles of leadership and followship were indiscernible!

Genesis 1:28 says that God blessed *them*... and told *them* to subdue the earth... and gave *them* dominion. They were actually co-regents on the earth—or "heirs together of the grace of life" (1Pe 3:7), both entrusted with ruling power in the physical kingdom of the earth (Gen 1:28). Marriage was a beautifully simple thing (Pro 18:22; 2Co 11:4). It is important to understand, however, that this unique love relationship and co-regency was made possible by each of them simply fulfilling their God-given roles (1Co 11:3,8-9).

What is often overlooked when the man and woman ate the forbidden fruit in Genesis 3:6 is that, inherent in their disobedience to God's clear command, was also a role reversal. Genesis 3:6 says, "And when the woman saw that the tree was good for food, and that it was pleasant to the eyes, and a tree to be desired to make one wise, **she took of the fruit thereof, and did eat, and gave also unto her husband with her; and he did eat**." Notice: he's not leading her— she's leading him (1Co 11:3). He's not providing for her—she's providing for him (1Ti 5:8). She's not with him—he is with her (1Co 11:8–9).

270

Chapter 9 — The Key of Association

Recognizing this obvious role reversal in the midst of their disobedience in Genesis 3:6 is of vital importance in comprehending one of the consequences of the ensuing curse God pronounced upon the woman in Genesis 3:16. Along with the curse of sorrow in her conception and child-bearing, God tells her at the end of verse 16: "…and thy desire shall be to thy husband, and he shall rule over thee."

At first glance, God telling the woman "thy desire shall be to thy husband" sounds like a rather pleasant thing. May I remind you though: this is God's *curse* upon the woman, which actually turns out to be a curse that hits at the very core of how God designed the marriage relationship between a husband and wife to succeed and flourish. As we employ the Key of Comparison (Chapter 5) to allow the Spirit of God to reveal His truth and wisdom to us, we see the actual meaning of this phrase. God uses the same terminology in the next chapter, Genesis 4:7, to explain to Abel the desire sin had to rule him. Because the woman's sin was in large part the result of her stepping out of her role as man's help meet by desiring to lead her husband, God is letting her know that as they moved forward in their relationship, she would continue to desire to lead her husband, and yet the end result would be that he would *rule over* her. No longer would her husband afford her a humble, tender, compassionate, loving headship—but rather a domineering and controlling *rulership*. This tension between a woman desiring to lead her husband in the marriage relationship, and the husband thus finding a way to rule over her, continues to be at the center of nearly every problematic marriage to this very day.

As God provides New Testament teaching concerning marriage, it is with this very tension in mind! He is actually providing us the exact instruction we need to be able to reverse the curse that came upon marriage in Genesis 3.

If husbands would simply be obedient to the very first and basic New Testament responsibility God gives them in the marriage relationship (to love their wives as Christ loves us), obviously, husbands wouldn't be seeking to exercise a dominating and

271

controlling *rulership* over their wives. Their obedience to this one command alone would bring a couple at least halfway toward the goal of being able to reverse the curse.

And if wives would simply be obedient to the very first and basic New Testament responsibility God gives them in the marriage relationship (to be in submission to their own husbands), as per God's original design (1Co 11:3), obviously, wives wouldn't be seeking to assume the *leadership* role over their husbands. And again, their obedience to this one command could bring couples the other half of the way toward the victory of reversing the curse.

But it's very apparent by the way God approaches the subject of a wife's submission in the New Testament that He knew the curse of Genesis 3:16 would cause this to be a difficult concept for a wife to *understand*, and maybe even more difficult *apply*. Because do you know what God does? Four times in the New Testament, God seeks to get the undivided attention of women who are married, calling them by name, saying: *Wives!* Four specific times! And you know what's crazy? Every time He calls their name, He gives them the same exact instruction.

Ephesians 5:22: "**Wives, submit** yourselves unto your own husbands..."
Ephesians 5:24: "Therefore as the church is **subject** unto Christ, so let the **wives** be to   their own husbands..."
Colossians 3:18: "**Wives, submit** yourselves unto your own husbands..."
1 Peter 3:1: "Likewise, ye **wives**, be in **subjection** to your own husbands..."

Now, I think you realize God doesn't repeat Himself because He suffers from amnesia—and He certainly doesn't waste space in His Bible! God uses repetition in the Bible as a point of emphasis. As He communicates His words to us, repetition is His way of slowing His voice down, and raising the decibel level, as it were. Perhaps we

Chapter 9 — The Key of Association

could say it's His way of highlighting or underlining key truths in His word.

But you know what's even more interesting than God simply repeating Himself every time He seeks to get the attention of wives? The fact that every time He gives the command for wives to submit in these verses, God follows the command with the little word *as!*

When it comes to this thing of wives submitting to their husbands, God knew the difficulty and the confusion that would cloud the issue (2Co 11:3). He knew that wives would want to know what He actually meant by it. He knew wives would want to know just how far He intended it to go. He knew they'd want to know what it actually looked like in real life. So you know what God did? Every time He gives the command for wives to submit to their own husbands, He **associated** it with something He knew wives *would* understand, helping them make the connection through His masterful and strategic usage of the word *as.*

Ephesians 5:22 Wives, submit yourselves unto your own husbands, **as** unto the Lord.

A Christian wife can legitimately pray a prayer that sounds something like this: "Lord, I'm not sure I know what submitting to my husband actually means!" And according to this verse, Christ's answer would be, "Well, you know how you willfully and joyfully submit to Me as your Lord? Well, that's the kind of submission I'm calling on you to exhibit toward your husband. You submit to him, just **as** you do to Me." Wow! That puts the standard way up there, doesn't it?

Ephesians 5:24 Therefore **as** the church is subject unto Christ, so let the wives be to their own husbands in everything.

This Christian wife may ask, "How far it should my submission be taken?" According to this verse, Christ's reply would sound something like this: "Well, do you know how far the church actually

273

The Keys of Bible Study

subjects itself to Me? My church subjects itself to me in absolutely everything. And that's how many things to which I'm referring when I say that a wife is to subject herself to her own husband... in everything."

Colossians 3:18: Wives, submit yourselves unto your own husbands, **as** it is fit in the Lord.

And here the Lord is letting us know that in order for a husband and wife to achieve the *oneness* that God both desired and designed their marriage to exhibit and enjoy, there is actually only one way to get the two entities to actually *fit*—and that is through each of the partners fulfilling their God-given roles. As we saw in 1 Corinthians 11:3,8-9, the husband must assume the position of the head, leading in the relationship, and the woman must willfully place herself under his headship in submission. To achieve the oneness God intended a marriage to enjoy, that's the only way it fits. We would fully comprehend that it would not be *fitting* for the church to be providing headship over our Lord Jesus Christ, and this verse is letting us know that, likewise, it would not be fitting for the woman to be providing headship over the man.

1 Peter 3:1 Likewise, ye **wives**, be in **subjection** to your own husbands.

I remember how excited I was years ago when I was first recognizing God's careful placement of the word *as* in these biblical admonitions concerning a wife's submission to her husband. I thought to myself—how masterful! And then, at the same time, I remember how disappointed I was when I got to 1 Peter 3:1, because as Peter provides this admonition about a wife's subjection, it wasn't followed by an *as*. The rest of verse 1 says, "...that, if any obey not the word, they also may without the word be won by the conversation of the wives." I thought to myself, "Man, how unlike God to break a biblical pattern like that—and how unlike God to miss the opportunity to send, what was in my mind, such a powerful message."

The problem was, however, that I just needed to keep reading a

274

Chapter 9 — The Key of Association

little further! God's careful placement of the word *as* to wives concerning their submission doesn't show up until verse 6: "...even **as** Sara obeyed Abraham."

The Spirit of God is here referencing a time in the marriage of Abraham and Sarah when Abraham was not being obedient to the word of God. The biblical account is laid out and for us in Genesis 20:1-16, when Abraham knew the men of the land would take Sarah into the king's harem for her beauty. As they were approaching the city, Abraham tells her to tell them that she was his sister so that they would take her to the king without feeling they needed to do away with him. As the story unfolds, Abraham tells the men she is his sister, and off she goes to the king's palace.

As I read this account from the book of Genesis, I must say, that though I was highly disappointed in Abraham's lack of faith in this instance (see also Gen 12:11-20), I was just as disappointed in Sarah's willingness to be a part of this deception—especially the vulnerable place into which it was placing her from a moral standpoint. But you know what I discovered? This passage in 1 Peter 3:1-6 actually serves as God's commentary on this whole debacle in Genesis 20. And you know why 1 Peter 3:5 says Sarah didn't open her mouth in this horrific instance when her husband was not obeying the word of God? This is beautiful! She did it, not because she was being deceptive, but because she was one of the *holy women* of old *who trusted in God*—even in the times when they couldn't trust their own husbands! She exercised faith in God, believing that if she would stay in her biblical role as submissive to her husband, God would both deal with him and the vulnerable situation into which he had placed her. And God holds her up here in 1 Peter 3:1-6 as the biblical exemplar of a wife who did it right.

How is a wife to operate when she has a husband who isn't obeying the word? Like the holy women of old, she is to remain in subjection to her husband, trusting that if she will remain in her God-given role, God will show Himself mighty on her behalf—even *as* with Sarah.

A Believer's WALK

The further we grow in our biblical understanding of the high calling of God concerning our daily walk as believers, we can actually get to a place that it can become rather overwhelming—leaving us to ask, "How will I ever be able to live out everything God is asking of me in His word?" Sometimes it seems that the more of the Bible we learn, the more we become aware of our failures and inability to obey it all.

Once again, God takes what seems confusing and even impossible and simplifies it all through His strategic usage of the simple word *as* in Colossians 2:6. The Spirit of God says through Paul, "**As** ye have therefore received Christ Jesus the Lord, so walk ye in him."

As believers, if there's one thing we know for sure, it's how we were saved! And that's what the Spirit of God is wanting us to have in our minds as we approach this subject of how we now walk as believers. In Colossians 2:6, He wants us to consider just how it was that we "received Christ Jesus the Lord."

I wasn't there when you received Christ, but based on how the book of Romans and other places in the New Testament lay out God's plan of salvation, I'm sure that though what we expressed to the Lord was worded somewhat differently, it certainly carried the same basic components and sentiment. We received Christ by recognizing and confessing our complete inability to do what needed to be done to save ourselves, and so we cried out for the Lord Jesus Christ to do for us through His death, burial and resurrection what we never could.

That's how we "received Christ Jesus the Lord"—and Paul tells us in Colossians 2:6 that it is also how we are now to walk as believers! We are to walk in the Christian life on a daily basis by recognizing and confessing our complete inability to do it on our own, crying out to the Lord for our death and burial with Christ to be so realized and appropriated that it will be by the risen life of Christ in us and through us that we can live in a way we could never live in the power of the flesh.

These are just a few of the monumental lessons we can learn through God's use of similitudes, identified by the simple word *as*. Recognize, however, that there are countless other powerful truths we can learn biblically through our understanding and application of the Key of Association.

THE KEY OF APPARENT CONTRADICTIONS

I would imagine that one of the top criticisms or objections to Christianity has to do with the notion that there are contradictions in the Bible. In fact, if you have sought to actively share your faith with others, you have no doubt had numerous people say to you, "I don't believe the Bible because it's full of contradictions!" In most cases, when people hurl this accusation, they couldn't actually find a contradiction in the Bible (even though it's "full" of them!) if their life depended on it. It's simply a convenient excuse to mask the fact that they want to live the way that they want to live without having to factor God into the equation. If they can discount the Bible because of all its so-called contradictions, they can then discount the God of the Bible.

But in terms of our personal Bible Study, how we approach the Bible is absolutely crucial and critical! For our spiritual eyes to be opened to the glorious treasures in God's word, we must approach it, both by faith and in faith. We must believe that because the Bible has been given to us by a holy and perfect God, and since His word mirrors His character, we must approach it believing that it, too, is holy and perfect—that it is completely without error or contradictions.

The Keys of Bible Study

The ninth key of Bible study:
Approach the Bible believing there are no contradictions, only apparent ones.

Even as we approach the Bible in faith, believing that there are absolutely no contradictions, we must recognize that there are going to be things we'll encounter in the word of God that will *appear* to be contradictions at first sight. As we dig deeper and deeper in the word of God, there will be things which surface from time to time that look like they don't actually add up. And that's the significance of this key of Bible study! By faith in God's perfect word, we continue to move forward trusting that it is only an *apparent contradiction*.

KEY THOUGHTS:

1. Always give the Bible the benefit of the doubt.

In other words, treat God and His book with the same respect you would treat a trusted and close friend. I doubt that any of us have a close friend who we feel like we have to question everything they say. We don't tend to pick our friends that way. And when it comes to the Bible and the God of the Bible, recognize that they are your greatest friends! So treat them with the same respect and dignity with which you would treat any of your friends. Always give the Bible the benefit of the doubt.

2. Always operate within the word of God with the conviction that the Bible is innocent until proven guilty.

I really can't stress the importance of operating with an innocent-until-proven-guilty mindset when it comes to God's word. As we are about to see, God places a premium on our by-faith belief and trust in His every word. Our understanding of God's word will be extremely limited without that mindset. But let me hasten to add that when it comes to how we operate with those who propagate God's word through preaching and/or teaching, we must always

280

Chapter 10 — The Key of Apparent Contradictions

approach them with the extreme opposite mentality! We approach them from the standpoint that they're guilty until proven innocent!

I realize that sounds like a completely negative approach, but I also want you to know that it is a positively biblical approach! God tells us in 1 John 4:1, "Beloved, believe not every spirit, but try the spirits whether they are of God: because many false prophets are gone out into the world." That is such an important verse, let's take a few minutes to make sure we've really captured its essence and weight.

John begins by saying: "Beloved, believe not every spirit..." Let's just stop right there and get our spiritual bearings. In other words, when somebody opens a Bible and begins to proclaim it, God tells us to begin by not believing a word they're saying just because they're saying it. And I would encourage you to begin developing that mindset with me! Don't believe a word I say in this book! And if I were to come to preach in your local church some Sunday, I would encourage you to listen carefully, but I would encourage you to not allow yourself to buy in to what I'm saying. Not without the next crucial part of God's instruction through John. He goes on in this verse to tell us that we are not to believe the spirit communicating the word of God to us until we "try the spirits whether they are of God." And this is another reason it is so important that we learn the keys of Bible study! They are not only for our own personal study of the word of God, but so that we have the tools we need to "try the spirits" when we're listening to someone impart the word.

And why does God tells us we must *try the spirits* before we believe them? The rest of verse 1 says it's because, "many false prophets are gone out into the world." And may I remind you that the Holy Spirit inspired John to write that in the first century! And already there were "many false prophets" all over. The Holy Spirit likewise told us in 2 Timothy 3:13 that "evil men and seducers shall wax worse and worse, deceiving, and being deceived." Things aren't going to get better and better over time—they're going to get worse and worse. So if there were *many false prophets* in the world in the first century, how many do you think there must be in the 21st century? That's why I said earlier: please begin to develop the

281

The Keys of Bible Study

mindset of "trying the spirits" by trying the spirit of my words to you. Then allow that mindset to extend to every person you listen to in every message you hear, regardless of how much you love the speaker, respect them, and/or have grown to trust them over the years.

In 2 Corinthians 11:2-4 , the Holy Spirit inspired the apostle Paul to write some very strong words to the Corinthians. His words, however, are just as pertinent and applicable for us as they were for them. In light of what we just saw from 2 Timothy 3:13 about things getting *worse and worse,* a great case could be made for this teaching to be even more pertinent and applicable for us than it was for them!

Paul say in verse 2, "For I am jealous over you with godly jealousy: for I have espoused you to one husband, that I may present you as a chaste virgin to Christ." Paul is likening the relationship we have with Christ in salvation to a bride being *espoused* to a husband. I find it interesting, that the only other time the word *espoused* is found in the New Testament in our King James Bible is when it is used to refer to Mary, who was *espoused* to Joseph (Mat 1:18; Luk 1:27, 2:5). And when it is used to refer to them in these passages, Joseph and Mary were already husband and wife, but the marriage had not yet been consummated. In that "espousal" period, though they were married, she remained a virgin until after the birth of Christ. And Paul is trying to get us to see this same thing, in terms of our marriage to Christ. He is our one husband and we are His bride, and yet our marriage to Him has not yet been consummated. And Paul tells us that when we make our appearance to Christ, our husband, that His desire is to find us in that day, like Mary, a *chaste virgin.*

But Paul had a very deep and very legitimate fear! He says in verse 3, "But I fear, lest by any means, as the serpent beguiled Eve through his subtilty, so your minds should be corrupted from the simplicity that is in Christ." He feared that Satan would somehow move us away from the simplicity that is in Christ, using the same strategy he did with Eve in the garden, and thereby cause us to lose our

Chapter 10 — The Key of Apparent Contradictions

chasteness as Christ's bride.

Then in verse 4, Paul takes this principle out of the abstract and into the specific, by letting us know what his actual fear was. He says: "For if he that cometh preacheth another Jesus, whom we have not preached, or if ye receive another spirit, which ye have not received, or another gospel, which ye have not accepted, ye might well bear with him." Paul is warning them that even if someone comes by and says that they're preaching Jesus, or the gospel, we ought not believe them blindly. He was afraid that the Corinthians would lend to that preacher credibility where credibility was not due. If the words someone preaches are not the words found in the Bible, they are not of God's Spirit, but of another spirit.

And just who are these people who preach such damnable and yet such subtle deception? Paul identifies them nine verses later. In verse 13, he says, "For such are false apostles, deceitful workers, transforming themselves into the apostles of Christ." They obviously don't come identifying themselves as false apostles and deceivers, but Paul tells us that that's who they are. He says that they transform themselves so that they appear to be what we think a minister of Christ would be.

He goes on in verses 14 and 15 saying: "And no marvel; for Satan himself is transformed into an angel of light. 15 Therefore it is no great thing if his ministers also be transformed as the ministers of righteousness; whose end shall be according to their works." And one of the first things I want you to notice from these two verses is that Satan has ministers! And they don't run around carrying Satanic bibles, living ghastly immoral lifestyles, and carrying out blood sacrifices! No, much to the contrary; he even refers to them as *ministers of righteousness!* Many times, and perhaps most often, Satan's ministers conduct themselves with high moral standards and righteous lifestyles, because Satan has found that he is tremendously more successful in gaining followers by posing to be Christ, rather than revealing himself for who he actually is. He has found the same to be true with his ministers. So we must not allow their "godly" lifestyle and demeanor to confuse us. After

283

The Keys of Bible Study

all, what better way to propagate *another Jesus*, *another spirit*, and *another gospel* than through a minister with an impeccable life, a godly demeanor, and a winsome personality?

The important point I want to make sure you see is that we must approach teachers and preachers of the word of God differently than we approach the word of God itself. When it comes to preachers and teachers, our mentality is that they're always guilty until proven innocent. When it comes to the word of God, our mentality is that it's always innocent until proven guilty (and, of course, it will never be proven guilty; we saw previously that the word of God is immutable). Additionally, when it comes to the Bible, the *attitude* with which we approach it is crucial.

KEY PRINCIPLE #1

Our APTITUDE in the word of God is directly commensurate with our ATTITUDE toward the word of God

When I talk about our "aptitude" in the word of God, I'm referring to the capacity we have to get into the word of God and actually understand it. The unique thing about our aptitude in the word of God, though, is that it's not about our intelligence or mental astuteness. Sure, we must have the ability to think and have some level of reasoning abilities. But the fact is, someone of very average intelligence who approaches the Bible believing that it is the very word and words of God... who trusts the Holy Spirit of God that lives in them to reveal His truth to them as they compare scripture with scripture... and who has already come to the conclusion that whatever the Holy Spirit of God reveals, they will obey... listen—that person of very average intelligence with that kind of an attitude toward the word of God will end up running biblical circles around most Bible college and seminary graduates—even those who have their Masters or Doctorate in theology! Because when we approach God's book the way He tells us to approach it, He will open to us the treasures of truth found in His holy word. But don't miss it: God places a premium on approaching His word

Chapter 10 — The Key of Apparent Contradictions

with an attitude of such reverence that we unquestionably believe it and unwaveringly trust it.

Let me show you this principle in several different places in the word of God...

Luke 24:25 Then he said unto them, O fools, and slow of heart to believe all that the prophets have spoken.

The context of Luke 24 is that Jesus had already died, been buried for three days, and risen from the dead. Early in the morning on that third day, several women had made their way to the sepulcher where the Lord had been buried, and became very perplexed to find that the stone had been rolled away and His body had been removed. In their distress, two angels appeared to them declaring that He had risen, reminding them of His promise to do so the third day. Mary Magdalene and Joanna make their way to inform the disciples of this incredible news, but when they heard it, the disciples thought they were nothing more than silly women telling idle tales.

Later that day, two of His disciples were walking on the road that led to Emmaus, glumly discussing the events of the previous several days concerning Christ's death and trying to make sense of it all, when all of a sudden Christ Himself approaches them. Though He is standing right in front of them, engaging them in a conversation, they simply don't have eyes to see that it is actually Him. Jesus asks them why they're so bummed, and they marvel that someone could possibly have been in that region and not been aware of all that had unfolded in recent days, so they recount the high points of it all for Him.

After they had given Him the play-by-play, rather than put His arms around them and speak sweet words of consolation and comfort to them in their distress, you know what Christ does? He rebukes them! He rebukes them for not believing Him... for not taking Him at His word!
And you know why Jesus said they didn't believe in verse 25? He said

285

The Keys of Bible Study

it was because they were *slow of **heart***. Notice, the problem wasn't that they were *slow of **mind***, but of ***heart***. And my brothers and sisters, our problem when it comes to knowing and understanding the word of God isn't our *intellect!* It's our *heart!* If God is ever going to open the eyes of our understanding to His word, we must have a heart attitude that tenaciously *believes* the word of God and *trusts* it. Without a heart attitude of belief, like these two disciples on the road to Emmaus, we can literally have the very truth of God staring us in the face and just totally miss it.

John 2:23–25 Now when he was in Jerusalem at the passover, in the feast day, many believed in his name, when they saw the miracles which he did. But Jesus did not commit himself unto them, because he knew all men, And needed not that any should testify of man: for he knew what was in man.

The simple but profound principle we glean from this passage is this: Jesus does not *commit* Himself to anybody who does not *submit* themselves to Him. As this passage says, Jesus knows what's on the inside of us. So when it comes to His word, He knows why we're really coming to it. He knows the real desire and motive of our hearts. If our motive for getting into His word is to gain *information* because we like how people look at us when we have Bible information, Jesus knows that! And it will affect what gets committed to us. But if the desire of our hearts is to gain *transformation* for His glory, He knows that as well! And with that submissive attitude toward God and His word, the truth He will commit to us will be astounding.

Luke 23:8-9 And when Herod saw Jesus, he was exceeding glad: for he was desirous to see him of a long season, because he had heard many things of him; and he hoped to have seen some miracle done by him. Then he questioned with him in many words; but he answered him nothing.

Verse 8 sounds so nice! I mean, here is Herod who has heard so

Chapter 10 — The Key of Apparent Contradictions

many wonderful things about Jesus that it says He was *exceeding glad* to finally meet Him... and that he had desired to do so for a long time. He even has great hope that, having audience with Him, he might personally witness Him perform a miracle. In his excitement, he riddles Christ with question after question, but interestingly enough, rather than celebrate Herod's apparent enthusiasm, the end of verse 9 says that Jesus "answered him nothing." Wow! If you didn't know better, it almost sounds as if Jesus is being rude to him! But the reality is that Jesus knows what's in Herod's heart. He understands that the source of Herod's desire, gladness, and excitement was his own self-serving and carnal intentions. And so you know what Jesus gives him? Nothing. Not so much as a word of response.

To this day, people continue to have all kinds of self-serving and carnal motives that make it appear they are desirous, glad, and excited about Christ and His word—but if the real motive of our hearts is not Christ's personal glorification and our personal transformation, we can, like Herod, expect to get nothing from the Lord.

1 Thessalonians 2:13 For this cause also thank we God without ceasing, because, when ye received the word of God which ye heard of us, ye received it not as the word of men, but as it is in truth, the word of God, which effectually worketh also in you that believe.

Paul lets us know here that something supernatural happens when we come to the word of God we hold in our hands, and by faith believe it to be, not simply the words of men, but the very word and words of God that don't need us or anybody else to change, correct, or mess with them in any way. Paul tells us in this verse that when we bring that kind of believing attitude in our approach to the word of God, that it will then *effectually* work in us. (*Effectually* means "producing an intended effect" — i.e. "a transformational work.")

The Keys of Bible Study

KEY PRINCIPLE #2

Never make the Bible conform to what you believe; always conform what you believe to what the Bible says.

That principle sounds like it should be the biggest no-brainer ever, but you'd be amazed to know how the things a person believes about the Bible dictates to them what they actually "see" in the Bible. It's true of those in what we've referred to as the "three Cs" earlier in the book—Catholics, Charismatics and Calvinists—and it's true of the Jehovah's (False) Witnesses, the Latter Day Ain'ts, the Church of Christ, and the Seventh Day Adventists as well.

But please be aware, it can just as easily happen to us! We must be very careful to never make the Bible conform to what we believe, but always conform what we believe to what the Bible says. As someone once aptly said, "It's what we think we know about the Bible that keeps us from learning."

KEY PRINCIPLE #3

Always be prepared to change whatever you've been taught, or whatever you've always thought to be true about the Bible, when it goes contrary to the Bible.

Now, you would think that principle would go without saying, but it most definitely needs to be said! Especially to people who think they know something about the Word of God—as in, people who have attended Bible college or seminary, or people who are in the ministry. It seems these are the people who are the most resistant to changing what they believe—because, of course, they are the ones who have the most to protect (their job, their pride, their friends, etc.).

I have been amazed through the years how it is possible to enter into a biblical discussion about a verse or a passage with people who claim to believe the Bible—having clearly established and

Chapter 10 — The Key of Apparent Contradictions

agreed upon the context and painstakingly compared scripture with scripture—and yet, if it all points to a biblical conclusion that goes against what they have always *thought* or been *taught*, they will invariably walk away continuing to believe what they've always believed. It is an amazing phenomenon, but what a person believes about the Bible can actually become bigger than the Bible in their lives. Which gets a little spooky when we consider the next Key Principle...

KEY PRINCIPLE #4

Be aware that God always gives us what we want.

Like so many principles in the word of God, this principle can be incredibly positive or incredibly negative. What determines which it is, of course, is what it is that we actually want. If we want truth, God will give us truth. But if our approach to the Bible communicates to God that what we really want is a lie, the fact is, He'll give us a lie! If we approach the word of God with our preconceived ideas, what God calls *idols*, He'll allow us to have enough spiritual rope to hang ourselves.

I realize that may sound a little unsettling, and maybe a little harsh. There may be some who will hear that and think to themselves, "Well, the God I know... or the way I envision God... or the way I imagine God to be... He would never do that! He would never give anybody a lie or give in to their preconceived ideas." And they're, of course, welcome to continue to think what they think, and believe what they want to believe, but the fact is: the Bible tells us something different! Let's go to the Key Verses so you can see where this principle is found in the Bible.

KEY VERSES:

Ezekiel 14:1-11

In the first three verses, Ezekiel says,

289

The Keys of Bible Study

> Then came certain of the elders of Israel unto me, and sat before me. 2 And the word of the Lord came unto me, saying, 3 Son of man, these men have set up their idols in their heart, and put the stumblingblock of their iniquity before their face: should I be enquired of at all by them? (Eze 14:1-3)

Notice that the religious big wigs in Ezekiel's day have come to sit before the prophet of God who speaks the word of God—and as they do, God whispers some information in Ezekiel's ear. He tells Ezekiel that the leaders are acting as if they want to hear God's words, but they'd already shrugged off what He had said long ago. The things they'd chosen to believe had become their heart's idols, and God wasn't going to play along with their charade.

God continues:

> Therefore speak unto them, and say unto them, Thus saith the Lord God; Every man of the house of Israel that setteth up his idols in his heart, and putteth the stumblingblock of his iniquity before his face, and cometh to the prophet; I the Lord will answer him that cometh according to the multitude of his idols; 5 That I may take the house of Israel in their own heart, because they are all estranged from me through their idols. 6 Therefore say unto the house of Israel, Thus saith the Lord God; Repent, and turn yourselves from your idols; and turn away your faces from all your abominations. 7 For every one of the house of Israel, or of the stranger that sojourneth in Israel, which separateth himself from me, and setteth up his idols in his heart, and putteth the stumblingblock of his iniquity before his face, and cometh to a prophet to enquire of him concerning me; I the Lord will answer him by myself: 8 And I will set my face against that man, and will make him a sign and a proverb, and I will cut him off from the midst of my people; and ye shall know that I am the Lord. 9 And if the prophet be deceived when he hath spoken a thing, I the Lord have deceived that prophet, and I will stretch out my hand upon him, and will destroy him from the midst of my people Israel. 10 And they shall bear the punishment of their iniquity: the punishment

of the prophet shall be even as the punishment of him that seeketh unto him; 11 That the house of Israel may go no more astray from me, neither be polluted any more with all their transgressions; but that they may be my people, and I may be their God, saith the Lord God. (Eze 14:4-11)

Wow! What an incredibly strong and indicting passage! This is why we must come to the Bible with an attitude that says, "Lord, I don't care what I've always believed. I want You to take your word and reveal its truth to me." Because it could be that what we've always believed may actually have become an idol in our heart that has become bigger than God to us. As this passage reveals to us, there is great danger in coming to the Bible with our preconceived ideas, because if that's what we want to see, that's exactly what God says He's going to allow us to see.

We find this same basic principle repeated in...

Isaiah 29:9-14

One of the characteristics of those in the Laodicean church in the first century and in the Laodicean Church Period in the 21st century (Rev 3:14–22) is spiritual and biblical blindness. We sometimes hear that and think to ourselves, "Oh that dirty Devil! He wants to blind us to the word of God and make the Bible a closed book to us, as if it had been sealed!" And the truth is, I'm quite certain he would love to do that! The only problem is—he can't! We don't need to concern ourselves with the *Devil* blinding us to God's truth. What we need to concern ourselves with, however, is *God* blinding us to His truth! Again, allow me to show you this.

Isaiah says,

Stay yourselves, and wonder; cry ye out, and cry: they are drunken, but not with wine; they stagger, but not with strong drink. <u>For the Lord hath poured out upon you the spirit of deep sleep, and hath closed your eyes</u>: the prophets and your rulers, the seers hath he covered. And the vision of all is become unto

The Keys of Bible Study

you as the words of a book that is sealed, which men deliver to one that is learned, saying, Read this, I pray thee: and he saith, I cannot; for it is sealed: And the book is delivered to him that is not learned, saying, Read this, I pray thee: and he saith, I am not learned. Wherefore the Lord said, Forasmuch as this people draw near me with their mouth, and with their lips do honour me, but have removed their heart far from me, and their fear toward me is taught by the precept of men: Therefore, behold, I will proceed to do a marvellous work among this people, even a marvellous work and a wonder: for the wisdom of their wise men shall perish, and the understanding of their prudent men shall be hid. (Isa 29:9-14)

Once again, God is showing that how we approach His word is very, very significant. These people had all of the outward form that caused them to look like they wanted to know what God's word said so they could do it, but their outward actions weren't actually reflective of what was in their hearts. Because of it, God struck them with spiritual drunkenness and spiritual blindness. God Himself poured out a spirit of deep sleep upon them which caused His own precious word to be a closed and sealed book. In the last verse of the chapter, God bottom-lines the real issue the people had which caused Him to take such drastic measures. He says that they "erred in spirit" (29:24). There was an error in their approach to His word, resulting in God no longer allowing them to even see His truth. Through how they approached God's word, they communicated to Him that they didn't really want it—so God gave them what they wanted.

2 Thessalonians 2:8–11

The context of this passage, of course, is after the Church has been raptured and the world has entered into the tribulation period. In that context, Paul says,

And then shall that Wicked be revealed, whom the Lord shall consume with the spirit of his mouth, and shall destroy with the brightness of his coming: 9 Even him, whose coming is

Chapter 10 — The Key of Apparent Contradictions

after the working of Satan with all power and signs and lying wonders, 10 And with all deceivableness of unrighteousness in them that perish; because they received not the love of the truth, that they might be saved. 11 And for this cause God shall send them strong delusion, that they should believe a lie. (2Th 2:8-11)

We see here the repetition of this same principle—that God gives to people what they communicate to Him they actually want. He talks in this passage about people who had the truth of God presented to them. They understood it, and in the full face of God's revelation of His truth, they chose to reject it. And in very simple and practical terms, if we reject God's truth, what are we actually communicating to God that we want? A lie. And so God says that during the tribulation period, that's exactly what these truth-rejectors are going to get.

Now, again, I present these very strong and negative examples of approaching God's word in unbelief or with impure motives as a warning to us. But with those warnings as a backdrop, we must allow our focus to be stayed on the reality of 1 Thessalonians 2:13— that if we approach the Bible in faith, wholeheartedly believing it is God's word and receiving its truth, it will transform our lives in ways that are nothing short of supernatural!

The reason we have taken the time to talk about the attitude with which we approach the Bible is because the further we plumb the depths of God's word, the more the Devil would love to do to us what he did to Eve (2Co 11:3), by getting us to question the word of God because of what appear to be contradictions.

KEY TRUTH:

Whenever the Bible appears to contradict itself, recognize that God is using it to get our attention so He can reveal to us a profound spiritual truth.

Now, be it known, as I mentioned previously, though most critics of

293

The Keys of Bible Study

the Bible who hurl accusations of contradictions couldn't actually take us to a single one—there are, however, numerous places in the word of God where the Bible *appears* to contradict itself. Again, they are not *actual contradictions*... they are *apparent contradictions*. And what we will discover if we will simply apply the principles of Bible Study to these passages is that God uses these places to get our attention so that He can reveal to us something profound.

KEY EXAMPLE:

There's no getting around the fact that there is an apparent contradiction between what the Bible tells us in 1 Kings 6:1 and Acts 13:16-22.

In 1 Kings 6:1 it says,

> And it came to pass in the four hundred and eightieth year after the children of Israel were come out of the land of Egypt, in the fourth year of Solomon's reign over Israel, in the month Zif, which is the second month, that he began to build the house of the Lord. (1Ki 6:1)

Take note, first of all, that the scripture says that Solomon is just coming into the fourth year of his reign. So at this time, he has three years under his belt. And this verse says, that at this point "he began to build the house of the Lord." So if we do the math from 1 Kings 6:1, we find that from the time of Israel's exodus to the time Solomon began to build the temple was 480 years. That's clearly what the verse says.

But that poses somewhat of a problem when we get to the New Testament and Acts comments on this same period of time. It records Paul's message as he preached in Antioch of Pisidia, saying,

> Then Paul stood up, and beckoning with his hand said, Men of Israel, and ye that fear God, give audience. 17 The God of this people of Israel chose our fathers, and exalted the people when they dwelt as strangers in the land of Egypt, and with high arm

294

Chapter 10 — The Key of Apparent Contradictions

brought he them out of it. (Act 13:16-17)

Notice that Paul is talking about the exodus, just like 1 Kings 6:1 mentions.

Then in the midst of Paul's message, he provides for us a timeline. As he continues preaching, verses 18 says, "And about the time of **forty years** suffered he their manners in the wilderness." So he lets us know that Israel was in the wilderness after the exodus for a period of 40 years.

He continues,

> And when he had destroyed seven nations in the land of Chanaan, he divided their land to them by lot. 20 And after that he gave unto them judges about the space of **four hundred and fifty years**, until Samuel the prophet. (Act 13:19-20)

So Paul tells us that the time from the wilderness to Samuel (during the time of the judges) was a period of 450 years. Then he adds in verse 21, "And afterward they desired a king: and God gave unto them Saul the son of Cis, a man of the tribe of Benjamin, by the space of **forty years**." So, after the judges, Saul was king for a period of 40 years.

Then he says,

> And when he had removed him, he raised up unto them David to be their king; to whom also he gave testimony, and said, I have found David the son of Jesse, a man after mine own heart, which shall fulfill all my will. (Act 13:22)

We know from the Old Testament (1 Kings 2:11, specifically) that David reigned over Israel after Saul for a period of 40 years. As we saw in 1 Kings 6:1, after David, Solomon began to build the Temple at the beginning of the fourth year of his reign. So we need to factor into our math from Paul's sermon in Acts 13:16-22 another three years.

295

The Keys of Bible Study

So if we go back into Paul's message to do the math, there was...

$$
\begin{array}{r}
40 \text{ years} \\
450 \text{ years} \\
40 \text{ years} \\
40 \text{ years} \\
+\quad 3 \text{ years} \\
\hline
\end{array}
$$

For a total of **573 years**

Now, that's a problem! Because the math from Acts 13 is 573 years, while 1 Kings 6 says it was 480 years. And it doesn't take a math whiz to figure out that between 573 years and 480 years, there is a 93 year discrepancy.

Can't you just hear the critics of the Bible gloating about this obvious contradiction in the Bible, saying, "My goodness! If we can't trust the Bible to give us a lousy timeline, how would we ever trust it to give us the truth we need to guide our lives, much less stake our eternal destiny on it?"

So, obviously, we have a 93 year problem. And I think it is more than apparent by the amount of years in question that the discrepancy must be in Acts 13:20, as it gives us the years the judges ruled, because 450 of the 480 years are taken up there.

So, maybe there's something in the book of Judges that can tell us why it is that, as the critics would say, there is this *obvious contradiction* in the Bible—and as we would say, this *apparent contradiction* in the Bible.

As we dive into the book of Judges, like we discussed in Chapter 8, this book is really nothing more than the record of a series of sin cycles that took place during the time of the Judges. Do you remember? The children of Israel would follow God... sin would lead them away from God... God would chastise them by allowing them to come under the oppression of their enemies... then they

296

would cry out to God in repentance... God would hear their cries and raise up a Judge to deliver them... they would defeat their enemies... and they would follow God once again.

Then, sin would lead them away from God... everything would fall apart again as God chastised them... and this sin cycle is repeated over and over throughout the book.

But as God gives us the record of these sin cycles in Judges, He is careful to provide for us a timeline throughout this book (please listen carefully to this!) of the amount of time the Nation of Israel spent under the control and domination of other peoples.

This is how it unfolds in the book...

Judges 3:8
Therefore the anger of the Lord was hot against Israel, and he sold them into the hand of Chushanrishathaim, King of Mesapotamia: and the children of Israel served Chushanrishathaim **eight years**.

Judges 3:14
So the children of Israel served Eglon the King of Moab **eighteen years**.

Judges 4:3
And the children of Israel cried unto the Lord: for he had nine hundred chariots of iron; and **twenty years** he mightily oppressed the children of Israel.

Judges 6:1
And the children of Israel did evil in the sight of the Lord: and the Lord delivered them into the hand of Midian **seven years**.

Judges 13:1
And the children of Israel did evil again in the sight of the Lord; and the Lord delivered them into the hand of the Philistines **forty years**.

The Keys of Bible Study

Alright, now let's add up these years.

$$
\begin{array}{r}
8 \text{ years} \\
18 \text{ years} \\
20 \text{ years} \\
7 \text{ years} \\
+ \underline{40 \text{ years}} \\
\mathbf{93 \text{ years}}
\end{array}
$$

And do you remember the Key Truth we just talked about? Whenever the Bible **appears** to **contradict** itself, recognize that God is using it to get our **attention**, so that He can **reveal** to us a profound spiritual truth. So, what is the profound truth God is trying to show us from this *apparent contradiction?*

God is revealing to us that when Israel was out of the land and under the control of other nations during the time of the Judges, His clock stopped! He stopped counting time. He counted time only when Israel was in control of the land that He gave them. That's why in 1 Kings 6, when God is giving the official record of the kings of Israel, it says 480 years—but when Paul comes along speaking in a Gentile-controlled area centuries later, he gives the chronological history of that same time period and says it was 573 years.

From a *biblical standpoint*, that's obviously a very important lesson to learn. But where it gets profound is the lesson it teaches us from a *practical standpoint!*

Sometimes when we try to find answers as we work through the problems in our lives, the math simply doesn't add up, if you will. When we factor all of the details of our life together and compare them to the promises we find in God's word, sometimes there certainly seem to be contradictions. So, what do we do in those times? How do we make sense of them?

298

Chapter 10 — The Key of Apparent Contradictions

Well, what God has just revealed to us through the example of Israel during the Judges, is that there are details we haven't yet seen that need to be factored into the equation of our lives to get it to all add up. And in the same way we that we believe and trust the word of God by faith in the face of an apparent contradiction knowing God's "got it"—we can, by faith, believe and trust God in the face the apparent contradiction in the circumstances of our lives... knowing God's "got that" as well!

KEY CONCLUSION:

As we come to the conclusion of the Keys of Bible Study with this example from the book of Judges, my hope and prayer is that for the rest of our lives it will cause us to approach God's word fully communicating to Him...

"Lord, I believe Your book. I believe it is Your truth. I believe every word of it. And from this day forward, by Your grace and power, I'm going to set my life to put into practice whatever You show me from it. I'm going to go to Your book not seeking information, but transformation. I want You to use Your word to make me like Your Son, the Lord Jesus Christ, that I might give to You through my life, the glory that is due Your name."

THE KEY OF LITERALITY

As Paul wrote his second epistle to the Corinthians, he expressed a very genuine concern he had in his heart for them and the body of Christ in general. In 2 Corinthians 11:3, Paul said: "But I fear, lest by any means, as the serpent beguiled Eve through his subtilty, so your minds should be **corrupted from the simplicity** that is in Christ." It is important to always keep in mind that God in His word constantly seeks to keep things simple. It is the Devil who takes God's simplicity and seeks to convolute it in an attempt to make it appear complicated and confusing. The final key of Bible study speaks, first and foremost, to God's *simplicity*.

The tenth key of Bible study:
Approach the Bible from a literal standpoint

KEY THOUGHTS:

The Bible is not a difficult book to understand. We make it difficult by not believing every word we read.

As we're reading and studying the word of God, the devil wants us to be intimidated. He wants to make us think that the Bible is over our heads, that it's complicated and difficult to understand, or that

The Keys of Bible Study

it takes someone with a theological degree to really understand the "deep things of God" (1Co 2:10). But again, God has made His word simple. As we come to any verse or portion of scripture, we must certainly keep in mind the first nine keys of Bible study—but then, the last key is to simply approach the Bible from a literal standpoint. We must force ourselves to not make Bible study more difficult than God intended it to be—we must simply believe what it says... where it says it... and how it says it!

Before trying to determine what any passage <u>means</u>, make sure you have clearly determined what it <u>says</u>.

One of the ways Satan has found to get us diverted in our Bible study is by getting us to approach a verse or a passage asking the wrong question. Almost by default, the first question most students of the Bible find themselves asking of a passage of scripture is: What does this **mean**? The question we must train our brains to ask, however, is very simply: What does it **say**? God really has made it that simple! You will be amazed how asking this simple question will unlock the treasure of the word of God. If we can lock in on what a verse or passage is *saying*, 99 times out of 100 we will know what it *means*. My brothers and sisters, we must apply the age-old K.I.S.S. principle: **K**eep **I**t **S**imple, **S**aints!

Now, that's certainly not to say that Bible study is *easy*. There is certainly a difference between something being *easy* and something being *simple*. God told us in 2 Timothy 2:15 that when it comes to His word, it requires **study**, which necessitates our being a **workman**. God talked in 1 Timothy 5:17 of elders who "**labour** in the word and doctrine." The fact is, real Bible study that leads to sound doctrine will require a lot of **labor** and hard **work**. And yet, the *labor* and the *work* is exerted in our diligence to *simply* apply the ten *simple* keys of Bible study.

KEY PRINCIPLE:

Take the literal sense of a verse or passage unless it doesn't make biblical sense.

What I'm referring to when I talk about something not making biblical sense is that if taking a particular verse or passage literally causes us to violate a clear command or teaching of scripture, we may need to apply the brakes and slow ourselves down to examine more closely what is actually happening in the particular verse or passage.

KEY QUALIFIERS:

Recognize that some principles in the Bible don't make logical sense, but they do make biblical sense.

God articulates this idea for us in Isaiah 55:8-9, saying: "For my thoughts are not your thoughts, neither are your ways my ways, saith the Lord. For as the heavens are higher than the earth, so are my ways higher than your ways, and my thoughts than your thoughts." In other words, God doesn't think the way we humans think. Something making logical sense, then, is not necessarily the standard by which God operates. Which means there will be times when we come to something in the word of God that simply does not make *logical* sense to us. What we must then determine is: does it make *biblical* sense?

God uses 1 Corinthians 2:4-7 to help us get our minds wrapped around how it is that something could make *biblical* sense, but not *logical* (or human) sense. Paul writes,

> And my speech and my preaching was not with enticing words of man's wisdom, but in demonstration of the Spirit and of power: 5 That your faith should not stand in the wisdom of men, but in the power of God. 6 Howbeit we speak wisdom among them that are perfect: yet not the wisdom of this world, nor of the princes of this world, that come to nought: 7 But

The Keys of Bible Study

we speak the wisdom of God in a mystery, even the hidden wisdom, which God ordained before the world unto our glory. (1Co 2:4-7)

God is obviously talking about wisdom in this passage—contrasting man's wisdom in verse 4 (which he calls the world's wisdom in verse 6)—with God's wisdom in verse 7. And Paul's whole point in this passage is that the wisdom of God is contrary to the wisdom of men and the wisdom of this world. So with that understanding, we must approach the Bible recognizing that there may be times that, because of God's wisdom, we may be dealing with a *biblical* principle that doesn't make *logical* sense to us.

But we must also recognize another key qualifier...

Keep in mind that though the Bible never contradicts itself, it often presents truth that is contrary to our natural inclinations.

Again, we must always approach the Bible literally. But we must also recognize that it will sometimes be difficult for us to do so, for the simple fact that our natural inclinations are often contrary to the truth of the word of God. For example...

- God plainly tells us that *the way UP is DOWN*.

James 4:10 says, "Humble yourselves in the sight of the Lord, and he shall lift you up." I can tell you that everything in my brain tells me something different than that! And yet, regardless of how *my mind* thinks, I must recognize that this verse reveals to me how *God's mind* thinks.

- God tells us that *in order to LIVE, we must DIE*.

In John 12:24, Jesus said, "Verily, verily, I say unto you, Except a corn of wheat fall into the ground and die, it abideth alone: but if it die, it bringeth forth much fruit." And again, though that principle

304

certainly runs contrary to our natural inclinations, it makes all the biblical sense in the world.

- In Acts 20:35, God tells us that *"It is more blessed to GIVE than to RECEIVE."*

Now, I can assure you: we're way more inclined to comprehend this principle after having grandchildren, and yet it is a principle that always makes biblical sense regardless of our season of life.

- In Luke 6:38, God also lets us know that *to RECEIVE, we must GIVE.*

Jesus says, "Give, and it shall be given unto you." Again, we simply must recognize that biblical sense doesn't always mean logical sense, and God's wisdom often runs contrary to our natural inclinations. That is why we always approach the Bible taking the literal sense, unless it doesn't make biblical sense.

KEY EXCEPTIONS:

God's usage of FIGURES of SPEECH

It is important for us to realize in our study of the Bible that in the same way we use figures of speech in the course of normal communication with one another, God does the same thing in His communication with us. When we use figures of speech, everybody readily recognizes it and nobody tries to force a literal interpretation of our words. Nor should we when God employs the same means of communication.

For example, Psalm 113:3 says, "From the rising of the sun unto the going down of the same the Lord's name is to be praised." Obviously, the point God is making through the psalmist is that His name is to be praised at all times, whether night or day. And yet, we all realize that the earth orbits around the sun, and that, technically, the earth actually rises on the sun. Are we to surmise

The Keys of Bible Study

by God's description in Psalm 113:3 that He is not aware of that? Certainly not! God knew that from our vantage point, every single day we watch the sun rise above the horizon in the east, and every single day we watch the sun go down in the west. So in His communication with us, He has simply chosen to talk the way we talk! He has chosen to use figures of speech just like we use them, and when He does, we ought simply to recognize it and not try to force a literal interpretation of His words.

The Bible does the same thing in Malachi 1:11. God says through Malachi, "For from the rising of the sun even unto the going down of the same my name shall be great among the Gentiles." Once again, God is obviously using a figure of speech! So what do we do? We give God the benefit of the doubt—and we thank Him that He has chosen to dispense His truth to us in a way that is relatable and in a way that we can comprehend it from our earthly vantage point.

God's usage of PARABLES

In our study of the Bible, it is likewise important that we comprehend just how it is that parables fit into our overarching understanding that God always *says* what He *means*—and *means* what He *says*—dictating that we approach the Bible literally.

In most Bible colleges and seminaries, the common definition of a parable is that it is simply an earthly story which has a heavenly meaning. The explanation typically goes on to say that Jesus used parables as teaching tools to help people to have a fuller or deeper understanding of the truth. But wait just a minute! Is that really what a parable is? And is that really why they are used? Let's take a few minutes to examine them biblically.

To fully grasp their usage, may I remind you that the first key of Bible study we talked about in Chapter One was the Key of Theme, which is simply this: **we must establish the theme of the author**. We discovered that the theme of the Bible is actually all about a kingdom that was promised all the way through the Old Testament to the Nation of Israel, in which the Lord Jesus Christ will rule from His throne in Jerusalem over all the world. In that literal kingdom, every person on this planet will bow their knee before Israel's king and will use their tongues to proclaim that He is Lord to the glory of God the Father. That is the theme of the Bible!

As Jesus began His ministry, it was this literal, physical kingdom that had been promised to the nation of Israel in the Old Testament that our Lord was proclaiming and offering to them. This is particularly clear through the content of Matthew's gospel—the gospel written to the Jews—that presents Christ as the King of the Jews. All the way through this book, it chronicles God's offer of the kingdom to the nation of Israel. It unfolds like this:

Chapter 1: The GENEALOGY of the King

God reveals to us the human lineage through which Christ had come, bringing it all the way back to the first human, Adam, who was the "son of God."

Chapter 2: The BIRTH of the King

In Matthew 2:1, the wise men say, "Where is he that is born **King of the Jews?**"

Chapter 3: The HERALD of the King

John the Baptist goes out before the King, publicly heralding His arrival.

Chapter 4: The TEST of the King

The King, the Lord Jesus Christ, goes out into the wilderness and is tested of Satan.

Chapters 5-7: The CONSTITUTION of the Kingdom

We typically refer to it as the Sermon on the Mount, but, more than a sermon, it is actually the declaration of the constitution of the kingdom.

The Keys of Bible Study

Chapters 8-9: The CONFIRMATION of the IDENTITY of the King

In these chapters, in rapid-fire succession, Christ performs a series of miracles. Though it appears He is just randomly making His way here and there, miraculously meeting people's needs, there is actually nothing random about it at all. Christ was taking Old Testament prophecies concerning the Jewish Messiah and very calculatedly fulfilling each one to the letter to let Israel know beyond any shadow of a doubt that their King had arrived.

Chapter 10: The OFFICIAL OFFER of the Kingdom

In this chapter, Christ calls the disciples to Himself (10:1), who at this point become the apostles ("sent ones" — 10:2,5), and He sends them to the lost sheep of the house of Israel (10:6). In fact, He clearly forbids them to go into the way of the Gentiles or into any city of the Samaritans. There would be time for that, but this was the time when the King and His Kingdom was being officially and exclusively offered to the house of Israel.

Chapters 11-12: The REJECTION of the King and His Kingdom

In these chapters, the Jewish Messiah has audience with the leaders in Israel who supposedly held the truth of the word of God and who supposedly spoke for God. And yet, having witnessed both Christ's ministry and His miracles, in Matthew 12:24 it says this: "But when the Pharisees heard it, they said, This fellow doth not cast out devils, but by Beelzebub the prince of the devils."

Wow! Do you understand what just happened there? In the face of the full biblical reality of who Jesus was, the religious leaders actually attributed the power by which Christ performed His miracles to Satan! Jesus responded in verse 31 saying, "Wherefore I say unto you, All manner of sin and blasphemy shall be forgiven unto men: but the blasphemy against the Holy Ghost shall not be

308

forgiven unto men." It is very important to see what happens next in the Gospel of Matthew.

Coming off of the heels of these Jewish leaders committing this blasphemy against the Holy Ghost, what happens next in chapter 13 is of key importance! Notice how Matthew 13:1 begins. Matthew tells us: "The same day..." That's going to be a significant piece of information, because we've learned through the Key of Context that we must always keep verses in their context. And for some reason, the Holy Spirit wanted us to know that what happens in chapter 13 happened on "the same day" that the Jewish leaders of Israel committed this heinous blasphemy against Him. It is more than apparent that God is wanting us to make the connection between what He's getting ready to do in chapter 13 with what had just happened in chapter 12. And not only is He wanting us to see the connection, but He wants us to see that what happens in chapter 13 is actually in response to what just happened in chapter 12. And so He begins in verse 1, saying, "The same day went Jesus out of the house, and sat by the sea side."

As we've talked about before, there is nothing in Jesus's ministry or in the Bible that is random. Jesus certainly isn't walking out of the house and making His way to the seashore because He thought it would make for a great photo op, or because He felt He needed a little change in scenery to clear His head. No; in the same way that Jesus wasn't simply going here and going there in chapters 8 and 9, let me assure you: Jesus isn't on this *same day* just randomly walking out of the *house* and just randomly going and sitting by the *sea*. This is actually a turning point in the Gospel of Matthew!

You see, one of the key themes all through the Old Testament is this thing of the *house*. Do you remember what Jesus told His disciples (apostles) as He was sending them forth in Matthew 10? He specifically told the to go *to the lost sheep of the HOUSE of Israel* (Mat 10:6). And one of the symbols we observe all the way through the scriptures is that the *sea* is representative of the Gentile nations.

But then, after Jesus goes out of the house and takes a seat by the

309

seashore, Matthew continues on in verses 2 and 3 saying, "And great multitudes were gathered together unto him, so that he went into a ship, and sat; and the whole multitude stood on the shore. And he spake many things unto them in parables." And you know what's tremendously significant about that? It's something He had never done before! This is the very first time Jesus has ever used a parable in His entire ministry! And much to contrary opinion, He's not doing it to illustrate or clarify His truth so that the people can understand. He's actually speaking in parables to *hide the truth* from those who could and should have understood it. He's speaking in parables to hide the truth from the group of people who just committed the unpardonable sin (Mat 12:24-31).

So in verse 3 He begins speaking this first parable, the one we refer to as the parable of the seed and the sower. And as He does, His disciples are no doubt thinking to themselves, "What in the world is He doing?" They're probably staring at each other with a look of, "Why is He talking this way?" They had never heard Jesus do anything like this.

Matthew lets us know that the parable ended in verse 9 with Jesus saying, "Who hath ears to hear, let him hear." And then, immediately in verse 10, the disciples storm the platform, as it were, and say, "Hey! What was that all about? Why were you talking like that?" Every other time they ever heard Him speak, it was always very straight forward and extremely clear. Jesus tells them in verse 11, "Because it is given unto you to know the mysteries of the kingdom of heaven, but to them it is not given." In other words, "I'm doing what I'm doing because I want you to understand all of the aspects of my literal, physical kingdom on the earth—but I'm going to hide it from these who have already proven by their smug and pompous rejection of Me that they don't really want the truth… or Me, their Messiah."

Jesus continues on, saying,

> Therefore speak I to them in parables: because they seeing see not; and hearing they hear not, neither do they understand.

Chapter 11 — The Key of Literality

And in them is fulfilled the prophecy of Esaias, which saith, By hearing ye shall hear, and shall not understand; and seeing ye shall see, and shall not perceive: For this people's heart is waxed gross, and their ears are dull of hearing, and their eyes they have closed; lest at any time they should see with their eyes, and hear with their ears, and should understand with their heart, and should be converted, and I should heal them. But blessed are your eyes, for they see: and your ears, for they hear. For verily I say unto you, That many prophets and righteous men have desired to see those things which ye see, and have not seen them; and to hear those things which ye hear, and have not heard them. (Mat 13:13-17)

Jesus makes it very clear to His disciples that because of their response to the truth, He was going to make sure they understood. But He also made it very clear that because of the response of the religious leaders, He was going to make sure they didn't.

Then notice what Jesus says to His disciples in verses 18, "Hear ye therefore the parable of the sower." And then He goes on in verse 19-23 to explain to His disciples every single detail of the truth that He had just hidden from the leaders of Israel.

The point we must see in terms of taking the Bible literally is that there are times when God speaks in parabolic language, or in a mystery form. But when He does this, He'll either do what He does here in Matthew 13 and explain every single detail of it, or He will explain it somewhere else in the word of God. By using the simple keys of Bible study we have learned together, we can understand His explanation of it, and take it very literally—just the way it is presented.

Now, just to throw a little spice into the dish, it is rather interesting in Matthew 13 that as Jesus comes *out of the house* (the Nation of Israel) and goes to *sit by the sea* (the Gentiles), He goes on to speak seven parables. And if we took the time to look at them, we would see that every one of them in their context hints at the fact that in Israel's rejection, He is going to turn from the house of Israel to the

311

The Keys of Bible Study

Gentiles. Each of the seven parables has a Gentile and Church-Age connotation—and all seven of them just happen to line up beautifully with the seven letters that Jesus wrote in Revelation 2 and 3 that are representative of the seven periods of church history!

It is also very interesting that there are five other parables that Jesus gives in the Gospel of Matthew, bringing the total number of parables to 12—which just happens to be the number associated with the Nation of Israel (as in the 12 tribes of Israel). These last five parables just happen to deal with what happens right after the Church Age is over—the tribulation period, when God will once again turn His attention to the Nation of Israel!

Now, if you don't understand all of that right now, don't panic! I brought it up to get you to realize that the Bible is like an onion. We remove one layer, only to find there's a deeper layer—and we peel that one back to find there's another layer... and another and another and another! That's why Paul referred to God's truth in Ephesians 3:8 as "the unsearchable riches of Christ." There is no end to its depth.

God's usage of SYMBOLISM

Another exception we need to factor into our literal approach to the Bible is its use of symbolism. We often hear people say that the reason they can't understand the Bible because of all the symbolism. Do you realize, though, there is actually very little symbolism in the Bible? This is true even of the book most people think is riddled with symbolism, the book of Revelation. Actually, there is very little symbolism even in this book—and with the few symbols that are used, they are all very easy to understand by simply applying the keys of Bible study. May I assure you: you have what you need to be able to go to the Bible and understand it!

Let me show you how simple this is. In Revelation 1:12-16, John says:

> And I turned to see the voice that spake with me. And being

312

Chapter 11 — The Key of Literality

turned, I saw seven golden candlesticks; And in the midst of the seven candlesticks one like unto the Son of man, clothed with a garment down to the foot, and girt about the paps with a golden girdle. His head and his hairs were white like wool, as white as snow; and his eyes were as a flame of fire; And his feet like unto fine brass, as if they burned in a furnace; and his voice as the sound of many waters. And he had in his right hand seven stars: and out of his mouth went a sharp twoedged sword: and his countenance was as the sun shineth in his strength. (Rev 1:12-16)

We sometimes tend to read a passage like that and allow ourselves to get overwhelmed with the symbolism. But with the keys of Bible study you now have in your hands, if you gave the time to study this passage, don't you think you could figure it out?

John says in verse 16, "Out of his mouth went a sharp twoedged sword." As you cross reference this in your head, doesn't Hebrews 4:12 quickly come to mind, where it clearly says that "the word of God is quick, and powerful, and sharper than any twoedged sword"? When Jesus speaks, what comes out of His mouth? Words! But because of who He is, those words are sharper than a twoedged sword. That's not difficult to understand!

John goes on to say, "...and his countenance was as the sun shineth in his strength." We've talked numerous times in our study about Malachi 4:2, where it talks about the fact that Jesus is the *Sun of righteousness,* and that when He is revealed for who He really is, He always shows up as blazing, blinding light. We've looked at when Christ was on the Mount of Transfiguration, revealing who He really was behind that veil of flesh and revealing the glory that will be His at His second coming. Matthew 17:2 says, "...and his face did shine as the sun." We're simply employing the Key of Comparison, comparing scripture with scripture, and God is revealing to us everything we need to be able to understand what John was seeing in Revelation 1.

Back in verse 12, John says, "I saw seven golden candlesticks," and

313

The Keys of Bible Study

then in verse 16 he says, "And he had in his right hand seven stars." And you may be saying to yourself, "Oh my! How will I ever figure that symbolism out? I can't think of any cross references!" Well, don't lose heart! Just keep reading! Because you know what God does for us in this passage? He reveals to us everything we don't pick up by comparing scripture with scripture somewhere else in the Bible right here in this very passage! Verse 20 says,

> The mystery of the seven stars which thou sawest in my right hand, and the seven golden candlesticks. The seven stars are the angels of the seven churches: and the seven candlesticks which thou sawest are the seven churches. (Rev 1:20)

Again I say to you, this isn't hard! The Devil wants to make us think passages like this are too deep and too difficult to understand. But if we'll simply work through the passage phrase by phrase utilizing the keys of Bible study, the Spirit of God will reveal His word/wisdom to us (1Co 2:10).

God's usage of METAPHORS

If you need a little reminder about what a metaphor is, it's "a figure of speech in which a word or phrase literally denoting one kind of object or idea is used in place of another to suggest a likeness or analogy between them."[2]

Let me provide a few examples: "The world is a stage"... "The man's house was his prison"... "She drowned in a sea of grief"... "A mighty fortress is our God." In real life, we know how to recognize a metaphor and distinguish between the literal and the figurative. Many "religious" people, however, can't do that.

There have always been lots of these kind of people—and there are lots of them today! They were around even way back in Ezekiel's day. Ezekiel had just preached his heart out, and by the time he's finished, he's just as frustrated as he can be! He cries out to God in

---

[2] "Definition of METAPHOR." Merriam-Webster, Accessed November 2019.

314

Ezekiel 20:49, saying, "Ah Lord God! they say of me, doth he not speak parables?"

Every time Ezekiel would preach something God wanted the people to hear and apply literally, they interpreted it as if God intended for them to understand it figuratively. And the opposite was also true. Every time he was speaking figuratively, they interpreted it literally! That's just what "religious" people do; they can't distinguish between the literal truth and a metaphor.

A classic example of this in a more modern application is what the religious system of Rome (the Roman Catholic Church) does to Jesus's discourse in John 6. In this chapter, Jesus is talking to the religionists of His day using the metaphor of eating His flesh and drinking His blood.

The religionists in the Roman system have taking Jesus's teaching in this passage and turned it into the damnable doctrine of transubstantiation. This doctrine of the Roman Catholic Church, based on a false interpretation of this passage, teaches that Jesus actually intended that we literally eat His flesh and drink His blood, and thereby receive Him into our lives. It is called *transubstantiation* because they believe that during the Mass, the priest has the mystical power to *transform* the *substance* of the bread and the wine in communion such that it becomes the literal body and blood of Christ. They teach that without taking part in this practice, your soul is not secure. Over one billion people alive in our world today have fallen prey to this damnable teaching because of a misunderstanding of Jesus's usage of what is clearly a metaphor.

But since there is so much confusion concerning this metaphor that over a billion people can be duped by it, we may need to spend a few minutes to talk about how—as students of the Bible seeking to identify from the scripture the key principles to be utilized in Bible study—we approach a passage such as this. Because after all, Jesus says in John 6:54, "Whosoever eats my flesh and drinks my blood hath eternal life." And Jesus was holding bread in His hands at the Lord's Supper in Matthew 26:26 when He said, "This is my

315

The Keys of Bible Study

body." And He was holding a cup with red liquid in it in His hand in Matthew 26:28 when He said, "This is my blood." And isn't the main point of this particular key of Bible study that the Bible is to be interpreted literally? You may be thinking, "Man! I'm not sure I have the ability to discern when to take the Bible literally, and when to understand it figuratively!"

Well, once again, please allow me to show you just how simple this really is.

In John 6, many of the people who appeared to be following Jesus weren't following Him because of who He was—they were following Him because of what He could do for them. They'd seen Him perform all kinds of miracles, which was obviously very entertaining. But not only was it a good show, they also knew that they might become one of the beneficiaries of one of His miracles.

In John 6:5-14, Jesus miraculously feeds 5000 of them at one time with just a little boy's lunch. And do recognize that the feeding of the 5000 was actually a whole lot more like feeding the 15,000, because the 5000 number was only inclusive of the men. By the time we factor in the women and the children, there would no doubt have been at least 15,000 people who had become a beneficiary of this miracle.

And so as we're coming into this discourse about the bread and the wine, we're first making sure we're applying the Key of Context, recognizing that the context is the feeding of the 5000. So, as we're making our way into this passage, we're realizing that just the day before, these people had eaten the literal bread of this miracle.

So on the following day, they again want to find Jesus so they can be the beneficiaries of more of His miracles. In John 6:26, Jesus faces them with their ulterior motives in following after Him, saying, "Ye seek me, not because you saw the miracles, but because ye did eat of the loaves, and were filled." They didn't want Jesus; they wanted the physical blessings He gave.

Chapter 11 — The Key of Literality

He then tells them in verse 27, "Labour not for the meat which perisheth, but for that meat which endureth unto everlasting life, which the Son of man shall give unto you." Jesus wanted them to concern themselves with spiritual things, not temporal, physical things like food.

Then down in verse 35 He tells them, "I am the bread of life: he that cometh to me shall never hunger; and he that believeth on me shall never thirst." And what Jesus continues to communicate in this verse and throughout this entire passage (6:36-40) is that the multitudes were following Him because they were hungry for physical bread, but they needed to address the real issue: the spiritual hunger and drought in their souls. That hunger is one that only Jesus can satisfy, and the thirst is one only He can quench.

But rather than humbling themselves before Jesus and receiving from Him the spiritual nourishment their souls so desperately needed, verse 41 says, "The Jews then murmured at him, because he said, I am the bread which came down from heaven." They understood that by Him saying He was the true bread that had come down from heaven, that He was claiming equality with God. They understood that He was claiming to be God in human flesh. And all the way through this passage, Jesus just keeps hammering that point! And do you know why He does? It's because believing that Jesus is God in human flesh is the beginning place of salvation. To be saved, we must come to grips with who Jesus Christ actually is (Rom 10:9). We call on His name for salvation, not because He is godly... not because He is a god... not because He is from God... we call on His name because He *is* God! He is God in a human body, in human flesh. That's why He keeps pressing the fact that He was the bread of life.

Watch how He continues to press them:

I am that bread of life. Your fathers did eat manna in the wilderness, and are dead. This is the bread which cometh down from heaven, that a man may eat thereof, and not die. I am the living bread which came down from heaven: if any man eat of this bread, he shall live for ever: and the bread that I will give is my flesh, which I will give for the life of the world. (Joh 6:48-51)

The manna their forefathers ate in the wilderness was just like the bread He fed them with in the wilderness the previous day. It was physical bread that sustained physical life. But God was not wanting them to partake of physical bread now; He wanted them to partake of spiritual bread—bread that is a person: Jesus.

And watch their reaction in verse 52. They totally miss the point! John says, "The Jews therefore strove among themselves, saying, How can this man give us his flesh to eat?" They're all freaked out of their minds because they're not equating the "eating and drinking" He's been talking about with believing. They're not understanding that "eating and drinking" is simply a metaphor.

To have missed that metaphor, you would have to have the blindfold of religion strapped completely around your head and over your eyes. Let me assure you that the most blinding thing in all the world is religion! A drunk, a drug addict, a pimp, or a prostitute know they need Christ. But religious people get themselves worked into the fabric of a system which misses the spiritual reality God intends for us to see, and just like the people here in John 6, they begin to take literal what was intended to be figurative—and take figurative what God intended to be literal.

Nine times in this passage Jesus lets us know that "eating and drinking" is simply the metaphor He is using to speak of *believing*.

Verse 29: "This is the work of God, that ye BELIEVE on him whom he hath sent."

Verse 30: "What sign showest thou then, that we may see, and BELIEVE thee?"

Verse 35: "…and he that BELIEVETH on me shall never thirst."

Chapter 11 — The Key of Literality

Verse 36: "…ye also have seen me, and BELIEVE not."

Verse 40: "And this is the will of him that sent me, that every one which seeth the Son, and
BELIEVETH on him, may have everlasting life."

Verse 47: "Verily, verily, I say unto you, He that BELIEVETH on me hath everlasting life."

Verse 64: "But there are some of you the BELIEVE not. For Jesus knew from the beginning   who they were that BELIEVED not…"

Verse 69: "And we BELIEVE and are sure that thou art the Christ, the Son of the living God."

One would think that, with that kind of repetition in a single discourse, there could be no possible way for the real intent and issue of Jesus's message to be lost. And even if the ninefold repetition of *believing* would still somehow leave someone doubting about whether Jesus intended for us to eat His literal flesh and drink His literal blood, surely verse 63 would seal it! Because in verse 63, Jesus just flat out says, "It is the spirit that quickeneth; the flesh profiteth nothing: the words that I speak unto you, they are spirit, and they are life." He tells us plain and clear that this whole discourse has been about spiritual realities.

The bread in John 6 is spiritually representative of who Christ is—the fact that He is God who came down to earth in a body of flesh. The blood in John 6 is spiritually representative of what Christ came to this earth to do—to shed His blood to atone for the sin of the world. But the issue all the way through the passage is *believing!* That's why the very next verse (verse 64) says, "But there are some of you that **believe** not."

John 6 is actually a very powerful chapter to point people to the *simplicity* that is in Christ: that salvation is simply a matter of *believing* that Jesus is who He says He is (God in a human body)

319

and that He did what He came to do (shed His blood to atone for man's sin, be buried, and rise again the third day).

What I hope you see in this chapter is that we ought always to approach the Bible from a literal standpoint. Of course, we do so recognizing that in God's communication with us, there are times when there are exceptions to the rule. He does use figures of speech, parables, symbols, and metaphors. And when He does, we would no more force a literal interpretation upon His usage of them than we would force a literal interpretation upon a friend who used them in their communication with us!

As we started this chapter, I emphasized the importance of not being moved away from the simplicity that is in Christ. Let's work at not making our study of the Bible more difficult than it needs to be! Approach the Bible from a literal standpoint, until God clearly demonstrates not to.

UNLOCKING IT ALL

Let's take a brief moment to review each of the keys we've learned about:

The first key of Bible study:
ESTABLISH THE THEME OF THE OF THE AUTHOR

If we will ever truly understand the Bible and interpret it properly, we must approach it recognizing that the Bible is not about me, you, the Nation of Israel, or the Church. As important as each of those are in the plan and purposes of God, they very simply are not the main subject or the main theme of God's book. The Bible is about Jesus! It's about every knee bowing before Him and every tongue confessing that Jesus Christ is Lord to the glory of God the Father. The whole of scripture is about Christ's kingdom glory, the glory that will be Christ's when He returns to the earth at His second coming and establishes His millennial kingdom on the earth. Keeping that simple theme before us as we study God's word will keep those of us living in these last days—who are so prone to be lovers of our own selves (2Ti 3:1-2)—from making ourselves the theme, or somehow reading into the Bible the notion that God exists for us, rather than us existing for God (Gen 2:2-3).

The second key of Bible study:
MAKE THE RIGHT DIVISIONS

Though the God of the Bible is extremely ordered, patterned, structured, and consistent, the fact is that in the process of fulfilling His "eternal purpose" (Eph 3:8), God works at different times in different ways, just as surely as He works with different people in different ways. It is, therefore, imperative that we understand where we are in the Bible at any given period of time and who the audience actually is, because these distinctions—or shall we say *divisions*—are the only way to accurately interpret scripture and be kept from entering into false doctrine (2Ti 2:15).

The third key of Bible study:
KEEP VERSES IN THEIR CONTEXT

There are many verses that appear to be teaching one thing when read on their own, but are actually teaching something completely different when they are put into the context of the particular passage, chapter, and book of the Bible in which they are found. Understanding the context of a verse is vital to proper and accurate biblical interpretation (2Pe 3:16).

The fourth key of Bible study:
UTILIZE GOD'S PRINCIPLE OF COMPARING SCRIPTURE WITH SCRIPTURE

God makes completely clear that the wisdom He presents in His word transcends our ability as humans to see, hear, or comprehend it. He tells us that the only ones who will be able to understand it are, first of all, those who have been brought to life spiritually (born again) by the Holy Ghost; and secondly, Spirit-filled believers who diligently employ the specific method the Holy Spirit utilizes in revealing His word to us—comparing spiritual things with spiritual, or comparing scripture with scripture. Something supernatural takes place in our understanding when we trust God to use His Spirit and His word to reveal His supernatural truth to us (1Co 2:13).

Chapter 12 — Unlocking It All

The fifth key of Bible study:
RECOGNIZE THE THREE LAYERS OF APPLICATION

Two of the these three layers of application are very common and familiar to most students of the word of God. The first is the Historical Application, which is very simply understanding that what we are reading really happened to real people at a very real point in history. The other commonly understood application is the Devotional or Inspirational Application, which is taking the details of the biblical account and seeing how they apply to our lives practically. The layer of application that is often overlooked, however, is the Doctrinal or Prophetic Application. This layer of application is about understanding that God has carefully recorded the events of history in the Old Testament so that they picture future events that are fulfilled in Christ's first or second coming, or picture doctrinal truths, principles, and concepts that are taught in the New Testament. Recognize that our Devotional Application will be very limited and lacking without also factoring into the Historical and the Doctrinal Applications. (1Co 10:6,11; Rom 15:4).

The sixth key of Bible study:
REALIZE THAT THE KEY TO THE *WORD* OF GOD— IS THE *WORDS* OF GOD.

If God had simply promised to communicate His thoughts, ideas, concepts, principles or precepts, that would certainly be His prerogative and we would have to approach His word accordingly. The fact is, however, that God was careful to tell us that He would not only *inspire* His very words but also *preserve* them. He has chosen to preserve His words for us because the *words* of God are the very power of the *word* of God. That's why Satan has calculatedly and consistently sought to attack God's words since the dawn of time (Gen 3:1). Tracing God's usage of words is one of the main ways we are able to employ the Key of Comparison that God uses to reveal His word to us (1Co 2:10,13).

323

The Keys of Bible Study

The seventh key of Bible study:
INTERPRET SCRIPTURE IN LIGHT OF GOD'S CONSISTENCY

Though all of God's attributes are of immense biblical importance, one of the most beautiful and far-reaching attributes is God's immutability—or the fact that He cannot change. Because God is totally consistent in His person, we can likewise expect Him to be totally consistent when it comes to His word (Joh 1:1,14). Though the Bible was written over a period of almost 1600 years over 60 generations with over 40 different writers from all kinds of different backgrounds; who wrote from three different continents and in three different languages; who lived in all kinds of different times and places; and who wrote on hundreds of controversial subjects—from Genesis to Revelation, the Bible is consistent, and reads as if it were written by one author. And, of course, it was... by God!

The eighth key of Bible study:
ALLOW GOD TO TEACH YOU BY ASSOCIATION

As God was in the midst of creating everything in existence, He did so in such a way that by its very design, creation would perfectly illustrate the truth He wanted us to be able to clearly see and understand (Rom 1:20). God created everything in His physical creation to teach us spiritual truth. Throughout His word, God takes spiritual truths and concepts that He knows may be difficult for us to understand and *likens* them, or *associates* them, to things in creation that He knows we do understand. This is why two of the most important words in the Bible are the simple words *like* and *as*.

The ninth key of Bible study:
APPROACH THE BIBLE BELIEVING THERE ARE NO CONTRADICTIONS, ONLY APPARENT ONES

Though we must approach teachers and preachers of the word of God as guilty until proven innocent (1Jo 4:1), we must approach the word of God itself as innocent until proven guilty (1Th 2:13).

324

Chapter 12 — Unlocking It All

As we approach the Bible in faith believing there are absolutely no contradictions, we must recognize that there are going to be things we encounter which *appear* to be contradictions at first sight. In these instances, if we will simply apply the principles of Bible Study, we will discover that God actually uses these places to get our attention so He can reveal to us something profound.

The tenth key of Bible study:
APPROACH THE BIBLE FROM A LITERAL STANDPOINT

One of the ways Satan has found to get us diverted in our Bible study is by getting us to approach a verse or a passage asking the wrong question. Almost by default, the first question most students of the Bible find themselves asking of a passage of scripture is: What does this **mean**? The question we must train our brains to ask, however, is very simply: What does it **say**? We must force ourselves not to make Bible study more difficult than God intended it to be. We must simply believe what it says... where it says it... and how it says it... taking a very literal approach.

With each of those keys fresh in our minds, let's revisit the very beginning of our time in *The Keys of Bible Study*. We began by talking about the fact that there is one key which is the most important key of all. It's the key that actually makes all of the other keys work. It is, of course, is the key of David.

We learned that this is a key which God gives to churches, because our Lord specifically says that He gave it to the church in Philadelphia in the first century (Rev 3:7) and to many of the churches in the Philadelphian period of church history in the 16th through 19th centuries. What's more, we learned that God also entrusts the key of David to individuals. We can look down through the annals of history and see men and women who possessed this key that supernaturally opened doors of access to the treasures in God's word (truth) and the treasures in God's work (souls).

Do you remember who it is that Jesus entrusts with this key? He entrusts it to people who possess the key ingredient found in

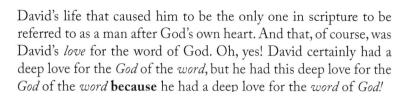

David's life that caused him to be the only one in scripture to be referred to as a man after God's own heart. And that, of course, was David's *love* for the word of God. Oh, yes! David certainly had a deep love for the *God* of the *word*, but he had this deep love for the *God* of the *word* **because** he had a deep love for the *word* of *God!*

With that in mind, as I bring *The Keys of Bible Study* to a conclusion in this chapter, I'd like to ask you to consider a very important question. Can you honestly say today that you possess a deep love for the word of God? Typically, when we're asked a question like that, our response is something like, "Well, I hope so!" Or, "I sure want to!" But we also typically wonder how we could ever really know that. Because after all, it does seem to be rather subjective, doesn't it?

Well, maybe it's not quite as subjective as we might initially think! Because in Psalm 119, under the inspiration and guidance of the Holy Spirit, David talks explicitly about his love for the word of God. As he does, he lets us know the very observable characteristics that his love for the word produced in his life. It would stand to reason, then, that if we love the word of God, those same characteristics would also be observable in our lives.

So, in this final chapter, I'd like for you to join me in seeking to determine whether or not we love the *word* of *God*—believing that when we do, we will certainly love the *God* of the *word*.

HOW TO BIBLICALLY KNOW WHETHER OR NOT WE LOVE THE WORD OF GOD

1. We know we love the word of God by what we *hate*.

That's right, my brothers and sisters! By what we *hate!*

We know that because David lets us know in Psalm 119 that His *love* for the word of God caused Him to *hate* three specific things. First of all, when we **love the word of God...**

A. We will hate every _false way_.

David says in Psalm 119:127-128, "...I **love** thy commandments above gold; yea, above fine gold. **Therefore** I esteem all thy precepts concerning all things to be right; and **I hate every <u>false way</u>.**"

Do you know why God is so strong about this? It's because the word of God is the **way <u>of</u> God**—and not only that, the Bible reveals to us the **way <u>to</u> God**! What we must realize, however, is that there are counterfeits! Listen to what Solomon said in Proverbs 14:12: "There is **a way** which seemeth right unto a man..." Notice, this is not _the way_ that God Himself _says_ is right. It's _man's way_ that _seems_ right—but isn't! That's why Solomon goes on to say in the rest of this verse, "...but the end thereof are the **ways of death.**" It is very simply a _false way_ that lands man in utter destruction! So I ask you, how could we not _hate_ it?

In Matthew 7:13, Jesus said: "Enter ye in at the strait gate: for wide is the gate, and broad is **the way, that leadeth to destruction,** and many there be which go in thereat." And again, that's the reason we have such a _hatred_ for all of the _false ways_—they lead people to destruction! And notice, Jesus said that _many_ people are on that _way!_

David reiterates this same hatred again in Psalm 119:104, where he says, "Through thy precepts I get understanding: therefore **I hate every <u>false way</u>.**" Notice that the passion ran so deep in David that it wasn't just that he didn't _like_ these false ways, or that he had _ill feelings_ toward these false ways. No, he flat-out **hated** them.

In the New Testament, when God came down from heaven to earth in the person of Jesus Christ, He told us something very significant about the **way <u>of</u> God** and **the way <u>to</u> God**. Jesus said in John 14:6, "I am **_the way_,** the truth, and the life: no man cometh **unto** the Father, but by me!" So, how many _ways_ to the Father are there? Jesus Himself said it: there's only one! Therefore, every other "way to God" or "way of truth" is a false way! And as we've already seen, false ways lead to _destruction!_ So how could we possibly say

327

The Keys of Bible Study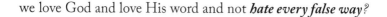

we love God and love His word and not *hate every false way?*

I know that sounds strong. It may even take a little bit of meditation for you to get your head wrapped around the Bible telling us to *hate*. In 21st-century Christianity, saying you *hate* something certainly doesn't sound like what we sometimes refer to as "Christian". But as "un-Christian" as it may *sound*—it is very consistent with the true nature of love! Because the fact is, if we're passionate *about* something, it automatically and necessarily means we're just as passionate *against* something! One of my dear pastor friends has a son who has been in a fierce battle for his life over the past year. Because he loves his son and is passionate about him, he automatically and necessarily hates the cancer that has been ravaging his body. Again, that's just how love works!

But somewhere along the way, we've acquired the mistaken idea that Christians are only allowed to talk about what they're *for*, but aren't allowed to talk about what they're *against*. We're free to talk about what we *love*, but we aren't free to talk about what we *hate*. Which leads to a very important concept I hope you will prayerfully consider...

We must learn to make a distinction between what is "Christian" and "spiritual" and what is biblical and scriptural.

Now, what do I mean by that? Well, by "Christian," I'm referring to what people subjectively expect to be consistent with what a *Christian* would *say* or *do*... or what people subjectively consider to be *Christian behavior*. By "spiritual," again, I'm referring to what people subjectively think fits the *demeanor* and/or the *language* of a devout believer.

By something being biblical, I'm referring to something concerning which we can objectively go to the Bible and get the principle from a specific biblical reference. By something being scriptural, I'm talking about an overarching biblical principle that we're able to glean from the *scriptures* as a whole. Though there may not be a *specific reference*, there is most definitely a *general inference*.

To illustrate the principle and the usage of these four words, let me reiterate a statement I made back in Chapter 5. I can honestly tell you: I *hate* the Roman Catholic Church. Notice I didn't say I hate Roman Catholics! Because I certainly don't hate *them;* I love them! But I *do* hate their church. And I could say the same thing about Jehovah's (False) Witnesses. I love Jehovah's (False) Witnesses themselves. But I *hate* their church.

But buddy, in the 21st century, if you make a statement like that, do you you know what most "Christians" are going to say? "Man, that certainly doesn't sound very *Christian!*" Or, "Brother, talking like that isn't very *spiritual!*"

However, if a person follows the teaching of the Roman Catholic Church or the teaching of the Jehovah's (False) Witnesses, are they going down a *false way* that will lead them to *destruction?* Absolutely! So, though *hating* their religion may not *sound* very "Christian" or "spiritual" by man's standard, it is most certainly *biblical* and it is most certainly *scriptural* according to God's standard.

And the fact is, folks, if the standard we use to make our assessments and determinations is based on what society deems "Christian" and "spiritual," it is a guarantee we're *not* going to make assessments and determinations that are *biblical* and *scriptural.*

Years ago when I was pastoring a church in Ohio, a representative of a very famous evangelistic organization called my administrative assistant to set up an appointment with me. As we met, he seemed to be a very friendly, kind, sincere, and loving gentleman. His purpose in setting up the meeting was to invite our church to an ecumenical crusade they were planning to have in our county, and to invite me to sit on the platform while the well-known evangelist preached. I asked the gentleman which pastors from other churches in the area would also be sitting on the platform, as well as what would happen in terms of follow-up with the people who might respond to the invitation to be saved. I was specifically asking whether the

329

The Keys of Bible Study

follow-up would be assigned to churches which added works of any kind to salvation or which taught that salvation was solely accessible through their church. He told me that in the name of fairness, the names of people who responded would be distributed to all of the participating churches, some of which matched those descriptions. I explained to him my personal doctrinal convictions and the doctrinal convictions of our church as graciously and respectfully as I could, and told him that we would have to decline the invitation.

The guy literally pleaded with me through tears to be part of this crusade, so that we could show the world our unity. Despite his sincere and passionate pleas, I told him that our church would not be participating.

Let me assure you: if every Christian in the world could have somehow been looking in on that meeting, I'm convinced that 95% of them would have said that I wasn't being very "Christian" and that I wasn't being very "spiritual." But I ask you: was my response to him biblical and scriptural? My dear brothers or sisters, for God's glory's sake, we must consciously and calculatedly determine that we will do what is biblical and scriptural, even when it appears that we are not being "Christian" or "spiritual."

Which leads us to the next point. If we truly do *love* the word of God, not only will we *hate* every *false way*...

B. We will hate *lying*.

David says in Psalm 119:163: "**I hate and abhor lying**: but thy law do I **love**."

At the end of Psalm 119:142, David says: "Thy law is truth." Jesus said the same thing in John 17:17. He said, "Thy word is truth." This means that anything that is *not according to* the word of God is a *lie*. Anything that is *contradictory* to the word of God is a *lie*. Anything that *subtracts* or suggests that something should be *removed* from the word of God is a *lie*. Anything that parades itself as something

330

that *needs to be added* to the word of God is a *lie*. Whether it be seven sacraments, as in Roman Catholic teachings; another testament, as in the Book of Mormon; the *Watchtower Magazine*, propagated by the Jehovah's (False) Witnesses; the so-called *Science & Health Key to the Scriptures* of the Christian Scientists—they're all lies. And if we *love* the word of God, like David, the man after God's own heart, we'll absolutely *hate* them.

I realize that this sounds extremely strong, and for some may even be a little unsettling. May I remind you, though, that as Jesus dictated His letter to the first-century church of Ephesus in Revelation 2:2, He commends them, saying: "…thou hast tried them which say they are apostles, and are not, and hast found them liars." And the fact is, folks, in the 21st century there are a lot of *lies* and *liars* out there! That's why John says in 1 John 4:1, "Beloved, believe not every spirit, but try the spirits whether they are of God: Because **many false prophets** are gone out into the world." There were a lot of *lies* and *liars* in the first century, and Paul says in 2 Timothy 3:13 that "evil men and seducers shall wax worse and worse." Since that be the case, just think how many lies and liars there are today!

The word of God is also very helpful in identifying just what a *liar* is *biblically*. Notice, I didn't say *culturally*… but *biblically*.

- **Proverbs 30:6 defines a liar as someone who adds to what God says in His word**

"Add thou not unto his words, lest he reprove thee, and thou be found a liar."

- **1 John 1:10 defines a liar as someone who says they don't sin**

"If we say that we have not sinned, we make him a liar, and his word is not in us."

- **1 John 2:4 defines a liar as someone who says they're saved, but isn't obedient to the word of God**

"He that saith, I know him, and keepeth not his commandments,

The Keys of Bible Study 🔑

is a liar, and the truth is not in him."

- **1 John 2:22 defines a liar as someone who doesn't believe that Jesus is God in a human body**

"Who is a liar but he that denieth that Jesus is the Christ? He is antichrist, that denieth the Father and the Son."

- **1 John 4:20 defines a liar as someone who says they love God, but hates his brother**

"If a man say, I love God, and hateth his brother, he is a liar: for he that loveth not his brother whom he hath seen, how can he love God whom he hath not seen?"

Folks, if we love the word of God, we will *hate* every *false way*. Secondly, we will *hate lying*. And then, thirdly...

C. We will hate *vain thoughts*.

David says in Psalm 119:113: "**I** *hate* *vain thoughts*: but thy law do I **love**." So, of course, the question is: "what are *vain thoughts?*"

Well, some of the other ways the word *vain* is translated throughout the Old Testament are: *lying, false, wrongful*, and *deceitful*.

Those words certainly provide us a general idea of what *vain thoughts* are, but in Psalm 94:11, God just flat out tells us what they are! The psalmist says: "The Lord knoweth the thoughts of man, that they are vanity." That's what *vain thoughts* are! God defines them as *man's thoughts!* The idea is man's thoughts versus God's thoughts; man's thoughts *as opposed to* God's thoughts; man's thoughts *apart from* God's thoughts; man's thoughts *without* God's thoughts; or man's thoughts *in the place of* God's thoughts.

To really get it, I think there are some concepts in 1 Corinthians 2 of which we must be reminded. As we have discussed previously, Paul takes this entire chapter to contrast man's wisdom with God's wisdom. In other words, how man thinks about life versus how

332

Chapter 12 — Unlocking It All

God thinks about life, or shall we say *man's thoughts* versus *God's thoughts*. By the time Paul gets to the end of the chapter, he says something monumental in verse 16: "For who hath known the mind of the Lord, that he may instruct him?" I mean, can you even possibly fathom being able to get into God's mind? But check out the last part of the verse. Paul says: "But we have the mind of Christ." Notice, Paul says we actually have it! We have access to and, as believers, actually possess God's mind. Do you know why and how? It's because the word of God has been revealed to us (2:9-10)! As we hold God's holy word in our hands, we're actually holding in our hands the very mind of Christ. That's what the Bible actually is—God's *thoughts* expressed in *words*. That's why David says that he hated man's thoughts, which don't begin and end with His word. And may I remind you that David was writing this approximately 3000 years ago! If David hated vain thoughts in the 10th century BC, just imagine what he would be feeling and expressing in the humanistic, man-centered days (2Ti 3:1-4) of the 21st century AD!

And before we move on from this point, I feel something else needs to be said. Many people think that with all of the religions in the world and all the various "brands" of Christianity that somehow we're all in this together, and we're all going to end up in the same place. My brothers and sisters, nothing could be further from the truth.

If your theology *accommodates* systems of thought that *oppose the Bible*, or if your theology is *tolerant* of systems of religion that *contradict the Bible*, I pray that the biblical realities we have been observing will become a divine wake-up call for you. As lovingly and graciously and as honestly as I know how to say it, you haven't gotten to this place of *accommodation* and *tolerance* because of your spiritual *maturity*—you've gotten there because of your spiritual *immaturity*. You haven't gotten there because you *love so much*, you've gotten there because you *love too little*.

David fell in love with *God's thoughts*, and it resulted in him automatically and necessarily hating *man's thoughts*. My brothers

333

The Keys of Bible Study

and sisters, when we fall in love with the word of God, the same thing will happen to us. Paul expressed the same sentiment in Romans 3:4 when he said, "Let God be true, and every man a liar." To love the word of God is to love God's *ways*, His *truth* and His *thoughts*—and when we do, the simple fact is, we will hate every *false way*, we will hate *lying*, and we will hate *vain thoughts*.

So, first of all, we know we love the word of God by what we <u>hate</u>.

2. We know we love the word of God by our extreme <u>*reverence*</u> for it.

David says in Psalm 119:140, "Thy word is very pure: therefore thy servant loveth it." He viewed God's word with an incredibly pure and holy attitude. And notice the way he said it in this verse. David didn't simply say, "Thy word is pure." I mean, that would have been awesome in itself! But David finds a way to even up the ante, saying, "Thy word is *very* pure." In other words, David was saying that the word of God is *totally pure...* it is *absolutely pure...* it is *completely pure...* it is *pure through and through!*

It's the same reverential attitude he expressed in Psalm 12:6 when he said, "The words of the Lord are pure words: as silver tried in a furnace of earth purified seven times." As we've talked about previously, the number seven is the number of perfection and completion in the word of God. It's also the same reverential attitude David's son expressed in Proverbs 30:5 when he wrote, "Every word of God is pure.

Is that the attitude you have toward the word of God sitting before you? If we believe it's pure, we'll love it. And if we love it, we'll believe it is pure. We'll have such a high and holy attitude toward it, such an extreme reverence for it, that we'll find ourselves crying out with David in Psalm 119:129, "Thy testimonies are wonderful; therefore doth my soul keep them." According to this verse, do you know why we often don't keep the testimonies found in God's word? It's because they're not wonderful to us. And do you know why they're not wonderful to us? It's because we don't love them.

334

Chapter 12 — Unlocking It All

Watch how David goes on to express his extreme reverence for the word of God. In verse 138, he says, "Thy testimonies that thou hast commanded are righteous and very faithful." In verse 161, he says, "...my heart standeth in awe of thy word." In verse 162 he says, "I rejoice at thy word, as one that findeth great spoil." All through this psalm, David finds every conceivable way to express the reverential attitude he had for God's word. In verse 164, he passionately declares, "Seven times a day do I praise thee because of thy righteous judgments." In other words, "Lord, I just find myself continually taking time out of my day to praise You for Your glorious book!"

We learn from David's testimony that there's a third way we know we love the word of God...

3. We know we love the word of God by what *consumes our thoughts*.

David says in Psalm 119:97, "O how love I thy law!" He goes on to tell us the characteristic that incredible love for the word of God produced in his life. He says, "It is my meditation all the day." In other words, "Lord, I just can't stop thinking about it! I can't get it off of my mind, and I can't get it out of my heart! Getting into Your word isn't simply something I do to start my day, it goes with me throughout the day!"

In any given 24-hour period, what do you think God would say it is that consumes your thoughts? What is your meditation all the day? Is it your job? Is it what you're going to do after work? Is it the next car or house you're hoping to buy, or some other earthly possession you're wanting to acquire? Would it be carnal, fleshly, or lustful thoughts? Or, like David, are you so consumed by and in love with the word of God that you just can't stop thinking about it? Do you find yourself continuously mulling it over in your head? How long do you think you go in a day's time *without* thinking about the word of God?

335

The Keys of Bible Study

This thing of continually thinking about and meditating upon the word of God isn't a *discipline*. It's not something we *train* ourselves to do. The fact is, we *think* about what's important to us. We *think* about what we *love!* And we'll know we love the word of God when we find that it consumes our thoughts.

4. We know we love the word of God by the *joy we receive from getting into it* and *it getting into us.*

David says in Psalm 119:47, "I will delight myself in thy commandments, which I have loved."

Folks, if we genuinely love the word of God, it'll become a fountain of joy for us! Taking the time to get into it won't be a drudge for us, or be something we dread, or something we have to force ourselves to do. It won't simply be our spiritual obligation to fulfill, or our Christian duty to perform. Oh my, a thousand times, no! Rather, we will find ourselves coming to the word of God simply because it is our delight! We'll get into it because we delight in *what* He says, and because we delight in *knowing* what He says, and because we delight in *doing* what He says. And we'll get into it because it has become what *fills* us, what *excites* us, what *satisfies* us, and what *gratifies* us. All the way through this psalm, David just keeps reiterating his *delight* in the word of God:

- 119:14: "I have rejoiced in the way of thy testimonies, as much as in all riches."
- 119:72: "The law of thy mouth is better unto me than thousands of gold and silver."
- 119:162: "I rejoice at thy word, as one that findeth great spoil."
- 119:103: "How sweet are thy words unto my taste! Yea, sweeter than honey to my mouth."
- 119:131: "I opened my mouth, and panted: for I longed for thy commandments."

336

Chapter 12 — Unlocking It All

We know we love the word of God because we love to get into it, but that's actually just half of it! Yes, we know we love the word of God *by the joy we receive from getting into it*. But just as surely, we know we love the word of God *by the joy we receive from it getting into us!*

A lot of people love getting into the word of God, not because they love the word of God, but because they love themselves. They're motivated to get into the word of God because they love the way they feel about themselves when they do, and they love the way they feel about themselves when others look at them with wonder because of how much they know about the Bible. Because of that self-motivation, however, the word of God never really impacts how they live. Though they've prioritized getting into the word of God, their motive in doing so ensures that the word of God won't be getting into them! This, my friends, is the missing link in answering why it is that so many Bible-believing, Bible-reading Christians can spend so much time in the Bible and know so much about it, and yet their lives are not really impacted by it.

There are others who have gotten into the word of God consistently on a daily basis, many of them for years on end, but they've never really seen the word of God have the profound and powerful impact it could be having because rather than getting into the word of God because it is their *delight*, they get into the word of God because it has simply become a *discipline*. It's just what they do. And so the word of God doesn't really get into them, again because their motivation isn't actually their love for the word of God. People who love the word of God, like David of old, delight in both! They delight in getting into the word of God, and they delight in it getting into them!

We find the beautiful reality of what it looks like for the word of God to actually *get into us* through what David expressed in Psalm 119:11. David said, "Thy word have I hid in mine heart, that I might not sin against thee." You see, the word of God had a profound and powerful impact in David's life because of what he did with it. He got into the word of God, grabbed ahold of what

337

God gave him, and he hid it. We hide things that are important to us. We hide things we treasure, like money or jewelry. And David very purposefully and very calculatedly hid it; you don't accidentally hide things! He hid it because he *delighted* in it, and he delighted in it because he *loved* it.

He also didn't just hide it in his mind. You see, a lot of people (like me!) use this verse to challenge people to memorize scripture (which you should most definitely do!). But all of us know many people who can quote all kinds of verses and have committed mounds of scripture to memory, yet their lives don't actually reflect the truths they've committed to memory. But David didn't say he'd hidden God's word in his mind, but rather his heart. Certainly, we must get the word of God into our mind before we can hide it in our hearts, but the truth is, without that 18-inch drop, we've not only missed the point—we've missed the power!

It is this same idea the Spirit of God was expressing through Paul in Colossians 3:16 when he admonished us to "Let the word of Christ dwell in you richly, in all wisdom." The key here is the word of Christ *dwelling* richly in us. The word dwell is defined for us biblically in 1 Kings 8:13 as a *settled place*. God is talking in Colossians 3:16 about us getting the truth of the word of God embedded in our hearts, so that it is dwelling in us. That it has found a settled place in us, has become a part of the fabric of who we are. It ought to be so much so that, as Colossians 3:17 says, it controls the words that come out of our mouth and the deeds we do in our bodies. The word hidden and settled in our hearts will lead to everything we say being spoken in Jesus's name and everything we do being done in Jesus's name. That's because it's Him speaking and living through us because of the place the word of God has in our lives!

5. We know we love the word of God by our <u>**complete surrender to it**</u>.

In Psalm 119:48, David says, "My hands also will I lift up unto thy commandments, which I have loved." Now, this isn't the venue to

Chapter 12 — Unlocking It All

do an exhaustive study on what the Bible teaches about the lifting up of our hands, but if we were to study it, one thing that would become obvious is that there is nothing spiritual in and of itself in the lifting up of our hands. What we find, however, is that it is to be *representative* of something spiritual. For example, in Lamentations 3:40-41, Jeremiah says, "Let us search and try our ways, and turn again to the Lord. Let us lift up our heart with our hands unto the God in the heavens." The lifting up of our hands to the Lord is to be representative of the surrender that is in our hearts.

What do the cops command when they have a suspect surrounded and want a peaceful ending to their pursuit? To come out with their hands up. And why do they want the perp's hands up? They want to make sure there isn't anything he's holding onto! And that's exactly what we're saying to the Lord when we lift our hands to Him. We're saying, in effect, "Lord, I lift my hands to you, because they reflect the fact that there's nothing in my heart I'm holding onto... and there's nothing in my heart I'm holding back! I lift my hands as the outward demonstration of the inward reality of the absolute surrender of everything in my life to You."

Now, for us to lift our hands and God to know that they're not really empty—for us to outwardly mime absolute surrender, yet inwardly avoid it—is actually an abomination to Him. God says in Isaiah 1:15, "And when ye spread forth your hands, I will hide mine eyes from you; yea, when ye make many prayers, I will not hear; your hands are full of blood."

But David lets us know in Psalm 119:148 that what is characteristic of those who love the word of God is that they approach it with their hands raised! Again, recognize, it's not a *hand* thing. That is, it's not a *physical* thing—it's a *heart* thing! It's a *spiritual attitude* thing! It's an attitude which says, "Lord, as I come to Your word, I already have my hands up. Before I even know what You're going to *reveal* to me today, before I even know what You're going to *ask* of me today, I can already tell You: the answer is an unequivocal yes, no questions asked. I'm not holding on to *my will... my wants...* or *my way.* There's nothing in my hands, Lord. There's nothing in my heart."

339

The Keys of Bible Study

My brother or sister, is that how you approach the word of God? It will be, if you love it!

6. We know we love the word of God by _our ability to experience extraordinary peace_ and by _our inability to be offended_.

David says in Psalm 119:165, "Great peace have they which love thy law: and nothing shall offend them."

It is a strange phenomenon that churches in the 21st century are filled with people who are anxious, nervous, worried, fearful, and fretful. And though I know you've probably read this verse or heard it quoted a thousand times, would you please seek to read it and hear it today with fresh eyes and ears? David says: "*Great peace* have they which love thy law..."

Notice, people who love the word of God don't just experience a *measure* of peace—David says they experience *great* peace! They experience that Philippians 4:7 kind of peace that passeth all understanding! They experience a peace so great that it defies *comprehension...* it defies *explanation...* it defies *description...* and it defies *communication.* The great peace he's talking about here, isn't a *natural* kind of peace. No, he's talking about a *supernatural* peace. And again, who is it that experiences this kind of peace? It is reserved only for those who *love* the word of God.

Why is this peace so great? Because it comes from such a great God! Our God is not just a *Champion* for peace. Rather, 1 Thessalonians 5:23 says He is the "very **God** of peace." He's not just the *Possessor* of peace; Isaiah 9:6 says He's the "**Prince** of peace." 1 Corinthians 14:33 says He's the "**Author** of peace." 2 Thessalonians 3:16 says He's the "**Lord** of peace." Not only is He the *Distributor* of peace, Ephesians 2:14 says, "He **is** our peace." Jesus said in John 14:27, "**My peace** I give unto you." Can you imagine the kind of peace Jesus had inside of Him? Well, *that's* the very peace Jesus said He'd give to you and me! Paul said in 2 Thessalonians 3:16, "Now the Lord of peace **Himself** give you peace." God doesn't *sub-contract*

340

Chapter 12 — Unlocking It All

or *delegate* the job. It's **His** peace He gives, and **He's** the One who gives it.

And notice something else in 2 Thessalonians 3:16. The peace He gives to us isn't ours sometimes or a good portion of the time or even most of the time. The verse says, "Now the Lord of peace Himself give you peace **always**..." Regardless of the circumstances in the world or in our lives, we can experience His peace! The verse goes on to tell us that the Lord of peace doesn't just have *a few means* of getting His peace to us, or even *a whole lot of means* of getting it to us. He possesses and uses "all means." The verse says: "Now the Lord of peace himself give you peace always **by all means**." God's peace comes by all means always and extends past sickness and suffering, persecution and prison, the mouth of the lion or the peril of the sword, economic recessions or depressions, and past all human and natural understanding. Hallelujah!

Listen, if I were David, I wouldn't call it "peace" either! I'd have to say with David: "That's **great peace!**"

And how is it that we are able to possess that kind of peace? Psalm 119:165 tells us it only comes by falling in love with the word of God. I know that there are some people more prone to anxiety, worry, and fear than others. If you are one of them, my heart sincerely goes out to you. Please don't allow the enemy to use what I'm about to say to put you on any kind of guilt trip. But all kinds of prescriptions are being written in the 21st century to give us peace. I certainly don't know what your situation is, and I'm not suggesting you do anything with your prescription other than take it! But I know the God of the universe and the God of the human anatomy wrote one whale of a prescription in Psalm 119:165: Take in massive doses of the word of God until you fall in love with it! He said that it would result in us receiving great peace.

Just how great is this peace? This is unbelievable! Psalm 119:165 tells us that it is a peace that is so great and runs so deep that it leaves us with the inability to be offended! Oh, please listen to it again: "Great peace have they which love thy law, and **nothing**

341

The Keys of Bible Study

shall offend them." And the word *nothing* in this verse is a very interesting word! It means… are you ready for this? It means nothing! As in, not a thing… no thing… nil… nada… nary a thang… zilch… zilch-o… diddly squat! I know that's extremely deep, but maybe we'll be able to understand it if we meditate on it for a while.

We're living at a time in these last days in which churches are full of people who are highly sensitive, overly petty, and easily offended. People who have a tremendous ability to *read into* what someone *said* or *didn't say,* or what someone *did* or *didn't do.* We have to walk on eggshells around them, because there are all kinds of potential landmines to step on. Somebody's always got them upset or hurt. Folks, the bottom line is this: if we are the kind of people who are easily offended, it's very simply because we don't love the word of God. When we fall in love with the word of God, the peace of God becomes so real, so deep, so abiding, so powerful and so overwhelming, Psalm 119:165 says it will cause us to become incapable of being offended. That, my friend, is some kind of peace!

Now, lest we all be working in our minds off of a different definition or understanding of what it is to be offended, perhaps it would be helpful to know that this word that is translated *offend* in Psalm 119:165 is the same word that is most often translated as *stumblingblock*. And obviously, a *stumblingblock* is something that trips us up. It is something that hinders our ability to walk. It keeps us from being able to walk in the Spirit. It hinders us from getting into the word of God, and hinders the word of God from getting into us. It causes us to stumble over prayer. It causes us to stumble over our area of service, or being fruitful in our area of service.

I'm not saying that people can't and won't say and do some incredibly hurtful, hateful, and spiteful things against us! I'm simply saying that when we *genuinely* and *passionately* love the word of God, those things won't trip us up! They won't become stumblingblocks, and we'll be able to maintain a holy walk. We'll keep walking in the Spirit. We'll keep hungering for the word of God. We'll keep humbling ourselves before God in prayer. We'll keep faithfully serving the Lord. Those potential offenses won't shut us down or

Chapter 12 — Unlocking It All

shut us up.

This is what Paul was talking about in Colossians 3:15 when he said, "Let the peace of God *rule* in your hearts." Something is always going to rule in our hearts, folks! Many Christians let people rule them. Some Christians let circumstances rule them. Some let their nerves rule them. Others allow anger, bitterness, hatred, jealousy, fear, lust, pride, greed, alcohol, drugs, depression or a zillion other things to rule them. When we love the word of God, however, that's when the peace of God is free to rule in our hearts.

There's one last way we know we love the word of God...

7. We know we love the word of God by *the desire in our innermost being to obey it*.

David says in Psalm 119:166-167, "Lord, I have hoped for thy salvation, and done thy commandments." (Note: this isn't *salvation* like we'd talk about "being saved" in the Church Age; he's talking about being saved or delivered out of his persecutions and trials.) That's verse 166. And if he stopped there, it might sound like he was obeying the word of God because of what God would do for him. But notice how that gets cleared up in the very next verse! David continues in verse 167: "My soul hath kept thy testimonies; and I love them exceedingly." Notice, the obedience he's describing here isn't obedience out of a grudging sense of duty. This isn't a case of, "I really want God to do *that* for me, so I'm gonna do *this* for Him." No! David says, "Lord, I love Your word with a love that exceeds what is natural, normal, expected, adequate, status-quo, or middle-of-the-road. And because I do, my very soul (my innermost being!) desires to obey it."

Perhaps the sentiment David is expressing here should cause each of us to consider: Do I obey the word of God because of what I believe God will do for me if I do? Because you see, that's not love for the word of God—it's actually the love of self masked in love for God and His word.

In that same vein, perhaps another question we should consider asking ourselves is: Do I obey the word of God because of what might happen to me if I don't? That's not love for the word of God, either—that's superstition. God wants us to obey Him because of the desire in our innermost being to obey Him—and that desire is the result of loving Him and loving His word.

Now that we've been able to observe biblically the characteristics the word of God produces in the life of someone who genuinely and passionately loves it, allow me to ask again: Does your life give evidence that you love the word of God? If so, praise the Lord! Keep doing what you're doing, and soldier on in the labour of study. If not, might I admonish and encourage you to join me in a lifelong pursuit applying *The Keys of Bible Study?* May we all be able to declare with the man after God's own heart, "O how love I thy law! it is my meditation all the day" (Psa 119:97). May God give unto each of us the key of David to unlock the unsearchable treasures of His word and the invaluable treasures of his work.